ADVANCING

Word 97

for Windows

CAROL MCKENZIE & PAT BRYDEN

Heinemann Educational Publishers,
Halley Court, Jordan Hill, Oxford OX2 8EJ
a division of Reed Educational & Professional Publishing Ltd

Heinemann is a registered trademark of Reed Educational
& Professional Publishing Limited

OXFORD FLORENCE PRAGUE MADRID ATHENS
MELBOURNE AUCKLAND KUALA LUMPUR SINGAPORE TOKYO
IBADAN NAIROBI KAMPALA JOHANNESBURG GABORONE
PORTSMOUTH NH (USA) CHICAGO MEXICO CITY SAO PAULO

First published 1998
2002 2001 2000 99
10 9 8 7 6 5 4 3 2 1

A catalogue record for this book is available from the British Library on request.

ISBN 0 435 45428 5

Designed by Moondisks

Typeset by TechType, Abingdon, Oxon

Printed and bound in Great Britain by The Bath Press, Bath

Screen shots reprinted with permission from Microsoft Corporation

▶ Contents

▶ RSA Text Processing Schemes

RSA Examinations Board has designed a suite of Text Processing Schemes at Stages I, II and III. The overall aim of these modular awards is to meet the business document production and presentation requirements of the discerning employer and to give candidates the opportunity to demonstrate competence in text processing skills to the level demanded for NVQ Administration.

Stage I shows that the candidate has sufficient knowledge or skill to begin employment, although further study would be beneficial.

Stage II indicates a sound understanding of and competence in the subject and a recommendation for employment. It also suggests that someone who holds such a certificate may well benefit from advanced studies.

Stage III indicates an all-round knowledge and understanding of the subject and, in the practical skills, a very high degree of proficiency.

At each stage, there is a *Part 1* examination, which assesses the core skills at that stage. A selection of *Part 2* examinations assesses skills in more specific applications such as word processing, typewriting or audio transcription.

There is a Text Processing Diploma at Stages II and III; this has been designed to recognise all-round achievement in text processing. The following modules that contribute to the Stage III Diploma are covered in this book:

Text Processing Stage III Part 1
Word Processing Stage III Part 2
Document Presentation Stage III Part 2.

The Diploma is awarded to candidates who demonstrate competence in the *Part 1* examination and in three *Part 2* examinations at the same stage. Additional modules include specialist applications of text processing, for example:

▶ typewriting

▶ shorthand transcription, and

▶ audio transcription.

Possession of Stage III Text Processing awards contributes significantly towards the evidence required for NVQ Administration Level 1, Element 7.1; Level 2, Elements 7.2, 13.1 and 13.2; and Level 3, Elements 13.2, 14.2 and 15.2.

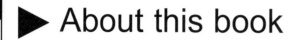

▶ About this book

This book has been written as a continuation to *Introducing Word 97 for Windows* and *Extending Word 97 for Windows*. It has been designed as a progressive course and is suitable for use in the classroom, in an open-learning workshop or as a private study aid.

This book has been produced to assist people who wish to gain advanced level accreditation through RSA Examination Board's Text Processing Schemes, using the Microsoft Word 97 for Windows software package. To get the most out of this book students should already have tackled intermediate standard.

Units 1–5 are designed for students preparing to take advanced examinations such as RSA Text Processing Stage III Part 1. These units are also suitable for the revision of text processing skills without taking an examination.

Units 6–10 are designed for students preparing to take intermediate examinations such as RSA Word Processing Stage III Part 2. These units are also suitable for students who wish to learn how to prepare multi-page documents, more complex tables and text in 'newspaper columns' without taking an examination.

Units 11–16 are designed for students preparing to take the RSA Document Presentation Stage III Part 2 examination. These units are also suitable for students who wish to extend their knowledge and skills to include advanced presentation skills without taking an examination.

A brief outline of the examination and examination practice for each stage of learning is included in Units 5, 10 and 16.

Format of the book

Printout checks for all exercises are given at the back of the book (pages 168–208). Use them to check your work.

The Progress Review Checklist (pages 166–67) helps you keep a record of progress, noting the number of errors made.

Command boxes for Word 97 functions are given when appropriate. Instruction is given on how to carry out the required function. The commands explain keyboard, mouse and menu operation.

The Glossary of Commands at the back of the book provides a comprehensive, alphabetically listed quick reference for all the Word 97 commands introduced in the book. The commands are shown for keyboard, mouse and menu users. Shortcut keys are included because many students prefer to use these methods, as they become more familiar with the program.

All exercise material is to be completed in Times New Roman point size 12 unless indicated otherwise.

Working through a unit

1   When you see this symbol, read all the information before you begin. You may also need to refer back to this information as you carry out the exercises.

2   When you see this symbol, carry out the exercises, following the numbered steps, eg **1.1**, **1.2**.

3   Use Word 97's spelling and grammar tool to check your document. Proofread the document carefully yourself – the spelling tool does not find every error.

4   Use the Print Preview facility to check that your document is going to be correct when printed. If it is, save your work on to your floppy disk (usually in A Drive) or into an appropriate directory. Then print your work.

5   Compare your document with the printout checks at the back of the book (pages 168–208). (If you are using this book in class, your tutor may also wish to check your work.) Correct any errors, which you find in your work. Print the documents again if required to do so by your tutor. (If you are working on your own, you may not consider this necessary.)

6   Complete your Progress Review Checklist. Then exit from Word 97 or begin work on the next unit.

Do not delete files from your disk – you may need them later!

unit 1

▶ Document formatting, page numbering and footnotes

By the end of Unit 1, you should have revised many intermediate formatting techniques. You should also have learnt how to:

▶ start page numbering from a given page number
▶ change the appearance of header and footer text
▶ insert footnotes to appear at the bottom of the page.

The techniques for revision listed below are included in Exercise 1A and also in Exercise 2A in the next unit. If you have problems with any of the techniques then you should go back to *Extending Word 97 for Windows*. If you do not have access to a copy of the book, then you can refer to the alphabetical glossary at the back of this book (pages 209–218) and ask your tutor to explain anything you are unsure about.

▶ Spelling and grammar, indenting text, setting margins, correction signs, consistency of presentation, page numbering, multi-page documents
▶ Locating information from another document
▶ Headers and footers
▶ Enumeration/bulleted points.

Note: The following types of errors are *not indicated* in the draft at Stage III. It is up to you to notice them and to correct them.

▶ Typographical errors
▶ Spelling errors
▶ Errors of agreement
▶ Punctuation errors, including apostrophes.

Word 97's spelling and grammar check will give you some help in correcting these but you should always proofread the text through very carefully yourself, as the spelling and grammar check will not pick up every mistake.

Exercise 1A ▶

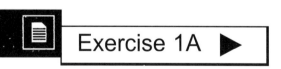

1.1 Open a new document and key in the following text. Format the document as follows:

▶ Single line spacing, except where indicated otherwise
▶ Ragged (unjustified) right margin
▶ Document line length of 13cm (5in)
▶ Insert a header: **SENSIBLE EATING** at the top right of each page
▶ Number the pages at the bottom right of each page.

The glossary at the back of the book will remind you of any commands you are not sure of.

EATING FOR HEALTH ← *Centre and bold*

Most of us [nowadays] [a~~c~~knowledge] that, to some ~~degree~~ extent, 'We are what we eat' and that we can only function to our full potential if we have a healthy body. Many common illnesses and health problems, including heart disease, are linked to our diet. — *double line-spacing*

~~Each and~~ every cell in our bodies needs ~~food~~ nutrients to be able to perform it's particular ~~job~~ function. Nutrients are extracted from the foods we eat. — *Copy to [A]*

The main food groups are:

close up
1 Proteins
2 Carbo~~h~~ydrates
3 Fats
4 Sugars
5 Alcohol

Many well-known phrases come to mind. *when giving advice on diet*

'VARIETY IS THE SPICE OF LIFE'

single
No ~~one~~ food or food group can provide the full range of nutrients required by the body.

a wide range of
Different foods supply different combinations of nutrients. Eating ~~plenty of different~~ foods helps to make sure that we get all the nourishment we need to stay healthy. *grow and*

Please make all headings like this one

'A BIT OF WHAT YOU FANCY DOES YOU GOOD'

The types of food we tend to use as 'treats' is unfortunately not very good in terms of nutrition – often being high in fats, sugars and salt, ~~which are not always apparent~~. However, in small amounts and eaten occasionally, they do not do us any harm. Alcohol and sugar are classed as foods but in fact contain no nutrients – just 'empty calories'. Malnutrition can result from excessive use of these. *especially if used instead of nourishing foods.*

Move this section to [B]

'KEEP IT IN PROPORTION'

In this country, most of us eat too much protein, fat and salt. The balance should be tipped more in favour of complex carbohydrates such as rice, pasta, bread, cereals, ~~and~~ potatoes and yams. These should be the main part of any meal or snack: ~~These foods are~~ [they are] low in fat and sugar and give us lots of energy, vitamins, minerals and fibre. Provided ~~you~~ [we] don't add too much fat or sugar when preparing dishes, we can all benefit from eating these foods. [starchy]

'Eat up your greens'

Vegetables, especially dark green leafy types, provide valuable vitamins, minerals and fibre. Poor storage, preparation and cooking practices deplete the vitamin content so it's best to buy and eat fresh – or grow yr own! 'An apple a day, keeps the doctor away' could also be an appropriate saying here as fresh fruit is equally important – and not only apples!

'PICK UP A PINTA'

Dairy products such as cheese, milk and yoghurt are rich in calcium. Low fat versions contain just as much calcium, protein and vitamins but less of the animal fats' we should avoid.

BODY BUILDING

Protein-rich foods such as meat, fish, beans, pulses, eggs and nuts also contain vitamins, minerals and fats. However, we tend to eat more of these types of food than we ~~should~~ [should be] need and care needs to be taken because of the high fat [possible] content. Meat should be lean, skin removed from poultry, and fish poached or [should be] grilled rather than fried. Vegetarians learn to combine foods to ensure good quality proteins.

[B]

'Moderation in all things'

[A]

Advertisments in the media make us beleive that it is necy to buy the manufacturers' latest food products to achiev a happy and healthy life for ourswelves and our family. Immed/accessibility [& convenent] to a wide range of attractively-packaged products is available to almost everyone. Obesity is increasing rapidly in this county altho millions of pounds is spent on health and nutrition education ~~so~~ it seems that we can have 'too much of a good thing'!   [info]

[by the government]

[Indent by 25mm at left]

1.2 Use the spelling and grammar tool to check your work, and proofread it yourself as well. Make sure that the format of the document conforms to the instructions on page 4. Save the document using the filename **EX1A** and print one copy. Check your printout with the printout at the back of the book. If you find any errors, correct them and print the document again, if necessary.

Number pages from a given page number

You have already learnt how to insert page numbering in Word 97 and how to select the position, alignment and format of the page number. Word 97 automatically numbers the pages using the number indicated in the status bar at the bottom of the document window.

For some documents, it may be necessary to start page numbering with a number other than 1, for example, if several introductory pages are to be inserted before the main text of the document. There are two methods of setting up this function in Word 97.

Insert method	View header and footer method
Select: Page Numbers from the Insert menu	Select: **Header and Footer** from the **View** menu
Select from the **Position and Alignment** options: As appropriate	Click: The **Format Page Number** icon on the Header and Footer Tool Bar
Click: **Format**	

The Page Number Format dialogue box is displayed on screen.

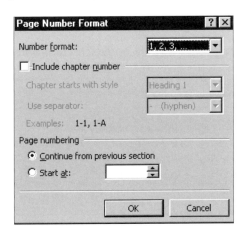

Figure 1.1 Page Number Format dialogue box

▶ Click: **Start at** in the **Page Numbering** section (black dot is displayed)
▶ Key in or select in spin box: The page number that you want your document to start from
▶ Click: **OK**.

Note: If necessary, you can also change the format of the page number in the **Number Format** dialogue box. You can choose from Arabic numbers (1, 2, 3), Roman numerals (I, II, III) or letters (a, b, c).

 # Change the appearance of headers and footers

You have already learnt how to insert headers and footers to appear on each page of a document and how to select the position and alignment of the text. You may be required to change the font, font size or format of the header/footer text to make it easily distinguishable from the body text of the document.

▶ Select: **Header and Footer** from the **View** menu
▶ Key in: The header or footer text or select the text if it is already there
▶ Select: **Font** from the **Format** menu
▶ Select: The required format from **Font**, **Font Style**, **Size**, **Underline**, **Color** and **Effects.**

The **Preview** box displays the text formatted as it will appear in the document.

▶ Click: **OK** to confirm the selections
▶ Click: **Close** to close the dialogue box.

 Footnotes ▶

Footnotes are used to explain in more depth, or provide references for, a particular point made within the body of the document text. A footnote comprises two linked parts:

1 a footnote symbol, such as an * or a superscripted character, eg [1] is placed as a reference mark in the body of the text next to the word, figure or phrase which needs further explanation, and
2 the same symbol is repeated later in the document with the explanatory text.

Note: A superscripted character is printed slightly above the standard line, eg 8.5^2

Example of footnote:

The special discount price for bulk orders[1] applies during the winter quarter[2] only.

1   Quantities of ten or more
2   December-February

Note: There is no space before the footnote reference mark in the body of the text. There should be at least one space between the footnote character and the explanatory text.

You can insert footnotes manually, using keyboard symbols or superscripted characters. Or you can use Word 97's automatic footnote command which automatically numbers footnote marks or allows you to create your own custom marks. With this latter method, Word 97 will automatically renumber the footnote reference marks if you add, delete or move any of them. The automatic method is not difficult to learn and when you have mastered it you will find it is more effective than the manual method.

 Insert a footnote using Word 97's footnote command ▶

To enter the footnote reference marker in the text:

Position the pointer: Immediately after the last character, word, figure or phrase requiring a footnote

Keyboard	Mouse and menu

Press: **Alt + Ctrl + F**

This command bypasses the dialogue box shown below and uses default settings. If you want to customise footnotes, use the mouse and menu method.

Select: **Footnote** from the **Insert** menu

The Footnote and Endnote dialogue box is displayed on screen.

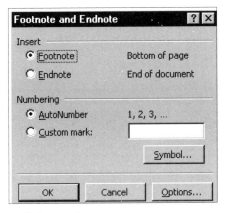

Figure 1.2 Footnote and Endnote dialogue box

▶ Select: **Footnote** in the **Insert** section
▶ Select: **AutoNumber** in the **Numbering** section to number the footnote(s) automatically.

 Customise the footnote marker as a symbol ▶

▶ Select: **Custom** mark in the **Numbering** section
▶ Click: **Symbol**
▶ Select: A symbol from the choice displayed (if necessary select another font from the **Font** drop-down menu)
▶ Click: **OK**.

 Modify the layout of a footnote ▶

▶ Click: **Options, All Footnotes**
    ▶ **Place at** – allows you to choose the position of the explanatory text – immediately **Beneath** text or at the **Bottom of page**
    ▶ **Number format** – allows you to select a different footnote display format, eg **a, b, c** or **i, ii, iii**
    ▶ **Start at** – allows you to specify from which character you want the footnote numbering to start
    ▶ **Numbering** – allows you to specify the printing of footnotes at different locations in the document
▶ Click: **OK** to confirm selections.

Enter the footnote explanatory text

When you exit the footnote and endnote dialogue box, Word 97 automatically prompts you to enter the explanatory text at the bottom of the page (or other specified location in the document). Word 97 automatically leaves space after the footnote number or symbol.

▶ Click: In the main document to leave the footnote and return to the main document.

 ## View footnotes whilst working on the main document text

▶ Double-click: The footnote reference mark in the text.

Note: In normal view, the footnotes appear in the **Footnotes** panel; in page layout view, the footnotes appear where they will be printed in the document.

 ## Move or delete a footnote

▶ Use normal cut and paste methods.

 ## Format a footnote

▶ Use normal text formatting commands, eg bold, italic, font size, etc.

 ## Remove the note separator

You may find that Word 97 inserts a short horizontal line above the footnotes in your document. RSA examinations do not require this separating line. However, you will not be penalised if you leave it in. You can remove it, in normal view, as follows:

▶ Select: **Normal** from the **View** menu
▶ Select: **Footnotes** from the **View** menu
▶ Select: **All Footnotes** in the **Footnotes** drop-down menu
▶ Click: **Footnote Separator** in the **Footnotes** drop-down menu
▶ Select: The separator line; *and*
▶ Press: **Delete**
▶ Click: **Close** to return to the main document text.

Insert a footnote using the manual entry method

To insert the footnote reference marker in the text:

You can use superscript characters or keyboard symbols for the footnote reference marker.

► Position the pointer: Immediately after the last character of the word, figure or phrase requiring a footnote.

Keyboard	Mouse and menu
Press: **Ctrl + Shift + Plus sign (+)** to change the font to superscript Key in: The footnote character (number, letter or symbol) Press: **Ctrl + Spacebar** to revert to normal text	Select: **Font** from the **Format** menu Select: The **Font** tab Click: The **Superscript** option in the **Effects** section to change the font to superscript Click: **OK** Key in: The footnote character (number, letter or symbol) Select: **Font** from the **Format** menu Select: The **Font** tab Click: The **Superscript** option in the **Effects** section to revert to normal text Click: **OK**

 # Enter the footnote explanatory text

► Position the insertion pointer: Where you want the explanatory text to appear – usually at the bottom of the page (footnote) or at the end of the document (endnote)
► Key in: The same footnote character that was used as a footnote reference mark (in the footnote section, this does not have to be in superscript)
► Leave at least one clear space between the reference mark and the footnote explanatory text
► Key in: The explanatory text.

 # Exercise 1B

1.3   Open the document **EX1A** if it is not already on screen. Save as **EX1B**. Make the following changes to the document format:

► Change the header font to Courier New, font size 10
► Change the header alignment to left alignment
► Change the page numbering to start from page 4
► Add a footer at the left in Times New Roman, font size 8, italic: Your name.

1.4 Referring back to the instructions on footnotes, insert a footnote reference marker in the form of an asterisk after the word **Fats** in the numbered list on the first page of **EX1A** as shown below:

```
1   Proteins
2   Carbohydrates
3   Fats*
4   Sugars
5   Alcohol
```

1.5 Insert the following text as the explanatory footnote (relating to the asterisk you have just inserted) to appear at the foot of the first page:

> Fats contain more than double the number of calories than proteins and carbohydrates.
>
> *Use Times New Roman size 10 Italic*

1.6 Add the following information at the end of the paragraph referring to dairy products:

> It is becoming apparant that many people are ~~allergic~~ intolerant of animal milks. Calcium-enriched soya milk provides a good alternative.

1.7 Add the following information at the end of the paragraph headed **VARIETY IS THE SPICE OF LIFE**:

> Malnutrition can arise on 'crash' diets and when food variety are restricted, despite the fact that the person may be overweight.

1.8 Use the spelling and grammar tool to check your work, and proofread it yourself as well. Ensure that the page break is sensibly positioned and that the document takes up only 2 pages. *You may find it necessary to reduce the top and/or bottom margins to do this.* Resave the document under the same filename (**EX1B**). Print one copy.

1.9 Check your printout with the printout at the back of the book. If you find any errors, correct them and print the document again, if necessary.

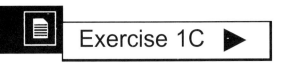

1.10 Open the document **EX1B** if it is not already on screen. Save as **EX1C**. Make the following changes to the document format:

▶ Change the header format to Arial, font size 10, underlined
▶ Change the header alignment to centred
▶ Change the page numbering to start from Page 1 and centre the page number
▶ Change the document line length to 14cm ($5\frac{1}{2}$ in)
▶ Change the text alignment to fully justified (except for the centred main heading).

1.11 Delete the existing footnote reference marker and footnote text.

1.12 Add the following footnote reference markers and footnote text to the paragraph headed **KEEP IT IN PROPORTION** as shown below. Ensure that the footnotes appear on the same page as the footnote reference.

'KEEP IT IN PROPORTION'

In this country, most of us eat too much protein, fat and salt. The balance should be tipped more in favour of complex carbohydrates[1] such as rice, pasta, bread, cereals, potatoes and yams. These should be the main part of any meal or snack: they are low in fat[2] and sugar[3] and give us lots of energy, vitamins, minerals and fibre. Provided we don't add too much fat or sugar when preparing dishes, we can all benefit from eating these starchy foods.

1   3.75 kcal/g (calories per gram)
2   9.00 kcal/g
3   4.00 kcal/g – 'empty calories' – no nutrition

retain same font style and size – Times New Roman size 10 italic

---

1.13 Change the numbered list on the first page to a bulleted list, using the bullet symbol shown below:

❑ Proteins
❑ Carbohydrates

1.14 Check your work carefully, ensuring that the formatting changes have been made and new footnotes added. Resave the document and print one copy.

1.15 Check your printout with the printout at the back of the book. If you find any errors, correct them and print the document again, if necessary.

1.16 Exit the program if you have finished working or continue straight on to the next unit.

unit 2

▶ Text formatting, spelling, grammar and specialised text

By the end of Unit 2, you should have revised more of the formatting techniques you learnt in *Extending Word 97 for Windows* – the second book in this series. You should also have learnt how to:

▶ use AutoCorrect for specialised text
▶ identify and correct errors in the use of apostrophes
▶ identify and correct spelling errors
▶ expand additional abbreviations
▶ interpret additional correction signs
▶ key in specialised text, including symbols, fractions, superscript and subscript.

Proofreading text

One of the main differences between Stage II work and Stage III work is that errors which were indicated for correction at Stage II will *not* be indicated at Stage III. You need to be much more careful at checking *all* text whether this is recalled text, manuscript text or keyed in by you.

Typescript containing typographical errors

In the Stage III examinations, you will be expected to carry out complex proofreading, text editing and formatting. Text editing may involve correcting any mistakes made in previous printouts. Watch out for uncorrected spelling errors and transposition errors. Remember, the errors in the draft will *not* be circled for you to correct – you must find them yourself.

Typescript containing spelling errors

Remember, Word 97 can help you with spelling because it has a built-in spelling and grammar tool which checks as you type for spelling and grammar errors. Word 97 will identify a spelling error with a red wavy line and a grammatical error with a green wavy line. However, you must also proofread the text yourself, as Word 97 will be unable to check many proper names (eg cities, surnames etc). Also, if you have keyed in the wrong version of a word, eg *their* instead of *there*, the spellchecker will not detect this as both versions are spelt correctly. In the RSA Stage III examination you will be expected to be able to spell a list of additional words.

Specialist text or frequently used words or names

Only you can tell if you have copied names of people or places, or specialist vocabulary, correctly and if a piece of information you were asked to find is correct. If Word 97 queries a word which you know to be correct, you can ignore Word 97's prompt to change it. If you are going to use an unusual word fairly frequently then you can add it to the Spellchecker dictionary.

Sometimes, to help you, an author may write unusual words in capitals in the margin and put a dashed line around the word. This is to indicate the correct spelling of the word only – you are not required to key in the word in capitals or to put a dashed line around it! You will find an example of this technique in Exercise 2B.

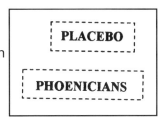

AutoCorrect

As you type, you may already have noticed that Word 97 automatically corrects some commonly misspelt words such as 'teh' instead of 'the' or 'adn' instead of 'and'. If there is a word that you often mistype or misspell, you can add it to Word 97's list of automatic corrections.

  AutoCorrect ▶

▶ Select: **Tools**, **AutoCorrect** from the menu
▶ Check that: The **Replace Text As You Type** check box is ticked
▶ In the **Replace** box, key in: The word that you often mistype/misspell, eg unusaul
▶ Key in: The correct spelling of the word in the With box, eg unusual
▶ Click: **Add**
▶ Click: **OK.**

Word 97 will also make the following corrections automatically:

▶ change the second capital letter to a lowercase letter if you accidentally type two capital letters at the beginning of a word;
▶ capitalise the first letter at the beginning of a sentence;
▶ capitalise the first letter of the days of the week; and
▶ reverse accidental usage of the cAPS LOCK key.

  Exercise 2A ▶

2.1 As you may already have realised, a good use of AutoCorrect is for replacing shortened versions of words which you find particularly difficult to spell. When you key in the shortened version, Word 97 will automatically replace it with the correct spelling for you. When working with specialist vocabulary, this feature can be a great help. Select **AutoCorrect** from the **Tools** menu. Enter the short version under **Replace:** and the full version, correctly spelt, under **With:**

Replace:	With:
SSD	SIGNED SEALED AND DELIVERED
PNI	Psychoneuroimmunology
NEWC	NEWCASTLE-UPON-TYNE
A&E	Accident & Emergency Department

2.2 To test your AutoCorrect entries, with a clear screen, key in the following, pressing the return key between each word:

SSD by the said James Maloney
PNI – an old wisdom under new scrutiny
A&E Staff Rota
Victoria Road
NEWC
NE2 7HG

If you have followed the instructions correctly for AutoCorrect, Word 97 should automatically have converted your entries to appear on screen as:

> **SIGNED SEALED AND DELIVERED by the said James Maloney**
> **Psychoneuroimmunology – an old wisdom under new scrutiny**
> **Accident and Emergency Department Staff Rota**
> **Victoria Road**
> **NEWCASTLE-UPON-TYNE**
> **NE2 7HG**

Note: AutoCorrect will only insert replacement entries exactly as they were entered. You would not, for instance, be able automatically to substitute the word 'psychoneuroimmunological' instead of 'psychoneuroimmunology'. You would either have to key in the whole word correctly, or edit the AutoCorrect entry as appropriate.

2.3 Close the file without saving, ready for the next exercise.

Apostrophes
Omission

In RSA Stage III examinations, you will be expected to know when to use an apostrophe and where it should be positioned in the word it relates to. One use of the apostrophe is where it indicates that a letter (or letters) have been left out, eg:

didn't	*(did not)*	aren't	*(are not)*
he'd	*(he had)*	we're	*(we are)*

2.4 Starting a new file, key in the following sentences, shortening the words underlined and putting the apostrophe in the correct place:

> We <u>are</u> leaving for our holiday today. The representatives said <u>they are</u> to meet us after <u>we have</u> landed at the local airport. Then <u>they will</u> take us to the hotel where <u>we are</u> going to spend the first 5 days. <u>There is</u> to be a trip to local beaches and although we <u>had not</u> booked, the representative said there <u>would not</u> be any problem in finding places as <u>there will</u> be some guests who <u>are not</u> able to take the trips.

Leave this work on the screen. Save the document using the filename **EX2A**, but do not close or print the file yet.

Possession

Apostrophes are also used to show possession – that something belongs to someone or something, eg:

Simon's house	*(the house belonging to Simon)*
The box's lid	*(the lid of the box)*
Next month's magazine	*(the magazine for next month)*
The week's work	*(the work of the week)*

If the word ends in 's', an apostrophe is added but there is no extra 's', eg:

The dress' hem	*(the hem of the dress)*
The students' folders	*(the folders of the students)*
The boys' mother	*(the mother of the boys)*
The dresses' hems	*(the hems of the dresses)*

2.5 Key in the following sentences below the previous task, rearranging the underlined words and inserting the apostrophes in the correct places:

> The heat of the sun when we land will surprise and delight us. We will need to use good sun protection creams to protect the skin of the children when they are playing on the beaches of the island. The toddlers like to sit at the edge of the water and squeal with anticipation as each crest of the wave approaches them. The plans of the older children are concerned more with the water in the swimming pool and they expect to join in the activities organised by the recreation team of the hotel. We parents hope to be able to enjoy the cuisine of the island, the poolside bar of the hotel, and the chance to unwind for a few days.

Resave the document using the same filename. Leave it on the screen. Do not print it yet.

Its and it's

In speech, 'its' can mean 'it is' (or 'it has') or 'belonging to it'. An apostrophe is used only when the full phrase of 'it is' (or 'it has') is shortened – the apostrophe shows that a letter has been missed out, eg:

It's hot	*(It is hot)*
It's reported	*(It is reported)*
It's your decision	*(It is your decision)*
It's been in my possession	*(It has been in my possession)*

But when showing possession, there should be no apostrophe, eg:

The chair has its leg broken.
We will amend its contents.
The house had its garden landscaped.

2.6   Key in the following passage, below the previous tasks, inserting apostrophes where necessary:

> The islands history shows that its culture has been influenced by many other civilisations. Its been invaded by neighbouring countries and its natural harbours have made it a valuable port of call for seafarers and merchants for centuries. This fact probably accounts for its cosmopolitan nature and its this aspect of its atmosphere that attracts its many annual visitors. Its not unusual to see traces of European, African, and Asian cultures within the architecture or the cuisine of its famous restaurants. Its one of the most popular holiday destinations for many of the northern European nations.

2.7   Resave the document using the same filename. Check your work on screen against the printout check at the back of the book. If you are unsure of the reason for the inclusion, position or omission of any of the apostrophes, refer back to the explanations in this unit. If you are working with a tutor, you may wish to discuss apostrophes with them too. Correct any errors and print a copy of your work.

Spelling in context

You will be expected to be able to spell correctly the following words, and their derivations where marked * (eg plurals, -ed, -ing, -ment, -tion, -ly, -able, -ible). New words for Stage III are shown in bold text:

access*	business*	expense*	recommend*
accommodate*	cancel*	experience*	responsible*
achieve*	client*	financial*	satisfactory*
acknowledge*	colleague*	foreign	separate*
advertisement*	committee*	government*	success*
although	correspondence	inconvenient*	sufficient*
apparent*	definite*	permanent*	temporary*
appreciate*	develop*	receipt*	through
believe*	discuss*	receive*	unfortunate*

2.8   Spend a little time making sure you know how to spell all the words listed above correctly – ask someone to test you! Learn four per evening and it will take you no time at all.

Exercise 2B ▶

2.9   Use AutoCorrect to prepare for the document by inserting the following shortened and full versions of words and phrases which will appear in the text:

Replace:	**With:**
psych	psychology
acu	acupuncture
allo	allopathic
ung	unguents

2.10 Starting with a clear screen, key in the following document, ensuring that you correct all spelling and grammar errors, use apostrophes correctly, and correctly reproduce the full versions of the words and phrases inserted into AutoCorrect in step 2.9 above.

▶ Insert the header COMPLEMENTARY THERAPIES to appear on each page
▶ Number all pages
▶ Insert your name in a footer
▶ Use fully justified margins
▶ Use single line spacing unless instructed otherwise
▶ Use a document line length of 12.5cm.

<u>PAST REMEDIES FOR TODAYS ILLS</u>

[double line-spacing]

Increasing interest is currantly been shown in complementary therapies by the allopathic sector of Medicine. Rigorous testing are required for westen orthodox Medicine to ~~beleve~~ rely on in the efficacy of therapies which uses herbs, plants, essentail oils, tinctures and so on. The sientific revolution of the early 19th century allowed chemists to isolate components in natures products, and then to acheive sucess in developing synthetic drugs for the treatment of disease. This lead in turn to the pharmaceutical ~~business~~ industry of today. The emphasis on logic and reasoning at that time tend to lead to a dismisal of the earlier experiance of the interdependance of medicine (or rather therapy) and psychology. [Although the placebo effect has been considered responsable for the success of complementary therapies, some medical researchers aknowledge, and have proved, that this ~~effect~~ affect is definitly important and apparant in all branches of medicine. ✓

[ANCIENT CHRONICLES]

Over 700 different substance's are listed in Indian Vedic literature. The Rig Veda classifies the use of these substances, such as — for example, cinnamon, myrrh, coriander and sandalwood, for both therapeutic and liturgical purposes. Chinese acupuncture combines with the use of herbs, and aromatic's such as ginger and opium were recommended for use in the 'Yellow Emperor's Book of Internal Medicine'. Egyptian papyrus manuscripts from the reign of Khufu, describe the use of 'fine oils and choice perfumes' by people who were experts in cosmetology. Traces of scented unguents ointments and oils such as cedar and myrrh which were employed in the embalming process, is still detectable today. ✓

[work on the meridians]

~~FEATURES~~ PASSING THE MESSAGE

The Egyptian's early practises and traditions were passed down thro the centurys via the Phoenicians, Greeks and

Romans to the Persians and Arabs.

A

and gifted

A famous ∧ Arabian physician and scholar, Avicenna (AD980-1037)
wrote over one hundred books and improved the art of distillation.

However, it was discovered in 1975 that ancient
~~that~~ inhabitants of the Indus valley had pre dated
his work by 4,000 yrs. A perfectly ~~to~~ preserved
distillation unit is on permanant display in a local museum.

PERFUMES OF ARABIA ← (delete underline)
During the Middle Ages, Europeans began to have acces to
the 'perfumes of Arabia' and also to experiment with the
[plants] native ~~to~~ of Europe such as sage, Rosemary and
Lavandar. The ∧fifteenth and /sixteenth centuries saw the ~~publication~~ printing ✓
of many famous 'herbals' giving detailed info on ~~herbs~~ herbs,
and recomending there use for most ailments. These books
are still refered to today and products bearing one
authors' name - that of Nicholas Culpepper - are available
for us to buy in the high street ~~today~~.

(LAVENDER)

Romans 'appreciated aromatic substances' (greatly) and used
perfumes categorised as:
• solid unguents (ladysmata)   UNGUENTS
• scented oils (stymₘata)   STYMMATA
• powdered perfumes (diaspasmata)

Move to A

Footnotes
1 around 2,000 BC
2 around 2,800 BC

2.11 Save the document using the filename **EX2B**. Use the spelling and grammar tool to check your work and proofread it yourself as well. Using the Print Preview facility, check your work with the printout at the back of the book. If you find any errors, correct them and print one copy of the document.

Typescript containing abbreviations

You will be expected to be able to expand the following abbreviations in examinations. You should key in these words in full whenever you see them, unless instructed otherwise. Additional abbreviations for Stage III are shown in bold text.

Note: In the RSA examinations, there are no 'full stops' after the abbreviations.

a/c(s)	account(s)	necy	necessary
approx	approximately	opp(s)	opportunity/ies
appt(s)	**appointment(s)**	org	organisation
cat(s)	catalogue(s)	poss	possible
co(s)	company/ies	ref(d)	refer(red)
dept(s)	**department(s)**	ref(s)	reference(s)
dr	dear	sec(s)	secretary/ies
gntee(s)	guarantee(s)	sig(s)	signature(s)
immed	immediate(ly)	temp	temporary
info	information	yr(s)	year(s)
mfr(s)	manufacturer(s)	yr(s)	your(s)
misc	miscellaneous		

Some abbreviations should be kept as they are, for example:

etc	**eg**	**ie**	**NB**
PS	**plc**	**Ltd**	**& (in company names)**

Note: Word 97's spelling check may suggest that some abbreviations such as ie and eg should have full stops, for example i.e. and e.g. In word processing, it is now common practice to omit the full stops in such instances. You can add the abbreviations without full stops to the spelling memory as follows:

▶ Key in: The abbreviations and run the spelling check
▶ When the spellchecker stops on the abbreviation, click: The **Add** button

Word 97 will then add this to its memory and will not suggest full stops for this abbreviation again.

You will also be expected to key in the following words in full:

▶ days of the week, eg Wednesday, Thursday
▶ months of the year, eg February, September
▶ words in addresses, eg Grove, Drive, Crescent
▶ complimentary closes, eg Yours faithfully/sincerely.

Typescript containing correction signs

You should already be familiar with basic text correction signs showing amendments required by the author. The following list shows **all** the correction signs you can expect to come across in advanced examinations such as RSA Text Processing Stage III Part 1:

Correction sign	Meaning
[or //	Start a new paragraph here
	Run on – join paragraphs or sections of text
⋏ ⋏ (word)	Insert a word (or words) here. The words may be immediately above the insertion sign or circled and joined to the insertion sign by an arrow or line

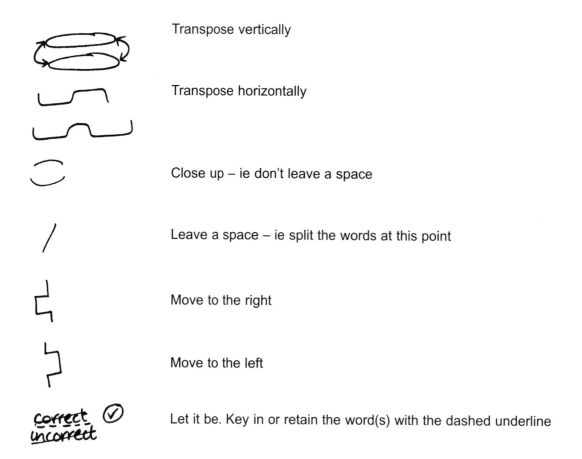

Transpose vertically

Transpose horizontally

Close up – ie don't leave a space

Leave a space – ie split the words at this point

Move to the right

Move to the left

Let it be. Key in or retain the word(s) with the dashed underline

Inserting additional text into an existing document

Text authors often require additional information to be incorporated into a document while it is being prepared or after it has been printed. In the RSA Text Processing Stage III Part 1 examination, the invigilator will simulate this by giving 2 additional pieces of information to candidates between 15 and 20 minutes after the start of the examination. In the examination, as you would at work, make sure that you have paper and pen ready to take down this information when it is given. Make sure that you insert the additional information in the correct positions. There will be gaps in the text to indicate these positions.

Working with specialised text

Stage III examinations include work likely to be given to a senior word processor operator and may also cover topics of a specialist business or technical nature. It is very important that you reproduce the text correctly, checking that all text is correctly spelt and that technical material is accurately keyed in. At work, if you are not sure of the correct spelling or interpretation, you should always ask for help and then make a note of any information which may crop up again in other pieces of work – so that you do not need to ask the same question again.

Adding characters not available on the keyboard

You may be required to reproduce symbols such as

► fractions, eg $\frac{1}{4}$, $1\frac{1}{2}$, $6\frac{3}{4}$
► accented letters, eg à, é, ñ, ä

Fractions

Word 97 automatically creates common fractions such as $\frac{1}{4}, \frac{1}{2}, \frac{3}{4}$ as you key in the numbers with the oblique stroke (solidus) between them: for example if you key in 1/4 Word 97 will convert this to $\frac{1}{4}$ Some other fractions such as 1/3 and 2/5 are not automatically converted in this way but are available by using the Insert Symbol function and selecting a font style which contains the fraction you require. You will learn about this function later in this unit.

 ## Fractions (using superscript and subscript) ▶

Some fractions are not available as symbols but can be reproduced by the use of superscript and subscript. Examples are $^2/_7$, $^1/_{52}$ and $^4/_{12}$ – representing 2 days, 1 week and 4 months respectively in medical 'shorthand'. Follow the instructions below to insert fractions not available as symbols:

Keyboard	Mouse and menu
Press: **Ctrl + Shift + Plus sign (+)** Key in: The first number (numerator), eg 1	Select: **Format, Font** Click: **Superscript** in the **Effects** box (√ in box) Click: **OK** Key in: The first number (numerator), eg 1

The number will be reduced in size and raised above the typing line.
Revert to normal text:

Press: **Ctrl + Spacebar** Key in: **/ (the solidus)**	Select: **Format, Font** Click: **Superscript** in the **Effects** box (no in box) Click: **OK**
Press: **Ctrl + = (equal sign)** Key in: The second number (denominator), eg 52	Key in: **/ (the solidus)** Select: **Format, Font** as above Click: **Subscript** in the **Effects** box (√ in box) Click: **OK** Key in: The second number (denominator), eg 52

The number will be reduced in size and lowered below the typing line

Revert to normal text:

Press: **Ctrl + Spacebar**	Select: **Format, Font** as above Click: **Subscript** in the **Effects** box (no √ in box) Click: **OK**

Accented letters

You may be required to key in text containing words from other languages and it is vital that these are accurately reproduced. Many languages use accents to indicate pronunciation and you must note these carefully and reproduce them correctly. You can access accented letters by using the **Insert Symbol** function and selecting a font style which contains the accented letter you require. For example:

Ç, Î, à, ö, ê, é, ñ, ø, ý, š, ÿ, À, È, Ï, Ô, ù

Insert Symbol function ▶

▶ Select: **Symbol** from the **Insert** drop-down menu
▶ Select: The **Symbols** tab on the dialogue box
▶ Select: **(normal text)** in the **Font** box

The Symbol dialogue box is displayed on screen.

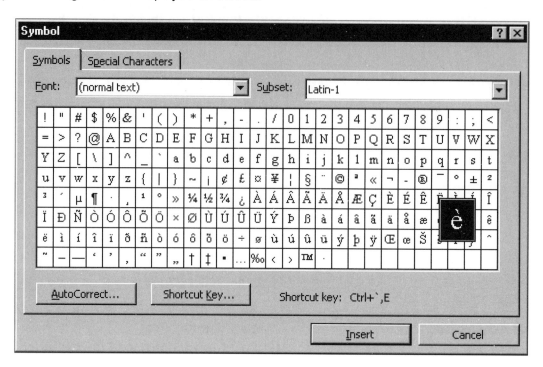

Figure 2.1 Symbol dialogue box

In Figure 2.1, the lower case letter e with a grave accent has been selected by clicking on the character. This allows you to check that this is the character you wish to use. (The shortcut (combination) keys you could use to reproduce the same character are also displayed.)

▶ Click: **Insert** to select this character and insert it into the text
▶ Click: **Close** to return to the document

Shortcut keys

As you saw in the Symbol dialogue box, you can also apply accents to text in other languages using the **combination keys** function (ie pressing two or more keys simultaneously):

Figure 2.2 shows the keys to be used to reproduce accented letters. (This table can be found in the Help menu under **Type international characters**. You could print a copy to keep for reference.)

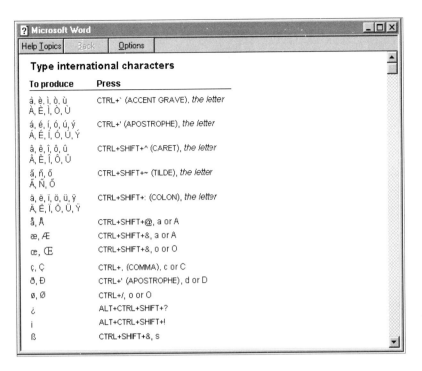

Figure 2.2 Type international characters

For example, when keying in the word **fricassée**, to produce the **é**:

▶ Press: **Ctrl + ' (apostrophe)**
▶ Press: **e**

To insert an accent with an upper case letter:

Press: The key combination
Press: **Shift** + the letter

For example, when keying in the word **NOËL**, to produce the **Ë**:

Press: **Ctrl + Shift + : (colon)**
Press: **Shift + E**

Other symbols

Note: You will find many other useful symbols such as ticks, fractions, arrows etc by investigating the different fonts in the Symbol dialogue box.

Some examples are:

¢¥°† □}❹≫→® ™
8§©V]"□▤✔♥✿∑→E

Experiment with these when you have some spare time. However, remember to confine your use of some of the more unusual symbols to your own work – do not use them in examinations!

2.12 Note the following information which will be needed for Exercise 2D:

> Braunsweig's book was written in 1527
> The oil burned in Roman Catholic mass is frankincense

2.13 Referring to the instructions on inserting symbols, key in the following text which is to accompany diagrams, copying the symbols exactly as shown. Use superscript/subscript for raised/lowered characters.

$A_1B = A_1B_1 = C_2B_2 = C_3B_3 = C_4B_4$
Invar expansion coefficient $= < 1 \times 10^{-6}$ per °C
Elinvar expansion coefficient $= 8 \times 10^{-6}$ per °C
The device is indexed through 30° or $^1/_{12}$ of a circle
If a_A and a_B were equal in value, then a_R would be zero as cos (180/2) = 0
SI is an abbreviation of Système International d'Unités
$y = 3.29x + 13.97$
Gauge accuracy can be taken as ±10%
Exchange rates - ¥197.25/US$1.635/NZ$2.6025/£1.00

2.14 Check your work very carefully against the above text and correct any errors. Save your work using the file name **EX2C** and print one copy.

2.15 Open the document **EX2B** if it is not already on screen. Save as **EX2D**. Make the following changes to the document format:

▶ Change the document line length to 13.5cm ($5\frac{1}{4}$ in)
▶ Change the main text to left justified
▶ Change the header alignment to right aligned
▶ Change the first two paragraphs to single line spacing.

2.16 Add the following text to the document as the second paragraph under the heading **PERFUMES OF ARABIA**. Copy the text as shown; do not correct the spelling.

Braunsweig's work in _____, 'The Vertuose Boke of Distyllacyon of the Waters of all Maner of Herbes' gives us the following quotation which demonstrates the respect afforded to 'herbes' at that time:

Indent at left — "Lerne the hygh and mervelous vertue of herbes ... use the effectes with reverence, and give thankes to the maker celestyall." — Indent at right

2.17 Add the following text to the document after the last paragraph:

<u>FROM AGE TO AGE</u>

The history of mans use of plants for medicine, food and cosmetics (perfume) go back to the earliest civilisations, from distillation in the Indus valley 3,000 years BC, through the Middle Ages where herbs were widely used in the household. (An illustration from 'Das Kerüterbuch oder Herbarius' in 1534 shows herbs being placed in a linen chest to scent the linen and also probably to keep away moths!)

Some practices remain to day. For example, in Tibetan temples, sprigs of juniper are burned for purification and _____ is used during Roman Catholic masses'. [Theraputic and religious] factor have frequently been combined in this way.

Most medicines and drugs, whether synthetic or 'natural', can be toxic and it is therefore vital that correct procedures are followed in their use. One important consideration is to ensure that the botanical name for a plant is used rather than the common name. Examples of these, related to some of the plants mentioned in this document, is given below:

Remember: some information for this document was given at 2.12

1   Rosemary - *Rosmarin officinalis*
2   Lavender - *Lavandula angustifolia*
3   Cinnamon – *Cinnamon zeylanicum*
4   Myrrh - *Commaphora myrrha* *[MYRRHA]*
~~8~~7   Ginger - *Zingiber officinale*
~~8~~5   Sandalwood - *Santalum album*
~~7~~6   Cedar – *Cedrus atlantica*

Ironically, just as the effectiveness of herbal medicines and aromatic therapys began to be proved by scientific methods, ~~the increased significance off technology and~~ the expanding synthetic drugs industry, ~~which placed more emphasis on the 'professional' approach,~~ lead to a decline in the use of 'natural' remedies.

~~In 1928,~~ a French chemist, René-Maurice Gattefossé, discovered the [3] the exceptional healing properties of the essential oil of lavender when he burnt his hand in the laboratory. ~~Many other examples of this type and more~~ *research* Recent ~~discoveries~~ have brought complimentary therapies/nearer to allopathic medicine and the ~~two~~ disciplines now often work together to great benefitt.

Such as homoeopathy, acupuncture, reflexology and aromatherapy

[HOMOEOPATHY]

[3] *in 1928*

2.18 Use the spelling and grammar tool to check your work, and proofread it yourself as well. If you find any errors, correct them. Resave the document and print one copy.

2.19 Exit the program if you have finished working, or continue straight on to the next unit.

▶ Producing business documents

By the end of Unit 3 you should have learnt how to:

▶ produce a business letter and a memorandum on pre-printed forms and templates using open punctuation and fully blocked style, with postdating and enclosure marks for multiple enclosures

▶ confirm facts by locating information from another document and including it where indicated

Note: Although Word 97 has an in-built Letter Wizard facility, it is not entirely suitable for RSA examination purposes.

Business documents – letters and memos

In the RSA Text Processing Stage III Part 1 examination you will be expected to produce a business letter and a memorandum either by printing onto a pre-printed form, or by using a template file. You will have learnt most of the requirements already at Stages I and II, but some details are repeated here as a reminder and for ease of reference.

Pre-printed forms or template files

As in Stages I and II, in the Stage III examination you will be asked to print business documents using either a pre-printed form or a template file stored on the computer. Refer back to either of the first two books of this series if you need to refresh your memory on this topic.

Multiple enclosures

In the Stage III examination you should read the text carefully to check if there is more than one enclosure. If there is only one enclosure, indicate this by typing **Enc** at the end of the letter or memo. If there is more than one enclosure you must type **Encs**. Failure to indicate multiple enclosures will result in penalties.

Page numbering

Second and subsequent pages of a letter or memo must be numbered.

Postdating

You should always date a letter or a memo with the date of typing, unless there is a specific instruction to do otherwise. There may be occasions when you need to postdate a business document – check the instructions carefully and enter the appropriate date.

Confirming facts

You will be asked to insert information that can be found in one document into another document. (At work you would be expected to consult paper files, computer databases, etc.) Take notice of the text as you are keying in. This way, it will be easier and quicker to locate and select the correct piece of information to make your document accurate.

Routing of copies

It is normal practice for the sender to keep one copy of a letter or memo for reference. Additional copies may be required for other people and this is usually indicated at the foot of the document, eg:

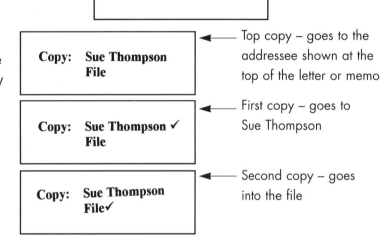

The routing indication is inserted at the bottom of the document (under any enclosure mark), eg:

When all the copies of the document have been printed, it is normal practice to indicate the destination of each copy by ticking, or underlining in coloured pen, or by using a highlighting pen.

Memorandum layout

A memorandum (memo) is a document sent 'internally' to convey information to people who work in the same organisation. At the top of the document, it is customary to enter **From** whom the document is being sent, **To** whom it is being sent, and also to include a **Reference**, the **Date** of sending and usually a **subject heading**. There is no complimentary close on a memo.

You should always insert a date – either the date of typing or a postdated date if specified. Some people like to sign or initial their memos but this is not necessary. Organisations have different ways of aligning and setting out the items on the memo. Two acceptable versions are shown in the examples in Figure 3.1.

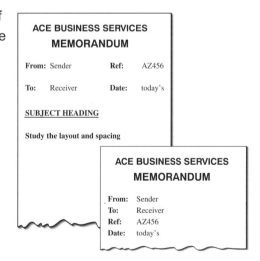

Figure 3.1 Memorandum layouts

Business letter layout

A business letter is written on behalf of an organisation and is printed or typed on the organisation's own letterhead. An attractive letterhead gives a good impression of the organisation and contains all the relevant details, for example, telephone, fax numbers and e-mail addresses. Only the name and address of the addressee (recipient) of the letter have to be typed because the sender's details are already printed on the letterhead. The company's letterhead may be stored as a template file (blueprint) on your computer – you can recall it whenever you need to complete a company letter.

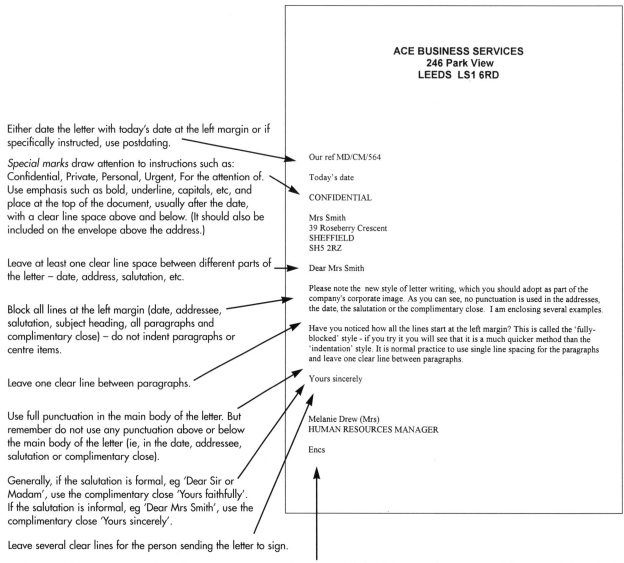

Either date the letter with today's date at the left margin or if specifically instructed, use postdating.

Special marks draw attention to instructions such as: Confidential, Private, Personal, Urgent, For the attention of. Use emphasis such as bold, underline, capitals, etc, and place at the top of the document, usually after the date, with a clear line space above and below. (It should also be included on the envelope above the address.)

Leave at least one clear line space between different parts of the letter – date, address, salutation, etc.

Block all lines at the left margin (date, addressee, salutation, subject heading, all paragraphs and complimentary close) – do not indent paragraphs or centre items.

Leave one clear line between paragraphs.

Use full punctuation in the main body of the letter. But remember do not use any punctuation above or below the main body of the letter (ie, in the date, addressee, salutation or complimentary close).

Generally, if the salutation is formal, eg 'Dear Sir or Madam', use the complimentary close 'Yours faithfully'. If the salutation is informal, eg 'Dear Mrs Smith', use the complimentary close 'Yours sincerely'.

Leave several clear lines for the person sending the letter to sign.

The letter shown reads:

ACE BUSINESS SERVICES
246 Park View
LEEDS LS1 6RD

Our ref MD/CM/564

Today's date

CONFIDENTIAL

Mrs Smith
39 Roseberry Crescent
SHEFFIELD
SH5 2RZ

Dear Mrs Smith

Please note the new style of letter writing, which you should adopt as part of the company's corporate image. As you can see, no punctuation is used in the addresses, the date, the salutation or the complimentary close. I am enclosing several examples.

Have you noticed how all the lines start at the left margin? This is called the 'fully-blocked' style - if you try it you will see that it is a much quicker method than the 'indentation' style. It is normal practice to use single line spacing for the paragraphs and leave one clear line between paragraphs.

Yours sincerely

Melanie Drew (Mrs)
HUMAN RESOURCES MANAGER

Encs

Enclosure marks (Enc or Encs) indicate that one or more item(s) should be included with the main document. Read the text carefully to check if there are multiple enclosures. If an enclosure is found to be missing, appropriate action can then be taken. The enclosure mark is usually placed at the end of a letter or memo with at least one clear line space above and below it. When using the open style of punctuation the mark Enc or Encs should not have a full stop after it.

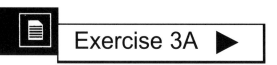

Exercise 3A ▶

3.1 Create a standard file for a business memorandum head. You will need to recall this memo template file later in this unit and in other units of this book. Starting a new file, key in the following text, centring both lines and using the text emphasis indicated. (If the Algerian font is not available on your computer, choose another from the Font menu.)

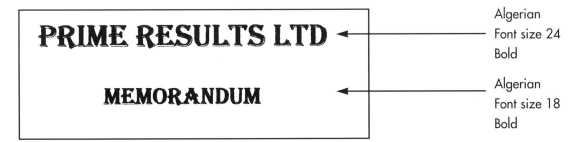

Algerian
Font size 24
Bold

Algerian
Font size 18
Bold

3.2 Save your document using filename **Memotemplate**. Close the file – you do not need to print at this stage.

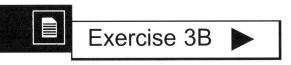

3.3 Create a standard file for a business letterhead. You will need to recall this letter template file later in this unit and in other units of this book. Starting a new file, key in the following text, centring all lines and using the text emphasis indicated.

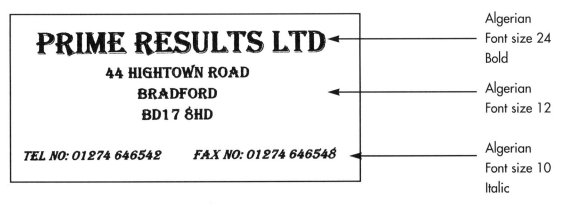

Algerian
Font size 24
Bold

Algerian
Font size 12

Algerian
Font size 10
Italic

3.4 Save your document using filename **Lettertemplate**. Close the file – you do not need to print at this stage.

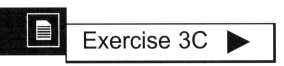

3.5 Starting with a clear screen, retrieve the **Lettertemplate** file which you saved at step 3.4. Using Times New Roman, font size 10, key in the rest of the letter details, following any specific instructions and correction signs. Remember to expand any abbreviations. Use the spelling and grammar tool to check your work, and proofread it yourself as well. If you find any errors, correct them. Save the document using the filename **EX3C** and print one copy.

Your ref 372/TRM

Dr Ms B——

(Please use the heading WORK EXPERIENCE SCHEME.
Mark the letter URGENT)

(Year Eleven)

In response to yr enquiry about work experience opps at this co for ~~fifthyr~~ students, I am delighted to advise you that we are ~~prepared~~ able to offer a total of five one-week placements in different depts. These ~~will~~ departments are ~~include~~ marketing, personnel, sales, computer services and finance.

Obviously we will rely on the school to match each individuals' career aspirations to ~~aspirations/with~~ the appropriate job placement. [As one of the largest employers in the area we recognise the value of investing in young people who may well be our employees of ~~tomorrow~~ the future. We hope ~~sincerely~~ that the placement will provide your students with a valuable insight into the needs of buisness. (and it's various functions)

I enclose a number of leaflets and info sheets which provides some background details about the orgs' ~~activities~~ activities. I will also ask each Head of Dept to contact you seperately with an outline of the activities yr students can expect to undertake in their ~~time~~ ~~week~~ with us

~~Each~~ Students will be assigned a 'mentor' who will be responsable for their daily workload and personal welfare. We will arrange an element of work shadowing with ~~of~~ senior employees so that the students can devellop an aprecaition of some of the more complex activities in the dept. // I trust these arrangements will be satisfactory and trust that you will contact me again shortly with a suggested start date.

Yrs sncly
Marie Potter
Personnel Manager

Letter to Ms Joan Brauthwaite,
Silverdale Grammar School,
Silverdale Way, SHIPLEY, SH3 4TU

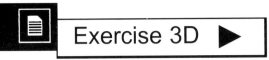
3.6 Starting with a clear screen, retrieve the **Memotemplate** file which you saved at step 3.2. Key in the rest of the memo details, following any specific instructions and correction signs. Remember to expand any abbreviations. Use the spelling and grammar tool to check your work, and proofread it yourself as well. If you find any errors, correct them. Save the document using the filename **EX3D** and print one copy.

Memo from Marie P— to Zafar Hussain. Ref MP/31CP

Following yr recent approval of the proposed work expereince scheme for school students, I have arranged for a Year Eleven student from S— G— School to spend a one-week placement with your staff in the Finance Dept. The placement will begin on Monday (give date of fourth Monday of next month).

I would be grateful if you could draw up a list of varied activities which the student will participate in and forward these directly to the school (a contact name and address is attached on a copy of their letter). Please include an element of work shadowing with a senior member of staff - I can reccomend Jane Griffiths as she has done this kind of thing before. [you will also need to arrange for a mentor to look after the pupil for the week that he/she is visiting us. The mentor will be asked to complete an evaluation a report at the end of the week reviewing the students achievements (and) progress. —

This should be counter-signed by yourself along with any further comments you may wish to make

As there will be five student on placement with us I will arrange for them all to have an induction - this will include a tour of the buildings and a meeting with the Health and Safety officer; [If their is any aspect of the placement you would like to discus with me, please do not hesitate to contact me on Extension 351.

first thing on Mon morning

3.7 Starting with a clear screen, retrieve the **Lettertemplate** file which you saved at step 3.4. Key in the rest of the letter details below, following any specific instructions and correction signs. Remember to expand any abbreviations. Use the spelling and grammar tool to check your work, and proofread it yourself as well. If you find any errors, correct them. Save the document using the filename **EX3E** and print one copy.

Letter to Dale, Green & Winters Ltd   432 Newberry Industrial Estate   Newberry   LEEDS   LS3 9GB
Our ref   HB/TDL
Use the heading CONFERENCE – EMPLOYEE SATISFACTION IN THE MILLENIUM

Your ref   556/BG

Dr Sir or Madam

I would like to draw yr attention to a special conference which we are holding on Wed, (give date of third Wed of next month). The conference will focus on employee ~~feelings~~ sattisfaction as a key corporate priority for bus sucess.

A major European Research Study has shown that altho' competitive levels ~~for~~ customer service are more likely to be acheived ~~there~~ with sattisfied employees, their are some significant trend of worker dissatisfaction. British workers are shown to be among the most discontented producing the lowest or ~~second~~ third ✓ lowest favourable response in a significant number of questionnaire categories;

pan-European
Statistics point to a/decline in employee perceptions of the security of their employment, with uk employees feeling less secure in their jobs than employees anywhere else in Europe. British attitudes towards the org and the efficiency of their work is said to be among the least favourable in europe and likely to have a ~~very big impact~~ profound effect on the employment contract. The full findings of this research, which includes refs to over 500 cos, will be presented at the conference (free of charge).

However, the main topic of the conference will be to introduce (problems) to these (solutions), with a positive framework for stimulating bus growth and financial stability thro' greater investment in human ~~resources~~ resources. [In addition ~~to the number of~~ ~~eminent speaker's who are~~ leading european who will be speaking at the conference authorities in this area], there will be a number of workshops where you will be able to exchange info and network with other bus managers who have a similar interest in the future of their workforce —

Their will also be an opportunity to discuss yr co needs+ with our specialised Human Resource Consultancy team.

I attach a conference cat giving ~~full~~ comprehensive details (/) of the days' events, along with a map showing how to get to the venue. A ~~application~~ booking form is also enclosed with the pack, Overnight acomodation is available on request.

As places is limited, we would reccomend an early booking to avoid disappointment.

Yrs ffly

Howard Benson
Conference Organiser

on an individual basis

Mark the letter : FOR THE ATTENTION OF THE HUMAN RESOURCES MANAGER

3.8 Starting with a clear screen, retrieve the **Memotemplate** file which you saved at step 3.2. Key in the rest of the memo details below, following any specific instructions and correction signs. Remember to expand any abbreviations. Use the spelling and grammar tool to check your work, and proofread it yourself as well. If you find any errors, correct them. Save the document using the filename **EX3F** and print one copy.

Memo from H __ B __ , Conference Organiser
to Hélène de Courcy, Public Relations Officer
Ref HB/342sw

Use the same heading as the letter in Exercise 3E and emphasise with bold

Top plus two copies Indicate routing - one to Marie Potter, one to File. Print out the copy to Marie Potter only.

The campaign to publicise the above conference is under way. I enclose a sample copy of the standard letter which I have sent out to all the Human Resource Managers on our mailing database. // it has occurred to me that we may need some additional copies of the conference info pack. Please can you arrange to have sufficient ~~copies~~ quantities printed as soon as poss.

Can you also order some name badges from the same mfr we used previously. My sec will be able to let you have there name and address from our conference correspondance file if you do not have all their details.

(in any new publicity material)

Also, can you check that the conference prices are updated immed. I will arranged for some new photographs and brief biographies of the speakers to be made available for the exhibition stands. [I have also made ~~some~~ arrangements with M __ P __ , Personnel Manager, for someone to assist you on a temp basis with the administration conference.

3.9 Exit the program if you have finished working, or continue straight on to the next unit.

unit 4 ▶ Consolidation 1

By the end of Unit 4, you should have revised and practised all the techniques and skills needed for the RSA Text Processing Stage III Part 1 award, and additional techniques and skills which will help you in the workplace and in preparation for the Part 2 awards.

Look at your Progress Review Checklist and at your completed exercises to remind yourself of what you have learnt so far and to identify any weaknesses. Then complete the following exercises as revision.

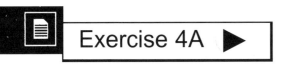

Exercise 4A ▶

4.1 Starting a new document, key in the following text which is later to form part of a larger report. Use an unjustified right margin and insert page numbering at the bottom centre. Use double line spacing throughout.

EMPLOYMENT ← (centre, underline and bold)

<u>General Comments</u>

Recent economical trends ~~show~~ give an encouraging picture although the Low Beck area suffered a major blow in the loss of over _____ jobs when Analogical Systems cut its work force last month.

A new superstore opened in Pine Valley and it is anticapated that the immed succes of (It should) this venture will have a permenant impact on shopping patterns in the Valley. ~~also~~ attract~~ing~~ shoppers from a wider area to experience the other amenities of the ~~area~~ town and bring the prosperity necy for the continued devellopment of small business enterprises. (As a matter of intrest, the store was opened by Herr Jürgen Freiwald, the 'Mayor' of Megèle, our twin town in Switzerland.)

broader   (regeneration)
Looking [to ~~wider~~ issues] and [further afield], we can report that work is going ahead on a final bid for funds to be submitted to the Goverment Office in ~~two~~ month's time. A poss decision is expected buy the end of the yr. In conjunction with this bid, the Council is very much involved ~~with~~ in the preperation of a Delivery Plan for a training and employment
the
initiative designed to help, unemployed to obtain work & [relevant] re-training to local industrial and comercial needs.

SOURCES (Please move to end of document)
1 Average house price: Castle Building Society
2 Unemployed claimants: Office # for National Statistics
3 Migration to and from borough: NHS Central Register

the
1 for Yorkshire &/Humber ← (footnote in font size 10 please)

Facts and Figures *(← use this style for all headings)*

A summary of the employment info is given below: *(definitely)*

- Despite the fact that numbers employ*ed* in manufacturing continued to drop – over 7,400 fewer in 1996 than in 1994 – the sector still *definitely* had an important role in the local economy accouting for a higher porportion of employees than at county, national and regional levels.

- Service sector employment rose by *8*,300 between 1994 and 1996.

- Part-time employment fell after 1994; full-time employment rose by nearly 4,100.

- In 1996, the total number of employees in the borough was estimated to be 84,550, over 4,250 more than in 1994.

- The average house prices rose in 1994 to £61,567 but fell in 1996 to £58,755. [• The trend towards increased migration out of the borough changed to a *positive* balance of ✓ 30 ~~migrating~~ *moving* into the borough in 1995.

Every ward *now* ~~have~~ increased levels of unemployment compared ~~to~~ *with* (give *this* ~~same~~ month last year, eg March 1998). The rising trend levelled out over the winter months.

Sector Changes
The number of Service Sector employes increased by ↑ ⅙ over the last 15 yrs, ~~and by~~ ⅓ over the last three yrs.
(compared with)

There has been a contrasting decline of over 8,000 jobs in manufactureing (⅕ of ~~the total~~) over the same 3 years. The construction industry, however, have suffered the largest dicline – allmost ~~½~~ half (5/12) the number of employees compared with 3 yrs ago. *(retain as a word)*

(retain fractions in this section, except for:)

(Over 350 jobs lost at how Beck)

4.2 Use the spelling and grammar tool to check your work, and proofread it yourself as well. If you find any errors, correct them. Save the document using the filename **EX4A** and print one copy.

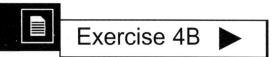

Exercise 4B ▶

4.3 Open the document you saved as **EX4A** unless it is already on screen. The document is to be incorporated into a larger report. Please make the following format changes so that the styles of the separate parts of the report are consistent:

▶ Use justified margins
▶ Use a left margin of 4cm (1½ in) and a right margin of 1.5cm (approximately ½ in)
▶ Change the position of the page numbers to the bottom right of the page and start the page numbering at page 6
▶ Move the header text to the footer and change it to Times New Roman, font size 10, italic and left aligned
▶ Add the following right-aligned header: **Employment Trends**
▶ Change to single line spacing except where otherwise indicated
▶ Move the paragraph headed **Sector Changes** to come immediately after the **General Comments** section and retain double line spacing for this paragraph.

4.4 Insert the following text before the **Facts and Figures** section.

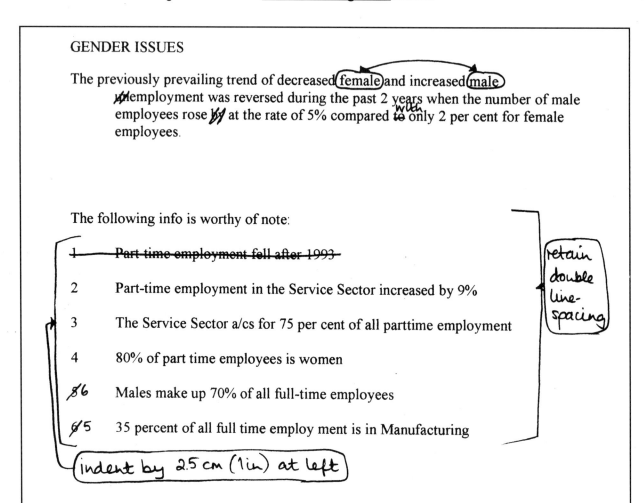

GENDER ISSUES

The previously prevailing trend of decreased female and increased male unemployment was reversed during the past 2 years when the number of male employees rose by at the rate of 5% compared to only 2 per cent for female employees.

The following info is worthy of note:

1   Part-time employment fell after 1993

2   Part-time employment in the Service Sector increased by 9%

3   The Service Sector a/cs for 75 per cent of all parttime employment

4   80% of part time employees is women

6   Males make up 70% of all full-time employees

5   35 percent of all full time employ ment is in Manufacturing

retain double line-spacing

indent by 2.5 cm (1in) at left

4.5   Add the following footnote symbols and footnote text to the section headed <u>Facts and Figures</u>.

<u>Facts and Figures</u>[1]

leave a clear line between each item

A summary of the employment information is given below:

- In 1996, the total number of employees in the borough was estimated to be 84,550, over 4,250 more than in 1994.
- Despite the fact that numbers employed in manufacturing[2] continued to drop – over 7,400 fewer in 1996 than in 1994 – the sector still definitely had an important role in the local economy accounting for a higher proportion of employees than at county, regional and national levels.
- Service sector employment rose by 8,300 between 1994 and 1996.
- Part-time employment fell after 1994; full-time employment rose by nearly 4,100.
- The average house price rose in 1994 to £61,567 but fell in 1996 to £58,755.
- The trend towards increased migration out of the borough changed to a positive balance of 30 migrating into the borough in 1995.

Every ward now has increased levels of unemployment compared to (same month last year). The rising trend levelled out over the winter months.

indent by 2.5 cm (1 in) at left

1 Analysis excludes the primary sector as reliable data is not available

2 Following re-classification of industries census figures prior to 1995 have been re-based

footnotes in font size 10 please

4.6   Check your work on screen against the printout check at the back of the book. Correct any errors, save as **EX4B** and print a copy of your work. Exit the program if you have finished working or continue straight on to the next unit.

▶ Examination Practice 1

By the end of Unit 5, you should have completed a mock examination for the RSA Text Processing Stage III Part 1 award.

RSA Text Processing Stage III Part 1

This examination assesses your ability to apply advanced text processing and production skills to produce, from handwritten and typewritten draft, a variety of standard business documents. The award demonstrates competence to the level demanded by NVQ Administration Level 3.

The examination lasts for $1\frac{1}{4}$ hours and you must complete 3 documents using a word processor or a typewriter. Printing is done outside this time.

Examinations are carried out in registered centres and are marked by RSA examiners. The centre will give you instructions regarding stationery.

Letters must be produced on letterheads (either pre-printed or template) and memos may be produced on pre-printed forms, by keying in entry details or by use of a template.

Examination hints

When sitting your examination:

▶ you may use a manual prepared by the centre or the software manufacturer
▶ you must put your name, centre number and document number on each document
▶ check your work very carefully before printing – proofread and spellcheck
▶ assemble your printouts in the correct order at the end of the examination.

You are now ready to try a mock examination for Text Processing Stage III Part 1. Take care and good luck!

The list of assessment criteria for this examination is long and detailed. To be sure that you have reached the required standard to be entered for an examination, you need to work through several past papers and have these 'marked' by a tutor or assessor who is qualified and experienced in this field.

Results

▶ If your finished work has 6 faults or fewer, you will be awarded a distinction
▶ If your finished work has between 7 and 17 faults, you will be awarded a pass.

Results are sent to the centre where you sit your examination.

Dr Mrs Wall

Letter to Mrs D S Wall   35 Winter Grove
BITTERTON Leicestershire   LE19 6 PV
Our ref PF/Wall/464. Please use
heading PURCHASE OF SQUIRREL VIEW
SOUTHLANDS LANE BITTERTON

Further to our telephone conversation, I am writing to inform you
that I have now perused the documents which have been forwarded
① by the ~~Vendors'~~ Purchasers' solicitors and I am pleased to report that they
appear to be ~~in order~~ satisfactory.   One or two minor queries arose and
my assistant is to request further info.↴ I have despatched
an application for Local Search and would ~~ap~~ anticipate
that the result should be recieved within 2 or 3 weeks.

By that ~~time~~ date, we should have instructions (also) from yr
mortgage lender. As discussed, I enclose the fixtures,
fittings and contents ~~list~~ for your attention.

I know that you are ~~anxious~~ keen to proceed as quickly
as possible and as soon as we have acess to all the necy
info, I will contact you to make an appt for us to go
through all the documents together. ~~At that time~~, I will
then take yr detailed instructions regarding exchange
of Contracts and completion. // I will be on holiday for
one week from (give next Monday's date) but my sec, Gemma white,
(Anne Müller,) will be able to answer any queries
which you may have. Anne or Gemma will telephone
you if necy.   Please do not hesitate to contact
Yrs sincly   ~~them~~ either of these members of
              my staff if any problems arise in
              my absence.

Paula Ferera
LICENSED CONVEYANCER

Information for Document 3:
① Telephone 0800-9786543
② £750 if sale and purchase involved.

Memo from Paula F___ to Anne Müller.
Ref PF/Wall/464.   Please mark URGENT

The purchase of S__ V__ , S__ L__ , B__ by
Mrs Wall is going ahead subject to a satisfactory
response from the mortgage lender, North East Building
Society, and 2 minor queries arising from the
documents received from the Vendors' solicitors. [The
prospective purchaser of Mrs Walls property at
35 Winter Grove are ~~putting some pressure on her~~
pressing for an early completion date, as the
co by whom he is employed relocated to the area
some months ago and / the ~~re~~ resulting ~~expense~~ (unfortunately)
(expence) and (inconvenence) of travelling long
distances, although temp, is definately causing
severe difficulty. // I have assured Mrs Wall that
we will do our best to expedite matters. To this end,
◀ I would be grateful if you would acknoledge all
                    letters
✓ ~~communications~~ from this client and from Stone & Co
immed they are received.

We require clarification on two matters from Stone
& Co:, with ref to the boundary fence on the north
and east sides of the land, and the proximity
of an electricity sub-station to the south.
(In my absence,) please obtain the documents from
Gemma and contact the Vendors solicitors as a
matter of urgency.

Double line spacing except where indicated

THE HOUSE TRANSFER BOND ← *centre this heading*

Vital information for yr protection ← *CAPS*

Most people remark after moveing house that they will never repeat the excercise! The vast ~~many~~ marjority of house sales, [removals] [and] [purchases] goes according to plan but, dispite this fact, it is a very stress~~ful~~ time for ~~everyone~~ at concerned ✓

← ———————— THE ~~HOUSE TRANSFER~~ BOND *when they instruct us to act for them.*

The HOUSE TRANSFER BOND is an insurance shceme available for buyer's and

sellers. If something does go wrong, the legal costs still have to be paid and you can

be left out off pocket with nothing to show for it. In order to help you, we

automatically issue an insurance certificate to all our clients. This covers you for up

fall

to £75 in re spect of our legal costs if the transaction ~~fa~~ through before exchange of

contracts. However, by paying an additional premium of £30*, the amount of cover

can be increased to £400** usually suffcent to cover all legal costs incured.

well take care of your bills. No complicated claim forms are necy. All we ask is that your pay the additional premium within 10 days of giving us your instruction to act for you.

* £55 if ~~we are~~ you have instructed us in a sale + a purchase

** £___ if sale and purchase involved

YOUR COVER

The cover applies to buyers if/

✗ (the seller withdraws

The cover applies to sellers if

✗ (the buyer withdraws for any reason expect:

3 ✗ because of a defect in your property

2 ✗ following an adverse survey on your property

1 ✗ an unreasonable delay on yr part.

WHAT COULD GO WRONG?

You ~~could~~ arrive at yr new home to find the
floor flooded because ~~of~~ the ~~seller~~ vendor disconnected
the dishwasher and damaged the plumbing.

The vendors removal firm did not turn up and they
are still in the house so you can't move in.

Legal problems mean the completion is
delayed and you have nowhere to stay in the
meantime.

The vendors cannot (or will not) move out

Single line spacing

What do you do then?

Simply telephone us/ on 0800 _____ we are open 7 days a week,
twenty-four hours a day. Our experts will solve
yr problems: booking hotels locating reliable
tradesmen, (organising transport,) recovering your car/
The ~~HOME~~ HOUSE TRANSFER BOND is the solution to your
problems. Make sure you're covered.

unit 6

► Advanced word processing

By the end of Unit 6, you will have revised many of the formatting techniques you learnt at the intermediate level. You should also have learnt how to:

► paginate a document following instructions
► follow a house style for the production of documents
► locate and select information to be included in a document.

The techniques for revision listed below are included in Exercise 6A. Before starting the exercise, refresh your memory by referring to the alphabetical glossary at the back of this book (pages 209–218) and ask your tutor to explain anything you are unsure about.

► Multi-page documents, widows/orphans
► Copy/move blocks of text, sort text in a list, search and replace text, move around the document – quick methods.

Pagination

In RSA Stage I and Stage II examinations, you were expected to be able to insert page breaks in documents in sensible places, ensuring that a new page started at a position in the text which did not leave fewer than two lines of text either at the foot of one page or at the top of another (widows and orphans). In Stage III examinations, you will be required to insert page breaks as instructed in the document even if this leaves a lot of space on the page.

Insert page breaks by pressing **Ctrl + ↵** (**return/enter**) in the appropriate position.

Following a house style

In the workplace, you may find that you are expected to produce documents to a certain format – eg margins, layout, enumeration, fonts etc. This format may differ from what you have learnt in this book or elsewhere. In addition to pre-printed letterheads and memos, your company may have a logo which appears on all communications. In large organisations, there will be an information or procedures manual setting out the standards required or a template stored on the network. In smaller organisations, you may have to look at previously-prepared documents on file and take note of the style used.

Exercise 6A ▶

6.1 Key in the following article for a staff magazine using the following format:

▶ Justified text
▶ Equal left and right margins
▶ Equal top and bottom margins
▶ Times New Roman, font size 12
▶ Single line spacing
▶ Blocked paragraphs
▶ Left-aligned headers using Times New Roman, font size 10
▶ Number all pages at the bottom left
▶ Centre the main heading and use capitals, bold and underscore.

Header: Investing in the community

Jeremiah's Heritage

Building on the philosophy of the founder of our co, the tradition of philanthropy continue to play an important part of in the culture of the Modern-day org

Jeremiah Turnbull's ideals are still converted into practical support for the local community and enviroment wherever the org operates in the world.

Copy to ✳ at end of doc

Over the past 150yrs, the development of the co has been linked to:

The Arts
Community welfare
Housing
Health
Education
Training
Environment
Technology

Sort into alphabetical order and indent 1.3cm (½ in) from left

In the competitive and proffesional enviroment of today, corporate giviing needs to be

well structured and based on efforts and themes with real impact. It is vital that we

never loose site of the fact that it is our employees who create the wealth, and that we

act on behalf of our share holders.

✳✳

Page 2 starts here

Jeremiahs' concerns regarding the work force at his Union Road mill in the middle of the last century made him a pioneer amongst employers of the time, many of whom where less than desireable characters.

The village he biult stands proud today as a symbol of community life. Every

weekend you will see the Central Hall and the Church, which he desinged with such

care, hosting social activities of all kinds and providing a focus for the local

~~people~~
✓ community.

In fact, he was probably the first industrialist to deserve the IiP award!

Move to **

At least 1.5% of our pre-tax profit is distributed in cash, in time or in kind to orgs, or communities or projects which reflect our aims and which are proven to be professionally managed.

In 1997 £6 million was contributed in cash

Educational involvement takes the form of national and local links with the aim of promoting ~~providing~~ the skills, [attitudes] and [understanding] necy for industry today and in the future. [Our priorities include:

(indent as before)
Curriculum materials
Teacher support packs
✓ Management training (Education)
School governor courses for our employees
Preparation for IiP ~~awards~~ standards ✓
Teacher placements
Student placements

(alphabetical order please)

(Page 3 starts here)

(Local support continues) J_T_ would be proud of the fact that ↓ only a few miles from his original mill in the Dean Basin. The aim is to bring the water of the estuary and river to a state where it is once again clean enough to sustain fish.

Already it is poss to see some encouraging signs such as the return of bird life.

Insert info regarding environment here please when we get it! Print draft now.

* Copy sentence here from first para

6.2   Save your document as **EX6A**. Check your work with the printout at the back of the book. If you find any errors, correct them and print a copy of your document.

Locating and selecting information

In RSA examinations, you are often required to insert information which is either contained in the same document, another document, or given to you by the invigilator. In the Word Processing Stage III Part 2 examination, the examination paper includes a **resource sheet** which can be detached from the main documents. The resource sheet contains information you will need to produce the documents, together with other information which is not needed. It is up to you to select the information which is needed and incorporate it into the documents in the correct positions as instructed.

It will help if you read the document you are working on very carefully so that you have an understanding of the topic. It will then be easier for you to extract the required information.

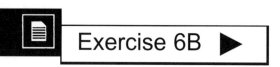

Exercise 6B ▶

6.3 Open the document **EX6A**. Save it as **EX6B** and make the amendments shown below. Refer to the **resource sheet** for Unit 6 (page 54) to find the necessary information.

Insert the following text after the listed items on Page 2:

Six of our sites are offering support ∧in conjunction with the U— B— l— programme: (in the form of workshops)

Please list the sites in alphabetical order here and indent consistently as other lists

Business simulations helps students to experience co decision-making skills and management processes. We are involved in ——, —— and —— projects throughout the country.

Please add correct project names to this sentence

Insert the following paragraph before the last paragraph of the document on Page 3:

The G— T— gives over — school lectures, —— field trips, and — weeks of residential courses in a typical year.

Please put correct figures in this sentence

6.4 Insert the following text into the document on screen (**EX6B**) at the point indicated by the symbol # in the manuscript for Exercise 6A (page 49).

Our stake holders [expect] [also] to be kept informed about our environmental policys and performance. ⌐In addition to reassurance regarding the wise distribution of profits,⌐

National organisations such as The Green Trust and The Stewardship Foundation benefits from our involvement on a partnership basis. Our support enables school lectures & field trips to be offered free of charge or at very reduced rates (IiP again!). We are also working towards the establishment of standards to ensure consumers have the right to chose products from sustainable sources.

Insert this text after ---
the return of bird life
and before The Green Trust

Please change IiP to
Investors in People
throughout document

Please change the header to become a footer at bottom right of page

Change 1st and last paras of document to double spacing

6.5 Check your work with the printout check at the back of the book. If you find any errors, correct them. Resave the document and print one copy.

Working in a specialist environment

If you are working in a specialist environment such as legal or medical, you may find that it is still the custom in your organisation to:

▶ Use the word **Re:** before the subject heading on letters and memos, for example:

> Re: Sale of property at 30 Vale View
> Re: Jenna BLACKFORD, DOB 21.07.92

▶ Have letters signed on behalf of the organisation but without identifying the signatory by name and designation, for example:

(No signatory name)

(No designation of signatory)

The reference at the top of the letter will usually identify the person who is dealing with matter, eg:

Our ref: PRW/JL/908978
This matter is being dealt with by P R Walton

Exercise 6C ▶

6.6   Open the document stored as **Lettertemplate** and change the alignment and format of the printed heading as shown below:

▶ Change the left margin to 3cm ($1\frac{1}{4}$ in) and the right margin to 2cm ($\frac{3}{4}$ in)
▶ Change the alignment to right aligned
▶ Put the telephone and fax numbers on separate lines.

The printed heading should now look like this:

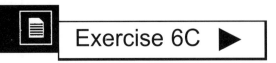

PRIME RESULTS LTD
44 HIGHTOWN ROAD
BRADFORD
BD17 8HD

6.7   Key in the letter below keeping to the following house style:

▶ Fully-blocked style with open punctuation
▶ Left aligned/ragged right margin
▶ Times New Roman, font size 12
▶ Subject heading: initial capitals; bold and underscore; font size 12
▶ Reference: author's initials/wp operator's initials (you)/Marketing/Ext 5056
▶ Complimentary close: **Yours faithfully**
                            PRIME RESULTS LTD

◀──────────── 4 clear lines for signature

Jennie Burton-Derby
MARKETING DIRECTOR

▶ Indicate multiple enclosures and their nature:
Enclosures: *list enclosures*

Our ref

Mrs C Pickard
Small Bus Publications Ltd
(address)
    Mrs P____   ['Prime Time' Staff Magazine]
Dr ~~Ciaran~~
With ref to our telephone conversation earlier this week,
I enclose 2 copies of previous 'Prime Time' publications.
                                                    workers
The magazine is distributed to all our ~~employees~~ quarterly.←

                                              (retain hyphen)
                    es
Our new management team wish to up date the content and design of the magazine to (profile)
appeal to the increasingley younger and more (technologically-minded) staff. Your design
for the new style magazine should incorporate the new co logo as a footer on each page.

[Insert hyphen (-)]

I enclose draught copy of an article entitled
'Jeremiah's Legacy'.←   (Please check this title)
We would like to incorporate photographs of J— T—,
Union Garden Village and schoolchildren enjoying
residential courses [funded partly] by the co. I hope to
discuss final details with you at our /meeting. (next)

I enclose hard copy of the logo, which I ~~think~~ you will
                             computer   understand
be able to scan into yr ~~equipement~~. We look forward
to seeing your designer's ideas at our meeting on
Thursday 24 (next month).

However, if you need ~~any~~ further info in the meantime
(please contact me).

Yrs ~~sincely~~ ffly

[Refer to Resource
Sheet for information]

[Please put Prime Time
in CAPS (PRIME TIME)
wherever it appears
in the letter]

[Ensure letter fits on one page by
adjusting margins if necessary]

6.8 Check your work with the printout check at the back of the book. If you find any errors, correct them. Save as **EX6C** and print one copy. Exit from the program if you have finished working or continue straight on to the next unit.

UNDERSTANDING BRITISH INDUSTRY

WORKSHOPS FOR SENIOR TEACHERS

SITE	DATE
Leamington Spa	24 October
Milton Keynes	25 November
Nottingham	12 December
Sheffield	9 September
Newcastle	26 September
Bury	1 October

BUSINESS SIMULATION PROJECTS

Schools involved in the Northern Region

NAME OF SCHOOL	PROJECT
Berry Road School, Bury	SELECT
St Bartholomew's High School, Bolton	PRISM
Durham Road School, Darnborough	PRISM
Ringway High School, Lentford	PROJECT ENTERPRISE
March Street School, Jarrow	SELECT
Hunckley Road School, Leeds	PROJECT ENTERPRISE
Moorfield Street School, Huddersfield	PRISM

❀❀❀THE GREEN TRUST❀❀❀

Responding to needs:

12,000 letters	2,000 phone calls	1,000 fax enquiries	per year

Providing experience:

10 weeks of residential courses	250 school lectures	25 field trips	per year

FOR ALL YOUR LOCAL PRINTING NEEDS

Precision Printing Plc	Small Business Publications Ltd		Ingley Design and Print
40A Bradshaw Street	First Floor, Wharfe Building		Unit 45
LEEDS	BRADFORD		Cross Lanes Business Park
LS5 8PO	BD2 4TH		SHIPTON SH12 3LK

unit 7

► Advanced text formatting

By the end of Unit 7, you will have revised some of the formatting techniques you learnt at the intermediate level. You should also have learnt how to:

► change font, font size and type of emphasis
► allocate space horizontally and vertically within a document
► format text in newspaper-type columns for the whole document and for a section of a document
► copy text from one document to another using the window option on the menu bar

Changing the font (typeface), font size and type of emphasis

The use of different fonts and font sizes is an effective way of emphasising text in a document. Throughout your work in this book, the main font you have used has been Times New Roman in font size 12. You should know how to increase or decrease the font size and you may have discovered that a range of other font styles is available to you.

Examples

This sentence is shown in Times New Roman font size 14 and italics
This sentence is shown in Courier New font size 10 and bold
<u>This sentence is shown in Arial font size 14 and underlined</u>
<u>This sentence is shown in Arial font size 12, underlined and highlighted</u>
THIS SENTENCE IS SHOWN IN COURIER NEW FONT SIZE 12 AND ALL CAPS
THIS SENTENCE IS SHOWN IN COURIER NEW FONT SIZE 12 AND SMALL CAPS

In RSA Word Processing Stage III Part 2 examinations, you will be asked to change the font style (typeface) and/or the 'pitch' (font size) for a portion of text.

Format fonts ▶

Dialogue box method

Keyboard	Mouse
Press: **Ctrl + D** Select: The **Font** tab	Select: **Font** from the **Format** menu

The Font dialogue box is displayed on screen.

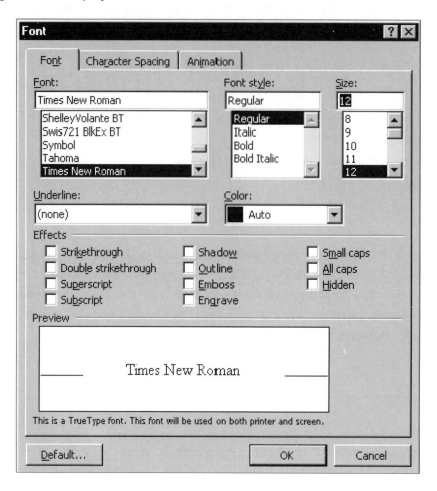

Figure 7.1 Font dialogue box

Select from the options shown below to format the font for selected portions of text:

▶ Select: The font you require from the **Font** list
▶ Select: The font style you require from the **Font style**, **Underline** or **Color** boxes
▶ Select: The font size you require from the **Size** list
▶ Select: The effect you require from the **Effects** list
▶ View: Your selection in the **Preview** box

Keyboard shortcut/mouse method

Format/emphasis	Keyboard	Mouse
Bold	Press: **Ctrl + B**	Click: The **B** **Bold** button
Italics	Press: **Ctrl + I**	Click: The **I** **Italics** button

Underline	Press: **Ctrl + U**	Click: The **U** **Underline** button
Colour		Click: The **A** **Font color** button
Change font	Press: **Ctrl + Shift +** Press: The ↑ and ↓ cursor keys to select a font from the list	Click: The `Times New Roman` **Font** button Select: A font from the drop-down grid
Change font size *Next larger point size:* *Next smaller point size:*	Press: **Ctrl + Shift + P** Press: The ↑ and ↓ cursor keys to select a size from the list Press: **Ctrl +]**, *or* Press: **Ctrl + Shift + >** Press: **Ctrl + [**, *or* Press: **Ctrl + Shift + <**	Click: The `10` **Font size** button Select: A point size from the list
Remove emphasis *(back to plain text)*	Select: The text to change back Press: **Ctrl + Spacebar**	Select: The text to change back Click: The appropriate button again, *or* Select: **Normal** in the **Style** box on the Formatting Tool Bar
Change case *Options:* ▶ *Sentence case* ▶ *lowercase* ▶ *UPPERCASE* ▶ *Title Case* ▶ *tOGGLE cASE*	Select: The text to be changed Press: **Shift + F3** until the required formatting is displayed	Select: The text to be changed Select: **Change case** from the **Format** menu Click: The required case in the **Change Case** dialogue box Click: **OK**
Change to all capitals	Select: The text to be changed Press: **Ctrl + Shift + A** Repeat: The command to reverse the action	Select: The text to be changed Select: **Font** from the **Format** menu Click: **All caps** in the **Effects** section *or* Select: **Change Case** from the **Format** menu Select: **UPPERCASE**
Change to small capitals	Select: The text to be changed Press: **Ctrl + Shift + K** Repeat: The command to reverse the action	Select: The text to be changed Select: **Font** from the **Format** menu Click: **Small caps** in the **Effects** section
Highlight text *(you can only highlight existing text)*		Click: The 🖊 **Highlight** button

Format text while typing

► Click: The appropriate command button (eg Click: The **Bold** button to switch bold text on)
► Key in: The text
► Click: The appropriate command button again to switch the emphasis off.

 Format existing text

► Select: The text to be changed
► Click: The appropriate command button.

 Margin alignments

Alignment	Keyboard	Mouse
Centre text *(between left/right margins)*	Press: **Ctrl + E**	Click: The **Centre** button
Align to left *(ragged right margin)*	Press: **Ctrl + L**	Click: The **Align Left** button
Fully justify *(justified left margin)*	Press: **Ctrl + J**	Click: The **Justify** button
Align to right *(ragged right margin)*	Press: **Ctrl + R**	Click: The **Align Right** button

 Line spacing

Keyboard	Mouse
Press: **Ctrl + 1** (single line spacing) Press: **Ctrl + 2** (double line spacing) Press: **Ctrl + 0** (to add or delete a line space)	Select: **Paragraph** from the **Format** menu Select: **Indents and Spacing**, **Line Spacing** Select: The appropriate line spacing from the drop-down menu

Consistency of presentation (fonts)

It is very important to ensure that text is presented consistently throughout a document. You should not be tempted to use too many different fonts within a document as this will usually look unprofessional. It is normal practice to use the same font, font size and type of emphasis for specific parts of a document (eg main text, headings, footnotes etc). To make this easier, you can use the **Style** command on the Formatting Tool Bar or copy the format from one block of text to another.

 ## Review formatting

(to check font and formatting of existing text)

Formatting Information boxes method	Formatting Tool Bar method
Press: **Shift** + **F1**	Select: The text to be reviewed
Click: The text to be reviewed	Check: The formatting options displayed on
Check: The details shown in the Formatting	the Formatting Tool Bar (eg font style, font
Information boxes	size, etc)
Press: **Shift** + **F1** again to reverse action	

 ## Use styles

Word 97 offers a range of pre-determined styles where a combination of font, font size and style of emphasis is collectively given a numbered heading style.

Note: The combination of features stored under any one heading may vary from one system to another.

Keyboard

Select: The text to be formatted to a
particular style
Press: **Ctrl** + **Shift** + **N** (Normal)
Press: **Alt** + **Ctrl** + **1** (Heading 1)
Press: **Alt** + **Ctrl** + **2** (Heading 2)
Press: **Alt** + **Ctrl** + **3** (Heading 3)

Mouse

Select: The text to be formatted to a particular style
Select: The style formatting option required from the
Style drop-down menu on the Formatting Tool Bar

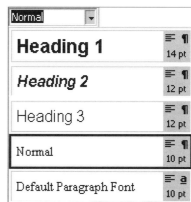

Figure 7.2 Style drop-down menu

Copy formats ▶

Keyboard

Position the cursor: In the block of text displaying the required format

Press: **Ctrl + Shift + C**

Select: The block of text where the required format is required *(The **Format Painter** brush symbol is displayed)*

Press: **Ctrl + Shift + V**

Mouse

Position the cursor: In the block of text displaying the required format

Click: The 🖌 **Format Painter** button on the Standard Tool Bar

To copy the format to one word:

Position the format painter brush symbol: On the word in the block of text where the format is required
Click: The left mouse button

To copy the format to a block of text:

Select: The text to be formatted
Click: The left mouse button

Exercise 7A ▶

7.1 Referring to the instructions in **Format fonts**, experiment with the different fonts available to you by reproducing the following text, ensuring that each line is shown in the font style and size given, and that you use the instructions given to obtain the desired effects:

> *Times New Roman size 12, bold, italics and underlined*
>
> Arial size 14, highlighted
>
> ARIAL SIZE 16, SMALL CAPS
>
> Courier New, Size 10, Title Case
>
> courier new, size 14, lower case, bold
>
> *Now key in the following text for each font available to you to create a list of the fonts for your future use:*

Copy the text in the second line to the position for the third line and then make the required formatting and text changes

Use the Format Painter to copy the format from the first line to these lines

7.2 Key in a line of text for each font which is available to you on your system, as follows:

> *(Name of font)* font, size 12, no emphasis

Key in this line of text and copy it for each font

Examples:

> Footlight MT Light, size 12, no emphasis
> **ALGERIAN, SIZE 12, NO EMPHASIS**

Select one line of text and change the font for that line

Change the font name in the text to show the correct font name for that line

7.3 Print a copy of your work and keep the sheet for reference. It will be useful when you need to choose a font for a document or part of a document.

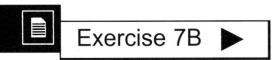

Exercise 7B ▶

7.4 Open the document you saved as **EX4B** and save as **EX7B**. Referring to the instructions in **Format fonts** and **Copy formats**, make the following font formatting changes to the document:

▶ Change the header text, **Employment Trends**, to Arial, font size 10
▶ Change the footer text to Arial, font size 8, italic
▶ Increase the font size of the main heading **EMPLOYMENT** by 2 points
▶ Change all other headings to Times New Roman, font size 14, bold
▶ Reduce the font size for the numbered items under the heading <u>Sources</u> to 10 points
▶ Change the last sentence of the second paragraph to italics.

7.5 Check your work on screen against the printout check at the back of the book. Before printing, review the text formatting by referring to the instructions in **Review formatting**. Correct any errors, resave the document and print one copy.

Exercise 7C ▶

7.6 Starting a new document, and referring to the instructions **Use styles**, key in the following notice using the styles shown.

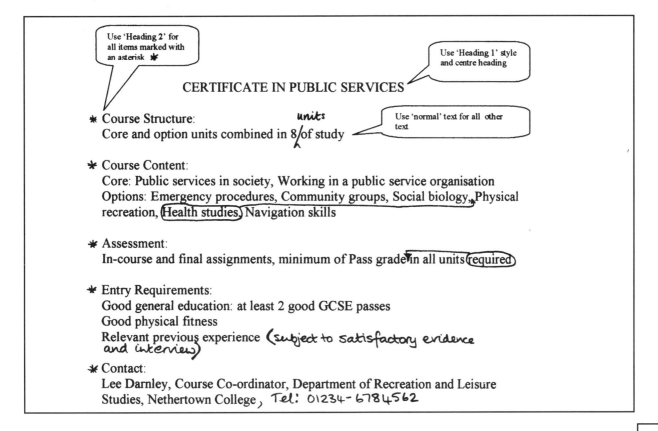

7.7 Save the document using the filename **EX7C** and print one copy. An example of the document is shown in Exercise 7E (page 65). However, your document may not look the same as the pre-stored styles may be different on your system. You should check that you have keyed in the text correctly, though.

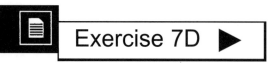

Exercise 7D ▶

7.8 Key in the following notice. Use fonts, font sizes and emphasis of your own choice in order to create an eye-catching display.

THE INTERNATIONAL MILLENIUM CHALLENGE

Conference to be held on Sat and Sun

(please insert dates for last weekend of next month)

in the
Central Civic Hall
SHEFFIELD

10.00 to 5 pm each day

Delegates:

Representatives of Department for International Development
International Banks ── *International Aid Agencies*
Private Sector
Voluntary Organisations
Environmental Organisations
Scientific Organisations
The Challenge:

(Partnerships)
Sustainable development of the planet
Eliminating poverty and establishing economic well-being
World health and human development
International trade and agriculture

The Debate:

A lively, well-informed debate is expected. Listen to the experts. Find out what is already being done. Decide on the best strategies. Learn what you can do. *(Consider the future options)*

TICKETS AVAILABLE FROM THE DEPARTMENT OF POLITICS, TOTLEY HALL, SHEFFIELD

Inset left Margin by 1.3 cm (½ in)

7.9 Save the document using the filename **EX7D** and print one copy. Compare your document with the printout check at the back of the book and correct any errors.

Allocate space

You may be required to leave space within a document for the later insertion of a picture or diagram. In RSA examinations the measurement required is usually only given in centimetres. In the Word Processing Stage III Part 2 examination, you will be given the minimum and maximum horizontal and vertical dimensions of the space.

 Allocate a horizontal space from the left or right margin

It is easiest to do this after the whole document has been keyed in.

▶ Select: The block of text which is to be positioned at the side of the space, *or*
▶ Place the cursor: Immediately before the first character of the block of text
▶ Move: The **Left Indent** or **Right Indent** marker to the required position on the horizontal ruler.

Note: It may be necessary to move the indent marker back to the left margin at the required point in the text.

 Allocate a vertical space across the full typing line

It is easiest to do this after the whole document has been keyed in.

▶ Delete: Any space already present before the first line of the text which is to come after the space
▶ Position the insertion pointer: Immediately before the first character of the text to come after the space
▶ Select: **Format**, **Paragraph**, **Indents and Spacing** from the menu bar
▶ In the **Before** box, key in: The measurement required. Word 97 will accept the measurement in centimetres, inches or points, and will then convert this into the unit of measurement currently in use (usually centimetres).

 Allocate a rectangular space within a document using a text box

The use of a text box without a border allows precise measurements to be used for the required space. This can be done during or after keying in.

If the Drawing Tool Bar is not already on screen:

▶ Select: **View**, **Tool Bars**, **Drawing**

The Drawing Tool Bar is displayed on screen:

Figure 7.3 Drawing Tool Bar

▶ Click: The 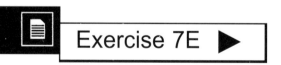 **Text Box** button on the Drawing Tool Bar
▶ Click: Anywhere in the document – a text box will appear on screen
▶ Select: **Text Box** from the **Format** menu (the text box must be selected for this option to be available)
▶ Click: The **Size** tab

In the **Size and rotate** section:

▶ Key in: The required measurements in the **Height** and **Width** boxes
▶ Click: The **Colors and Lines** tab

In the **Line** section:

▶ Select: **No line**
▶ Click: The **Wrapping** tab

In the **Wrapping** style section:

▶ Select: **Square**
▶ Click: **OK**
▶ Drag: The **Text Box** to the required position in the document.

The document text should now wrap around the box leaving a space of the required dimensions.

Note: You must position the text box very carefully. If the required space is to be measured from the left margin, you must line up the left-hand side of the text box exactly with the left margin of the text.

You should also use a ruler to double-check the space allocation dimensions when you have printed out the document.

Exercise 7E ▶

7.10 Open the document you saved as **EX7C** and save as **EX7E**. Referring to the instructions in **Allocate a horizontal space from the left or right margin** and **Allocate a vertical space across the full typing line**, allocate spaces in the document as shown below.

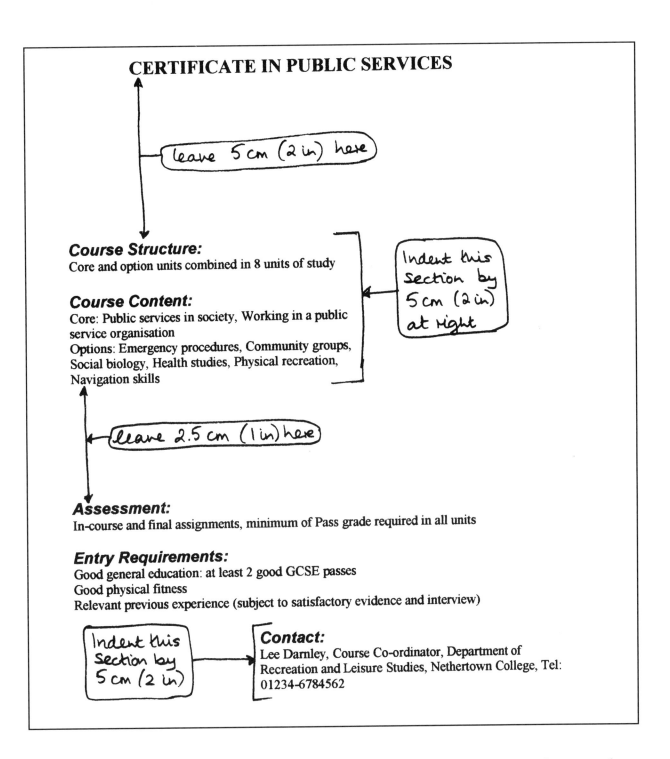

CERTIFICATE IN PUBLIC SERVICES

leave 5 cm (2 in) here

Course Structure:
Core and option units combined in 8 units of study

Course Content:
Core: Public services in society, Working in a public
service organisation
Options: Emergency procedures, Community groups,
Social biology, Health studies, Physical recreation,
Navigation skills

Indent this section by 5 cm (2 in) at right

leave 2.5 cm (1 in) here

Assessment:
In-course and final assignments, minimum of Pass grade required in all units

Entry Requirements:
Good general education: at least 2 good GCSE passes
Good physical fitness
Relevant previous experience (subject to satisfactory evidence and interview)

Indent this section by 5 cm (2 in)

Contact:
Lee Darnley, Course Co-ordinator, Department of
Recreation and Leisure Studies, Nethertown College, Tel:
01234-6784562

7.11 Resave the document and print one copy. Compare your document with the exercise above to confirm the proportions of the allocated spaces. Remember that your printout may not show the same styles. Use a ruler to double-check you have used the correct space allocations.

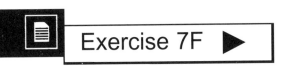

Exercise 7F ▶

7.12 Open the document you saved as **EX7C** and save as **EX7F**. Referring to the instructions in **Allocate a rectangular space using a text box**, allocate spaces in the form of unruled text boxes in the document as shown below.

CERTIFICATE IN PUBLIC SERVICES

Course Structure:
Core and option units combined in 8 units of study

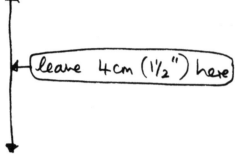

Leave a space here 3.5 cm high × 2.5 cm wide (½" × 1"). Do not rule the box.

Course Content:
Core: Public services in society, Working in a public service organisation
Options: Emergency procedures, Community groups, Social biology, Health studies, Physical recreation, Navigation skills

Assessment:
In-course and final assignments, minimum of Pass grade required in all units

leave 4 cm (1½") here

Entry Requirements:
Good general education: at least 2 good GCSE passes
Good physical fitness
Relevant previous experience (subject to satisfactory evidence and interview)

Leave a box here 3.5 cm (1½") high × 5 cm (2") wide. (Do not rule the box if you use the text box method)

Contact:
Lee Darnley, Course Co-ordinator, Department of Recreation and Leisure Studies, Nethertown College, Tel: 01234-6784562

7.13   Resave the document and print one copy. Compare your document with the exercise above to confirm the proportions of the allocated spaces. Remember that your printout may not show the same styles. Use a ruler to double-check you have used the correct space allocations.

Newspaper columns

A newspaper column format is often used to make a document easier to read and less formal in layout. It is often used for documents such as leaflets, newsletters and bulletins.

In the RSA Word Processing Stage III Part 2 examination, you will be required to display one document in a two-column format throughout. In the RSA Document Presentation Stage III Part 2 examination, you will be required to display a section of a document in two-column format.

Bulletin

Format columns for the whole document ▶

▶ Check: That you are in **Page Layout** view (select **Page Layout** from the **View** menu)
▶ Select: **Select All** from the **Edit** menu if the document has already been keyed in
▶ Select: Columns from the **Format** menu

The **Columns** dialogue box is displayed on screen:

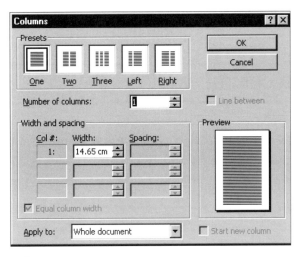

Figure 7.4 Columns dialogue box

▶ Select: The required number of columns in the **Presets** section of the **Columns** dialogue box, *or*
▶ Key in: The required number in the **Number of columns** section
▶ Check: Your selected column display format in the **Preview** box
▶ Click: **OK**

OR

▶ Click: The **Columns** button on the Standard Tool Bar
▶ Drag: The cursor across the grid to select the required number of columns.

Format columns for a specific section of a document ▶

▶ Check: That you are in **Page Layout** view (select **Page Layout** from the **View** menu)
▶ Select: The section of text which is to be changed to a newspaper-column format
▶ Select: **Columns** from the **Format** menu
▶ Select: The required number of columns in the **Presets** section of the **Columns** dialogue box, *or*
▶ Key in: The required number in the **Number of columns** section
▶ Check: Your selected column display format in the **Preview** box
▶ Check: That the **Apply to** box shows **Selected text**
▶ Click: **OK**

Insert a column break to force text into the next column

▶ Position the cursor: Where you want the new column to begin
▶ Select: **Break** from the **Insert** menu
▶ Click: **Column break**

The text will move to the top of the next column.

 Change the column widths

▶ Check: That you are in **Page Layout** view (select **Page Layout** from the **View** menu)
▶ Position the cursor: In the section to be changed
▶ Move: The column markers on the horizontal ruler to the required position

Note: You may specify measurements for each column width and the spacing between columns in the Column dialogue box. If the **equal column width** box in the dialogue box is ticked, you cannot change the column widths individually.

 Insert vertical lines between columns

▶ Check: That you are in **Page Layout** view (select **Page Layout** from the **View** menu)
▶ Position the cursor: In the section to be changed
▶ Select: **Columns** from the **Format** menu
▶ Click: The **Line between** box so that it is ticked

 Remove column formatting

▶ Check: That you are in **Page Layout** view (select **Page Layout** from the **View** menu)
▶ Position the cursor: In the section to be changed
▶ Click: The ▦ **Columns** button on the Standard Tool Bar
▶ Drag: To select one column

OR

▶ Select: **Columns** from the **Format** menu
▶ Select: One column in the **Presets** section of the **Columns** dialogue box, *or*
▶ Key in: **1** in the **Number of columns** section
▶ Check: Your selection in the **Preview** box

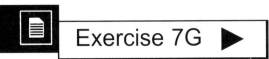

Exercise 7G ▶

7.14   Starting a new document, key in the following text displaying the whole document in a two-column newspaper column format, using Arial, font size 14.

THE ART OF CONVERSATION

The literal meaning of the word conversation indicate an activity where individuals 'turn or change together' in the sense of responding, co-operating and being interactive. Most of us learn to converse through experiance ~~and practice~~. However, in the modern age when there seems to be so much emphasis on transmitting a message, we seem to have lost the art of listening. Without this basic skill, we cannot hope to enjoy satisfactry conversations.

If a person join in a conversation with the aim of scoring points or applying pressure, then the listening aspect, and usually the enjoyment, is lost. Each person needs to feel that they can express there ideas and explain their thoughts and needs without having another person 'step on their toes'.

Conversation is our way of getting to know another person and finding out what is going on in their mind. Each of us lives to some extent in our own world which has been built up from the circumstances' and influences' which have shaped our lives. It is all too easy to assume that we know what another person feels or thinks, but unless we listen we will never really find out. We will be making assumptions based on our own ideas and experiences and not the other person's.

We rely on open conversations to establish good relationships. As well as listening to others and being open to their opinions, we need to be open ourselves and explain what is on <u>our</u> minds. If we do this, then guesses and assumptions will not cause confusion and misunderstanding.

Words <u>can</u> harm us considerably despite the old adage 'Sticks and stones may break my bones but words can't hurt me.' and can affect our self-esteem to a great extent. Negative emotions can build up if we are criticised constantly Even the first few words of a conversation can create a permanant barrier which may never be overcome between the people involved.

7.15   Save the document using the filename **EX7G** and print one copy. Check your printout with the printout at the back of the book. If you find any errors, correct them and print the document again, if necessary.

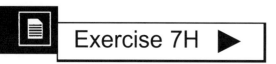

Exercise 7H ▶

7.16 Open the document you saved earlier as **EX7C** and save as **EX7H**. Insert the following text as indicated. Format the document as follows:

▶ Referring to the instructions in Format columns for the whole document, change the whole document to a two-column newspaper column layout

▶ Use the same style formats for headings and body text as in Exercise 7C

▶ Use justified margins

▶ Insert a column break immediately before the section headed Entry Requirements so that this section starts the second column.

Please insert the following text after the Assessment Section

Career progression:
The Certificate is the first step towards a career in the public services. Successful completion provides access to a range of advanced courses. Career opportunities exist in the health and social services, the emergency services, the armed forces and the prison service.

METHODS OF LEARNING:

An experieced team of lecturers provides a balanced programme of lectures and hands-on activities. Work placement is a large feature of the programme and you will be expected to carry out research projects and work-based assignments. Specialist speakers from the services will be used where appropriate and there is a wide range of opportunities for supervised – and supervising – recreation and leisure pursuits within the local community.

7.17 Resave the document and print one copy. Check your printout with the printout at the back of the book. If you find any errors, correct them and print the document again, if necessary.

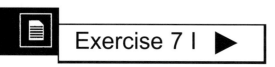

Exercise 7 I ▶

7.18 Open the document **EX7H** unless it is already on screen and save as **EX7I**. Referring to the instructions in **Allocate space**, leave spaces in the document as shown on the next page. Change to a ragged right margin.

CERTIFICATE IN PUBLIC SERVICES

Course Structure:
Core and option units combined in 8 units of study

Course Content:

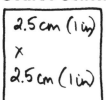
2.5 cm (1 in) x 2.5 cm (1 in)

Core: Public services in society, Working in a public service organisation
Options: Emergency procedures, Community groups, Social biology, Health studies, Physical recreation, Navigation skills

Assessment:
In-course and final assignments, minimum of Pass grade required in all units

Career progression:
The Certificate is the first step towards a career in the public services. Successful completion provides access to a range of advanced courses. Career opportunities exist in the health and social services, the emergency services, the armed forces and the prison service.

Methods of learning:
An experienced team of lecturers provides a balanced programme of lectures and hands-on activities. Work

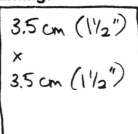
3.5 cm (1½") x 3.5 cm (1½")

placement is a large feature of the programme and you will be expected to carry out research projects and work-based assignments. Specialist speakers from the services will be used where appropriate and there is a wide range of opportunities for supervised, and supervising, recreation and leisure pursuits within the local community.

Entry Requirements:
Good general education: at least 2 good GCSE passes
Good physical fitness
Relevant previous experience (subject to satisfactory evidence and interview)

Contact:
Lee Darnley, Course Co-ordinator,
Department of Recreation and Leisure Studies, Nethertown College, Tel: 01234-6784562

5.0 cm (2 in) high x 2.5 cm (1 in) wide

Please insert unruled rectangular spaces as shown

7.19 Resave the document and print one copy. Check your printout with the exercise above. Use a ruler to double-check the space allocations. If you find any errors, correct them and print the document again, if necessary.

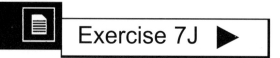
7.20   Open the document you saved earlier as **EX7G** and save as **EX7J**. Referring to the instructions in **Format columns for a specific section of a document**, reformat the text as shown below.

THE ART OF CONVERSATION

Leave a space 2.5 cm (1 inch) high by 4.5 cm (1¾ inch) wide here. Do not rule box.

The literal meaning of the word conversation indicates an activity where individuals 'turn or change together' in the sense of responding, co-operating and being interactive. Most of us learn to converse through experience. However, in the modern age when there seems to be so much emphasis on transmitting a message, we seem to have lost the art of listening. Without this basic skill, we cannot hope to enjoy satisfactory conversations.

If a person joins in a conversation with the aim of scoring points or applying pressure, then the listening aspect, and usually the enjoyment, is lost. Each person needs to feel that they can express their ideas and explain their thoughts and needs without having another person 'step on their toes'.

Two-column display

Conversation is our way of getting to know another person and finding out what is going on in their mind. Each of us lives to some extent in our own world which has been built up from the circumstances and influences which have shaped our lives. It is easy to assume that we know what another person feels or thinks, but unless we listen we will never really find out. We will be making assumptions based on our own ideas and experiences and not the other person's.

We rely on open conversations to establish good relationships. As well as listening to others and being open to their opinions, we need to be open ourselves and explain what is on <u>our</u> minds. If we do this, then guesses and assumptions will not cause confusion and misunderstanding.

Despite the old adage 'Sticks and stones may break my bones but words can't hurt me.', words <u>can</u> harm us considerably, and can affect our self-esteem to a great extent. Negative emotions can build up if we are constantly criticised. Even the first few words of a conversation can create a permanent barrier between the people involved which may never be overcome.

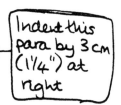

Indent this para by 3 cm (1¼") at right

7.21   Resave the document and print one copy. Check your printout with the exercise above. Use a ruler to double-check the space allocations. If you find any errors, correct them and print the document again, if necessary.

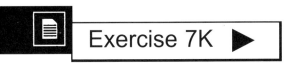
7.22 Open the document you saved earlier as **EX7D** and save as **EX7K**. Referring to the instructions in Format columns for a specific section of a document, reformat the text as shown below. Make sure that the two-column display resembles that shown below by inserting a column break if necessary.

THE INTERNATIONAL MILLENNIUM CHALLENGE

Conference to be held on Saturday and Sunday
(dates inserted)

in the
Central Civic Hall
SHEFFIELD

2-column format for these sections

10.00 am to 5.00 pm each day

Delegates:

Representatives of Department for
International Development
International Banks
International Aid Agencies
Private Sector
Voluntary Organisations
Environmental Organisations
Scientific Organisations

The Challenge:

Sustainable development of the planet
Eliminating poverty and establishing
economic well-being
World health and human development
Partnerships
International trade and agriculture

The Debate:

A lively, well-informed debate is expected. Listen to the experts. Find out what is already being done. Consider the future options. Decide on the best strategies. Learn what you can do.

TICKETS AVAILABLE FROM THE DEPARTMENT OF POLITICS, TOTLEY HALL, SHEFFIELD

*Please leave a space here :-
4 cm high × 5 cm wide
(1½" × 2").
Do not rule the box.*

7.23 Resave the document and print one copy. Check your printout with the exercise above. Use a ruler to double-check the space allocations. If you find any errors, correct them and print the document again, if necessary.

Copy text from one document to another

You have already learnt how to copy text from one position to another within the same document. The facility to copy blocks of text from one document to another document is a very useful one in practice.

This technique forms part of the RSA Word Processing Stage III Part 2 examination. The method is very similar to that for copying text within the same document. The additional step is to switch from the source document to the destination document using the **Window** option on the main menu bar.

 ## Open the source document ▶

▶ Check: That you have opened both the source and the destination documents
(Word 97 allows you to have several documents open at one time)
▶ Select: **Window** from the **Menu** bar

The **Window** drop-down menu is displayed on screen.

Figure 7.5 Window drop-down menu

▶ Select: The document containing the text to be copied

The selected document will come to the front so that you can work on it.
(Other documents listed under Window remain open.)

 ## Select the text to be copied ▶

▶ Select: The text to be copied using the normal copying techniques.

 ## Switch to destination document ▶

▶ Select: **Window** from the **Menu** bar

The **Window** drop-down menu is displayed on screen.

▶ Select: The document where you want the text to appear

The destination document will come to the front so that you can work on it.

| | Paste the selected text into the destination document ▶ |

▶ Move the insertion pointer: To the position where the text is to be inserted
▶ Paste: The text into position using the normal pasting techniques.

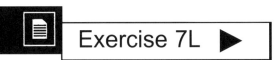

Exercise 7L ▶

7.24 Open the following documents and check under the Window menu that they are all listed:

▶ EX7B   ▶ EX7C   ▶ EX7H

7.25 Starting with a new document, key in the following document, using a single-column format and justified margins. Copy the text from the other documents as instructed.

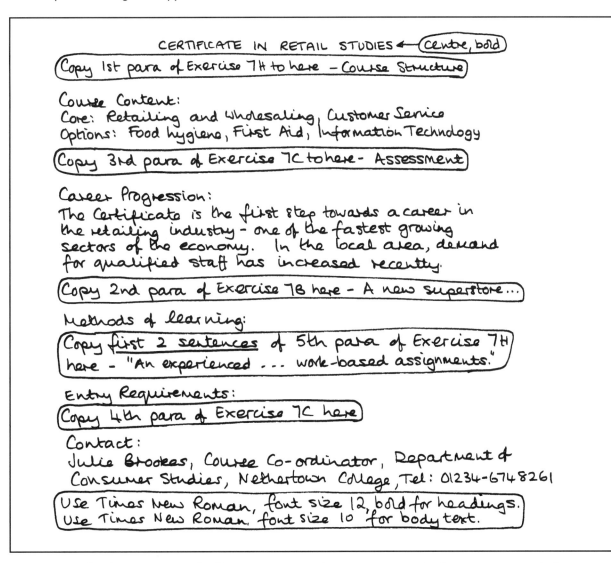

CERTIFICATE IN RETAIL STUDIES ◀── (Centre, bold)

(Copy 1st para of Exercise 7H to here – Course Structure)

Course Content:
Core: Retailing and Wholesaling, Customer Service
Options: Food hygiene, First Aid, Information Technology

(Copy 3rd para of Exercise 7C to here – Assessment)

Career Progression:
The Certificate is the first step towards a career in
the retailing industry – one of the fastest growing
sectors of the economy. In the local area, demand
for qualified staff has increased recently.

(Copy 2nd para of Exercise 7B here – A new superstore...)

Methods of learning:
(Copy first 2 sentences of 5th para of Exercise 7H
here – "An experienced ... work-based assignments.")

Entry Requirements:
(Copy 4th para of Exercise 7C here)

Contact:
Julie Brookes, Course Co-ordinator, Department of
Consumer Studies, Nethertown College, Tel: 01234-6748261

(Use Times New Roman, font size 12, bold for headings.
Use Times New Roman, font size 10 for body text.)

7.26 Save the document using the filename **EX7L** and print one copy. Check your printout with the printout at the back of the book. If you find any errors, correct them and print the document again, if necessary. Exit the program if you have finished working or continue straight on to the next unit.

▶ Ruled tables in landscape format

By the end of Unit 8 you should have learnt how to:

▶ apply ruling to a table
▶ produce a table in landscape format
▶ produce a table with subdivided and multi-line headings
▶ produce a table using different column layouts in specified sections
▶ set, delete and change the position of different tab settings within a table
▶ complete table data using a house style reference sheet

Using tabs for column work

Data is often presented in columns within letters, memos and reports to convey information quickly and clearly. Tabulated columns of information are also used for separate tables and accounts.

If you align text on screen by pressing the **spacebar** it may not line up when you print, so it is better to set tab stops at appropriate points on the ruler line. On some keyboards the tab key is labelled **Tab** and on others shown as ⬕ .

In Word 97 the tab settings are normally defaulted (ie previously set) to every 1.27cm ($\frac{1}{2}$ in). Each time you press the Tab key you indent the line by 1.27cm ($\frac{1}{2}$ in). You can often display text in columns satisfactorily using the default tabs. There will be times, however, especially if you are typing a table with columns containing a lot of data or where space is limited, when you will need to *set*, *delete* or *change* the position of the default tab settings.

You may also need to set a tab to apply a different alignment to the table data, ie a left-aligned, right-aligned, centred or decimal tab.

It looks better if you leave equal amounts of space between columns but this is not absolutely necessary. If you decide to use default tabs the spaces will probably be unequal. You should leave at least one clear line after the tabulation work before continuing with any further portions of text.

ITEM	CODE	COLOUR	PRICE	UNIT
Pencils	PY/34	mixed	5.50	hundred
Rubber	RF/673	grey	1.20	dozen
Ruler	RL/112	clear	2.25	dozen
Ringbinder	RB/95	marine blue	0.65	each

Leave sufficient space between headings to allow for the longest line of each column

Use capitals or underlining to emphasise column headings

Leave a clear line space between a heading and the information below it

Key in columns in double or single-line spacing according to the instructions provided or the amount of space available on the page

Set a tab stop for the longest line in each column, in the appropriate places, remembering to include at least 3 blank spaces between columns.

Types of tab setting

Depending on the type of display, you can choose a:

► left-aligned tab (to block entries to the left)
► right-aligned tab (to block entries to the right)
► decimal tab (to align decimal numbers at the decimal point)
► centred tab (to centre each entry around the tab stop).

You can set a combination of different types of tab stops within the document and even on the same line if appropriate. For example:

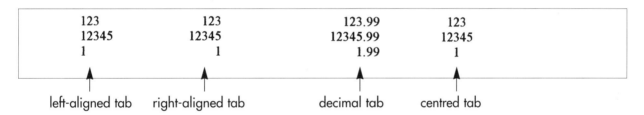

123	123	123.99	123
12345	12345	12345.99	12345
1	1	1.99	1

left-aligned tab   right-aligned tab   decimal tab   centred tab

Tabs ►

To add, delete or change tab stops in Word 97:

► select all the paragraphs in which you want to edit the settings
► make your tab stop changes.

Mouse and ruler method

Add a tab   Click: The Tab Alignment button at the far left of the horizontal ruler until the type of tab alignment you want is displayed:

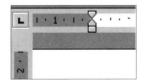

left-aligned tab	L	decimal tab	⊥
right-aligned tab	⌐	centred tab	⊥

Click: The mouse pointer on the horizontal ruler at the place where you want to set the tab stop

Delete a tab	Click: The tab marker and drag it off the horizontal ruler Release: The mouse button
Move a tab	Click: The tab marker and drag it to the right or left on the horizontal ruler
Change tab alignment	Delete: The tab; *then* Follow the instructions for adding a tab

Mouse and menu method

▶ Select: **Format, Tabs**

The **Tabs** dialogue box is displayed on screen.

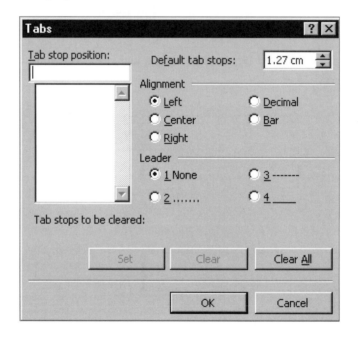

Figure 8.1 Tabs dialogue box

Add a tab (repeat this step for each tab you want to set)	Key in: The required position in the **Tab stop position** box (eg 2.54cm (1in)) Select: The type of tab alignment from the **Alignment** box options (eg Left) Click: **Set** Repeat for the next tab stop if appropriate Click: **OK**
Delete a tab	Select: The tab to be deleted from the **Tab stop position** box Click: **Clear**
Delete all tabs	Click: **Clear All**
Move a tab	Delete: The tab; *then* Follow the instructions for adding a tab

Change tab alignment	Highlight: The tab to be changed in the **Tab stop position** box
	Select: The new tab alignment from the **Alignment** box options
	Click: **Set**
Reset default tab stops	Select or key in: The distance you want between all tab stops on the horizontal ruler in the **Default tab stops box** (eg 1.27cm ($\frac{1}{2}$ in))
	Click: **OK**

Exercise 8A

8.1 Set tabs to every 1.27cm ($\frac{1}{2}$ in) if these are not already set by the program default (check the **Format**, **Tabs** dialogue box). Starting a new file, key in the following exercise (using the default tab settings, press the Tab key to enter the months of the year in the correct positions and before each numerical entry on the table):

SALES IN THE YORKSHIRE AND HUMBERSIDE REGION

<u>White Products</u>

	<u>Jan</u>	<u>Mar</u>	<u>Jul</u>	<u>Oct</u>	<u>Dec</u>
WASHING MACHINES	76	56	63	89	33
TUMBLE DRYERS	54	67	24	108	79
REFRIGERATORS	23	38	103	82	34

you may retain the abbreviations for the months of the year

add underscore separately to each month while keying in or after

---

8.2 Press ↵ (return/enter) several times to leave a gap before the next piece of work.

8.3 Refer back the instructions given on setting tabs (pages 77–78). Set a left-aligned tab stop at **4.5 cm** (**1$\frac{3}{4}$ in**) and **9 cm (3$\frac{1}{2}$ in)** only. Check that you have set the tab stops in the correct position by pressing the Tab key twice. The cursor should move across the screen to positions **4.5 cm (1$\frac{3}{4}$ in)** and **9 cm (3$\frac{1}{2}$ in)** on your ruler line.

8.4 Key in the main heading and the column headings shown in the next piece of work. Press ↵ (return/enter) so that your cursor is at the left margin.

8.5 Delete the left-aligned tab at **9 cm (3$\frac{1}{2}$ in)**. Set a decimal tab at **9.5cm (3$\frac{3}{4}$ in)**. Key in the rest of the columns using the tab key to move between the entries.

MORNING ROTA - TUESDAY

STYLIST	ACTIVITY	TIME
Lisette	Permanent wave	9.00
Deborah-Jane	Shampoo/set	9.45
Vanessa	Semi-permanent rinse	9.45
Sue	Cut/blow	10.00

8.6   Press ↵ (return/enter) several times to leave a gap before the next piece of work.

8.7   Set tab stops for the following exercise in the appropriate places and delete existing tab stops. Use a decimal tab for the first column where required. Key in the following exercise.

XMAS SHOPPING LIST

Price each (£)	Description	Quantity
1.75	Packs mens socks	4
20.00	Negligee	1
0.25	Paper plates	25
0.30	Sheets wrapping paper	10

8.8   Press ↵ (return/enter) several times to leave a gap before the next piece of work.

8.9   Set the tab stops as appropriate for the column entries below (ie column a = left-aligned; column b = centred; column c = right-aligned; column d = decimal). Then key in the exercise.

NEW ITEMS IN STOCK

Item	Material	Number	Price (£) each
Blouse	Polyester-nylon	5	9.99
Coat	Mohair	18	125.50
Dressing-gown	Towelling	147	19.50

8.10   Save the document using the filename **EX8A**. Check your work with the printout at the back of the book. If you find any errors, correct them. Resave your work and print one copy.

8.11   Reset the tabs to left-aligned tab stops every 1.27cm ($\frac{1}{2}$ in).

8.12   Clear your screen ready for the next exercise.

Complex table layouts in landscape format

Instructions about how to use Word 97's Table facilities were provided in *Introducing Word 97 for Windows* and *Extending Word 97 for Windows*, the first two books of this series. If you can't remember, or don't know, how to use Word 97's Table facilities, either check with your tutor or consult the earlier books in this series.

In the Stage III examination you will be required to produce a ruled table using subdivided and multi-line headings. The layout will be more complex than in the Stage II examination, with sections of the table displaying different numbers of columns and/or rows. You will also need to refer to a **Resource Sheet** – supplied as a separate document – to obtain the data for the table. There may be occasions when you will need to use different tab settings inside the table.

In the Stage III examination, you will be asked to produce the table in landscape format – ie, with the longest edge of the paper at the top.

Apply ruling (borders) to a table

As you have already learnt, Word 97 automatically produces tables with pre-ruled lines/borders around each cell. Previously, you have had to remove the cell lines/borders, but for the Stage III examination you should leave the ruling on.

There may be occasions when you want to alter the appearance of ruled cells in a table. To do this:

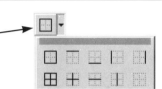

▶ Select: The cell(s) to which you wish to apply a border, or no border
▶ Click: The ▢ ▾ **Borders** button on the Formatting Tool Bar ——
▶ Select: The required border from the choices in the drop-down grid.

Set tabs inside a table

Tabs can be set inside a table where you want to specify a particular alignment. This is often useful when you want a column to display decimal figures.

To add, delete or change tab stops in a table:

▶ Select: The column in which you want to edit the tab settings
▶ Make your tab stop changes in the normal way – see page 78, earlier in this unit.

To move between tabs in a table:

▶ Press: **Ctrl + Tab**

Note: Pressing the Tab key alone moves to the next row or column.

Exercise 8B

8.13 Starting a new document, reproduce the following table:

▶ Merge the cells to produce the required format shown in the table exercise below.
▶ Centre the cell heading **STOCK DESCRIPTION**.
▶ Left-align the **ITEM** and **CODE** columns.
▶ Centre the **COLOUR** column.
▶ Centre the cell heading **SELLING PRICE (£)**.
▶ Insert a decimal tab setting for the rest of the data in the **SELLING PRICE** column as shown.
▶ Right-align the **PROFIT %** column.
▶ Adjust column widths as appropriate to improve the presentation.

NEW STOCK ITEMS

STOCK DESCRIPTION		COLOUR	SELLING PRICE (£)	PROFIT %
ITEM	CODE			
Lamp	LP45	Green	6.99	50%
Candleholder	CH321	Red multi	3.99	40%
Wardrobe	WD223	Pine	369.99	100%
Drawers	DW12	Pine	139.99	80%

8.14   Save the document using the filename **EX8B**. Check your work with the exercise above. If you find any errors, correct them. Resave your document and print one copy.

 ## Change the paper size to landscape orientation ▶

▶   Select: **Page Setup** from the **File** menu
▶   Select: The **Paper Size** tab
▶   Click: **Landscape** in the **Orientation** box
▶   In the **Apply to** box check that: **Whole document** is shown
▶   Click: **OK**

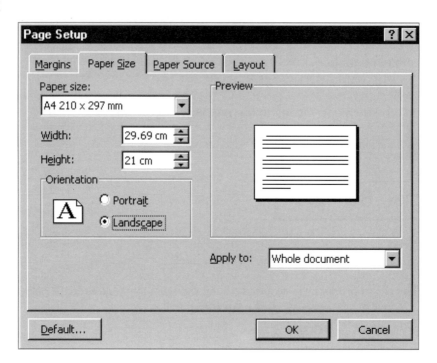

Note: Check the paper orientation by selecting **Whole Page** from the **Zoom** spin box on the Standard Tool Bar. The longer edge of the page should appear at the top. Alternatively, you can use the **Print Preview** facility to view the layout of the page.

 ## Complex table layouts ▶

Word 97 offers several different methods of producing a complex table layout. Practise the methods described below to see which one you feel most comfortable with.

Use the **Insert Table** facility to design the basic layout of the whole table.

Then merge the appropriate cells to achieve the correct number of columns and move the column dividers to reposition the columns in the bottom section.

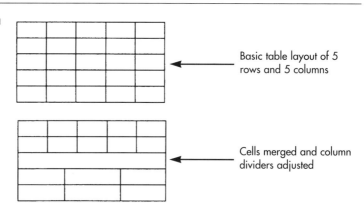

Basic table layout of 5 rows and 5 columns

Cells merged and column dividers adjusted

Use the **Insert Table** facility to design each section of the table separately, ie produce a separate table for the top section and one for the bottom section.

Then join the two tables by deleting the line space between.

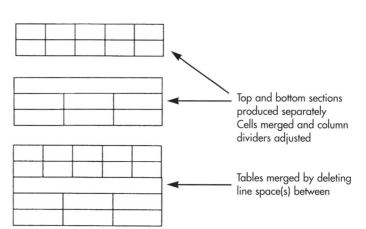

Top and bottom sections produced separately
Cells merged and column dividers adjusted

Tables merged by deleting line space(s) between

Use the [✏] **Draw Table** facility to draw the table layout – this is easiest in **Whole Page** view.

▶ Draw: The table outline first
▶ Draw: The row and column dividers
▶ Enter: The data in the usual way
▶ Adjust: The row and column dividers as appropriate.

Exercise 8C ▶

8.15 Starting with a clear screen, follow the instructions **Change the paper size to landscape orientation** on page 83 and change the paper size to landscape format. Use the **Print Preview** facility to check that the layout of the page is correctly set.

8.16 Study the table layout of the following table carefully. Note that the bottom section of the table contains a different number of columns from the top section, and that the column dividing lines are positioned in different places. Read the section on **Complex table layouts** on pages 83–84.

8.17 Reproduce the table layout shown below using your preferred method of working.

▶ Enter the data as shown
▶ Follow the column alignment indicated.
▶ Set a decimal tab to enter the data in the **TOTAL HOURS CONSULTANCY** column
▶ Using Print Preview, check your work with the exercise in this unit.

Rule as shown.
Save and print a copy of the document
using the filename: FX8C

FREELANCE CONSULTANTS – YEAR END REPORT

NAME	SPECIALIST AREA	TOTAL HOURS CONSULTANCY	IDENTITY CODE	DATE STARTED
Beddows, Jack	Marketing	37.00	P3337Z	14 March
Bray, Lorraine	Information Systems	64.00	P3476Z	3 February
Dennis, Maria	Sales	100.50	P4325Z	14 January
Ellwood, Liam	Sales	97.00	P3346Z	21 January
Hodge, Steve	Marketing	42.50	P3214Z	3 June
Klein, Jessica	Information Systems	76.00	P3187Z	17 February
Laine, Nicci	Public Relations	55.50	P3227Z	17 June
McLaughlin, George	Marketing	28.00	P3451Z	10 June
Simpkins, Vera	Information Systems	136.50	P3276Z	6 August

DETAILS OF CONSULTANCY OUTPUTS

ITEMS	JANUARY-JUNE PERIOD	JULY-DECEMBER PERIOD
Number of businesses contacted	32	46
Number of secondary referrals	173	205
Number of follow-up enquiries	96	116
Number of new customer accounts	61	90

8.18 Save the document using the filename **EX8C**. Check your work on screen with the exercise in this unit. If you find any errors, correct them. Resave the document and print one copy.

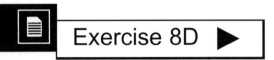

Exercise 8D ▶

8.19 Starting with a clear screen, key in the table shown below. Save the document using the filename **EX8D** and print one copy with the longest edge at the top. Rule as shown.

HOLIDAY SPECIALS – SUMMER OFFERS (FROM MANCHESTER AIRPORT) ← (Centre this heading)

RESORT	DEPARTURE DATE	ACCOMMODATION TYPE	NUMBER OF NIGHTS	PRICE
Turkey - Alanya	3 July	2AA/SC	7	£229.00
Malta - Valletta	4 July	3A/HB	7	£339.00
Tenerife - Playa de Las Americas	10 July	2A/BB	14	£329.00
Majorca - Palma Nova	12 July	2A/HB	14	£389.00

Refer to the Resource Sheet Information for Exercise 8D at the end of this unit to complete all the remaining details of this table. Follow the layout given here.

OFFER DETAILS

ACCOMMODATION	ADDITIONAL COSTS	CONDITIONS OF BOOKING
HB = Half Board	Insurance @ £38 per person for 14 days	All prices are subject to availability.
SC = Self Catering	Insurance @ £22 per person for 7 days cover.	Prices are per person and based on 2
BB = Bed and Breakfast	to per person booking fee for telephone bookings.	Full Fare passengers sharing. The
RO = Room Only	Credit card surcharge of 1%.	company reserves the right to withdraw this offer without notice.

8.20 Check your work with the printout at the back of the book. If you find any errors, correct them and print the document again, if necessary.

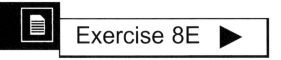

Exercise 8E ▶

8.21 Starting with a clear screen, key in the table shown below. Save the document using the filename **EX8E** and print one copy with the longest edge at the top.

GARDENING TELE-DIAGNOSTIC LINES – NEW SERVICE LINES ← Centre this heading

LINE TYPE	TOPIC	AVAILABILITY DATE	CALL DURATION	TELEPHONE NUMBER
FRUIT	Plum, pear and cherry problems	4 June	2.0 minutes	0645 68 5081
FRUIT	Raspberry and blackberry problems	4 June	3.0 minutes	0645 68 5082
FRUIT	Strawberry problems	4 June	2.5 minutes	0645 68 5083
VEGETABLES	Carrot/parsnip problems	6 June	1.0 minutes	0645 68 5221

Refer to the Resource Sheet Information for Exercise 8E at the end of this unit to complete all the remaining details of this table. Follow the layout given here. Rule as shown

NEW SERVICE FEATURE – ALL LINE TYPES

WHAT	REQUIRED ACTION	HOW
We have added a special feature to all our tele-diagnostic lines. Callers will be able to pause, slow down, speed up, rewind and repeat particular sections of the message. To access this special facility callers must have a touch-pad telephone.	Slow the message down	Press 1
	Speed the message up	Press 2
	Pause the message	Press 3
	Restart the message	Press 5
	Rewind the message by 30 seconds	Press 7

8.22 Check your printout with the printout at the back of the book. If you find any errors, correct them and print the document again, if necessary.

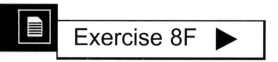

Exercise 8F ▶

8.23 Starting with a clear screen, key in the table shown below. Save as **EX8F** and print one copy with the longest edge at the top.

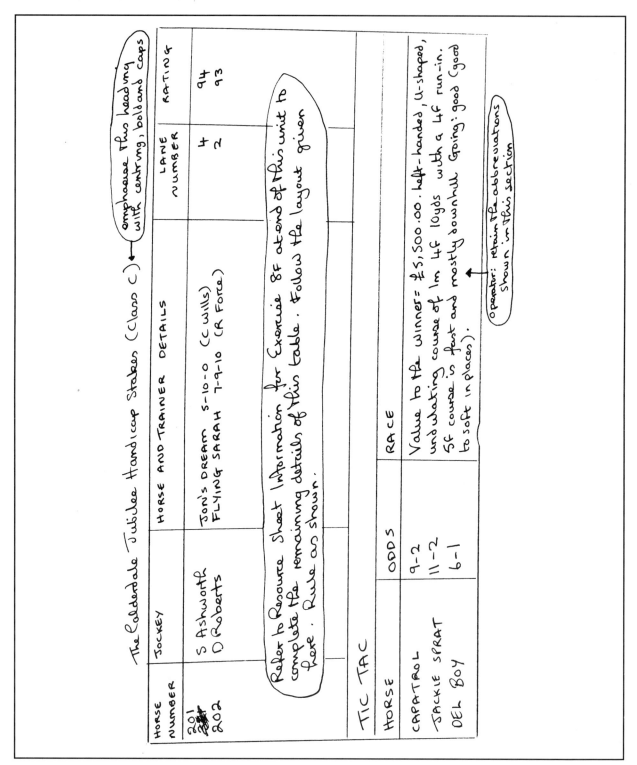

The Calderdale Jubilee Handicap Stakes (Class C) — *emphasise this heading with centring, bold and caps*

HORSE NUMBER	JOCKEY	HORSE AND TRAINER DETAILS	LANE NUMBER	RATING
201	S Ashworth	Jon's Dream 5-10-0 (C Wills)	4	94
202	D Roberts	FLYING SARAH 7-9-10 (R Force)	2	93

Refer to Resource Sheet Information for Exercise 8F at end of this unit to complete the remaining details of this table. Follow the layout given here. Rule as shown.

TIC TAC

HORSE	ODDS	RACE
CAPATROL	9-2	Value to the winner= £5,500.00. left-handed, U-shaped, undulating course of 1m 4f 10yds with a 4f run-in. 5f course is flat and mostly downhill. Going: good (good to soft in places).
JACKIE SPRAT	11-2	
DEL BOY	6-1	

Operator: retain the abbreviations shown in this section

8.24 Check your printout with the printout at the back of the book. If you find any errors, correct them and print the document again, if necessary.

8.25 Exit the program if you have finished working or continue on to the next unit.

 Resource Sheet for Exercise 8D

Resort	Departure Date	Price	Nights	Type of accommodation
Costa Blanca – Benidorm	16 July	£299.00	14	3A/SC
Portugal – Villamoura	21 July	£249.00	7	2A/BB
Ibiza – San Antonio	30 July	£329.00	14	3A/RO
Costa del Sol – Marbella	2 August	£239.00	7	2A/RO
Cyprus – Paphos	12 August	£369.00	14	2A/SC
Gran Canaria – Puerto Rico	14 August	£349.00	14	2A/HB

 Resource Sheet for Exercise 8E

LINE TYPE	DATE	CALL TIME	TOPIC	TELEPHONE NUMBER
VEGETABLES	6 June	1.5 minutes	Courgette problems	0645 68 5222
VEGETABLES	7 June	12.0 minutes	Potato problems	0645 68 5223
PEST CONTROL	7 June	7.0 minutes	Greenfly, whitefly and blackfly problems	0645 68 5342
PEST CONTROL	7 June	5.0 minutes	Leaf spots and leaf scorch problems	0645 68 5343
LEGAL	9 June	10.0 minutes	Lawn mower servicing	0645 68 5442
LEGAL	10 June	3.5 minutes	Mail order rights	0645 68 5443
LEGAL	10 June	2.0 minutes	Returning goods to garden centres	0645 68 5444
LEGAL	11 June	5.0 minutes	Overgrowing weeds from neighbour's garden	0645 68 5445

HORSE NUMBER	JOCKEY	LANE NUMBER	RATING	HORSE AND TRAINER DETAILS
203	Carl Peters	7	99	CAPATROL 4-9-7 (R Bass)
204	D Paige	5	96	LEE-VIT-OUT 8-9-7 (B Jake)
205	Jim Hunter	1	89	KATHALIAN 6-9-7 (P Caroma)
206	V Lowry	3	92	MY GOOD WILL 4-9-5 (P Terre)
207	Martin Vell	9	90	BEN 'M' 7-9-10 (C Mawdsley)
208	Will Smithies	11	88	CARLORAC 4-9-0 (D Range)
209	M Briggs	6	95	DEL BOY 7-9-10 (C McKenzie)
210	C Davies	10	91	JAUNTY JESS 4-8-6 (J Riley)
211	Darren Bounce	8	98	JACKIE SPRAT 5-8-3 (C Boot)

unit 9

▶ Consolidation 2

By the end of Unit 9, you should have revised and practised all the techniques and skills needed for the RSA Word Processing Stage III Part 2 award as well as additional techniques and skills which will help you in the workplace.

Look at your Progress Review Checklist and at your completed exercises to remind yourself of what you have learnt so far and to identify any weaknesses. Then complete the following exercises as revision.

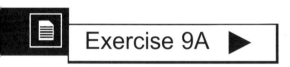

Exercise 9A ▶

9.1 Open the file you saved as **EX7G** and save as EX9A. Make the following formatting changes:

> ▶ Change to one-column layout throughout
> ▶ Change the font size to 12
> ▶ Change to double line spacing for the whole document unless otherwise indicated.

9.2 Format and amend the text as shown below:

[Handwritten box:] Please use document line length of <u>13 cm</u> (5 in) and a justified right margin. Using 10 pitch, insert a <u>header</u>: AURAL COMMUNICATIONS and a ~~footer~~: AC/Course Notes 3/name of author. Please refer to the Resource sheet to confirm spelling of header text and name of author etc – as shown for Module 3(3). Use 12 pitch for document text. Start numbering from <u>Page 14</u>

THE ART OF CONVERSATION *[Handwritten: ← Centre, bold, underline, increase font size]*

[Handwritten: Copy sentence to ✱]

The literal meaning of the word conversation indicates an activity where individuals 'turn or change together' in the sense of responding, co-operating and being interactive.//Most of us learn to converse through experience. However, in the modern age when there seems to be so much emphasis on transmitting a message, we seem to have lost the art of listening. Without this basic skill, we cannot hope to enjoy satisfactory conversations. *[Handwritten: fundamental]*

If a person joins in a conversation with the aim of scoring points or applying pressure, then the listening aspect, and usually the enjoyment, is lost. Each person needs to feel that they can express their ideas and explain their thoughts and needs without having another person 'step on their toes'.

[Handwritten left margin: Single line-spacing]

Conversation is our way of getting to know another person and finding out what is going on in their mind. Each of us lives to some extent in our own world which has been built up from the circumstances and influences which have shaped our lives. It is easy to assume that we know what another person feels or thinks, but unless we listen we will never really find out. We will be making assumptions based on our own ideas and experiences and not the other person's.

[Handwritten box:] At least one party in such a conversation does not particularly want to hear what the other has to say.

[Handwritten box:] Please leave 2.5 cm (1 in) before this paragraph

We rely on open conversations to establish good relationships. As well as listening to others and being open to their opinions, we need to be open ourselves and explain what is on <u>our</u> minds. If we do this, then guesses and assumptions will not cause confusion and misunderstanding.

Despite the old adage 'Sticks and stones may break my bones but words can't hurt me.', words <u>can</u> harm us considerably, and can affect our self-esteem to a great extent. Negative emotions can build up if we are constantly criticised. Even the first few words of a conversation can create a permanent barrier between the people involved which may never be overcome.

[Handwritten box:] *[Handwritten: keep at end of document]*
- Is the art of conversation really lost?
- If so, what factors have contributed to this loss?
- What strategies can we use in our own conversations?
- How can we help others to ~~perfect~~ master the art of conversation?

9.3 Add the following text to the end of the document, using the same font and font size as the first part. Follow all other formatting and text amendment instructions.

(replace party with participant throughout whole document)

The resulting hurt or anger can lead to withdrawal or attack, none of which leads to a helpful outcome. It is therefore important that we learn to create the right conditions for things to go well.

(PAGE 3 starts here)

During a conversation, one person is often explaining something while the other person is trying to understand. The roles change throughout a conversation. Each can help the other by really listening, by paraphrasing what the other person said to receive confirmation of understanding, and by asking questions (but not too many!) to help the other person to give a clear explanation.

(move to top of PAGE 4)

We all know how it feels to be threatened or patronised. Other people almost certainly feel exactly the same so whats needed is a way of ensuring that each party can treat the others with respect. From time to time we all need to say things which other people might not want to hear. If we try to anticipate the feelings which the other person may have, we can attempt to put across the point in a way which leaves each party feeling that their feelings and opinions are respected, even if they do not agree on the subject under discussion. We can prepare for a productive conversation by considering at the beginning/outset what the other person hopes to achieve/get out of it. Is he or she wanting some help in sorting out his or her own thoughts; is he or she anxious and needing reassurance; is he or she aiming to get an agreement on an issue; is he or she wanting to get to know you better; or is he or she simply wanting a chat for company. If we know the purpose of the conversation, we can try to make sure that it succeeds.

(PAGE 4 starts here)

Box (unruled) 5cm x 5cm (2" x 2") here   During a ... ←
✳ (Copy sentence from Page 1 here)   (replace he or she with s/he throughout document)

9.4 Save the document using the filename **EX9A** and print one copy. Check your printout with the printout at the back of the book. If you find any errors, correct them and print the document again, if necessary.

Exercise 9B ▶

9.5 Open the file you saved as **EX7K** and save as **EX9B**. Make the following format changes:

▶ Delete the text box which you used to allocate a space at the bottom right of the document
▶ Use a two-column format for the whole document
▶ Use a justified right margin.

THE INTERNATIONAL MILLENNIUM CHALLENGE

Conference to be held on Saturday and Sunday
(dates inserted)

in the
Central Civic Hall
SHEFFIELD

<u>10.00 am to 5.00 pm each day</u>

<u>Delegates:</u> *(Change headings to upper case)*

Representatives of Department for International Development
~~International Banks~~
International Aid Agencies
Private Sector
Voluntary Organisations
Environmental Organisations
Scientific Organisations

(leave 5.0 cm (2") here)

<u>The Challenge:</u>

(Re-arrange these lists in alpha-betical order and add bullets in the style of your choice)

Sustainable development of the planet
Eliminating poverty and establishing economic well-being
World health and human development
~~Partnerships~~
International trade and agriculture

(Start 2nd column here)

<u>The Debate:</u>

A lively, well-informed debate is expected. Listen to
the experts. Find out what is already being done.
Consider the future options. Decide on the best
strategies. Learn what you can do.

(Increase font size for this paragraph)

(add text here)

(leave 3.8 cm (1½") here)

<u>TICKETS AVAILABLE FROM THE
DEPARTMENT OF POLITICS, TOTLEY HALL,
SHEFFIELD</u>

(Capitals, no underline)

9.6 Add the following text where indicated and follow the formatting instructions given.

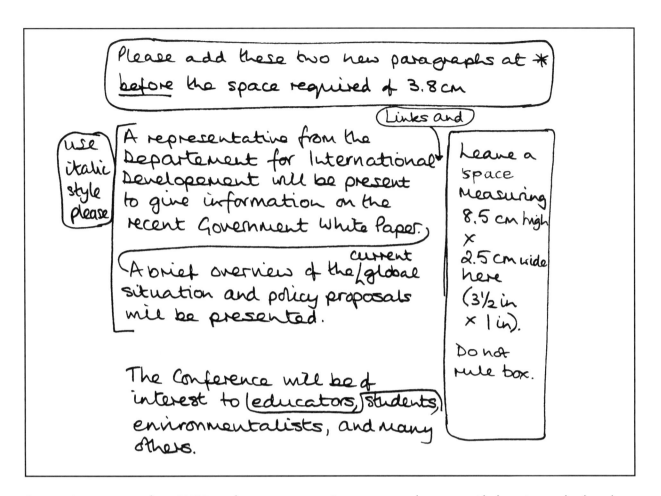

Please add these two new paragraphs at *
before the space required of 3.8 cm

Links and

use
italic
style
please

A representative from the
Department for International
Development will be present
to give information on the
recent Government White Paper.

current
A brief overview of the /global
situation and policy proposals
will be presented.

The Conference will be of
interest to educators, students,
environmentalists, and many
others.

Leave a
space
Measuring
8.5 cm high
X
2.5 cm wide
here
(3½ in
X 1 in).

Do not
rule box.

9.7 Save your work as **EX9B** and print one copy. Compare your document with the printout check at the back of the book and correct any errors.

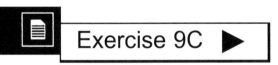

Exercise 9C ▶

9.8 Key in the following table in landscape format, referring to the Resource Sheet at the end of this unit (page 97) for the extra information.

9.9 Save the document using the filename **EX9C** and print one copy. Check your printout with the printout at the back of the book. If you find any errors, correct them and print the document again, if necessary. Exit the program if you have finished working or continue straight on to the next unit.

→ TOTLEY HALL COLLEGE, SHEFFIELD

SECTION	COURSE	CO-ORDINATOR	MODULE	TOPIC	TUTOR
Politics	World Politics	L D Forrester	1 (1)	The Pacific Rim	H K Kamara
"	European Studies	H Fürstenberger	2 (1)	The New Europe	H F ____
Economics	World Economies	J Mandanos	4 (1)	The Middle East	H Razahan

←———————————————— COURSE TUITION FEES

Section	Module(s)	Session(s)	Fee (£)
Economics	1, 2, 3, 4	Semester 1 – Oct to Jan	550.00
Humanities	3, 4, 5, 7, 8, 9	Semesters 1 and 2 – Oct to Jan, Feb to ~~June July~~	450.50
Politics	1, 2, 6, 10	Semester 1 – Oct to Jan	1,050.00

✓

TOTLEY HALL COLLEGE, SHEFFIELD

SECTION	COURSE	CO-ORDINATOR	MODULE	TOPIC	TUTOR/ AUTHOR
Politics	World Politics	L D Forrester	1(1)	The Pacific Rim	H K Kamara
Politics	European Studies	H Fürstenberger	2(1)	The New Europe	H Fürstenberger
Economics	World Economies	J Mandanos	4(1)	The Middle East	H Razahan
Economics	World Economies	J Mandanos	4(2)	The Far East	H K Kamara
Economics	World Economies	J Mandanos	4(3)	The New Europe	Elsa Granby
Humanities	Social Psychology	O J Cananga	3(3)	Oral Communications	J Welsh
Humanities	Social Psychology	O J Cananga	3(1)	Barriers to Communication	O J Cananga

unit
10

▶ # Examination Practice 2

By the end of Unit 10 you should have completed a mock examination for the RSA Word Processing Stage III Part 2 award.

RSA Word Processing Stage III Part 2

This examination assesses your ability to apply advanced word processing and production skills to produce a variety of business documents from handwritten draft, typewritten draft and recalled text and also using supplementary information. The award demonstrates competence to the level demanded for NVQ Administration Level 3.

The examination lasts for $1\frac{3}{4}$ hours and you must complete 4 documents using a word processor. Printing is done outside this time.

Examinations are carried out in registered centres and are marked by RSA examiners. The centre will give you instructions regarding stationery: letters must be produced on letterheads (either pre-printed or template) and memos may be produced on pre-printed forms, by keying in entry details or by use of a template. The invigilator will give you instructions concerning the recalling of stored files.

Examination hints

When sitting your examination:

▶ you may use a manual prepared by the centre or the software manufacturer
▶ put your name, centre number and document number on each document
▶ check your work very carefully before printing – proofread, spellcheck
▶ assemble your printouts in the correct order at the end of the examination.

You are now ready to try a mock examination for Word Processing Stage III Part 2. Take care and good luck!

The list of assessment criteria for this examination is long and detailed. To be sure that you have reached the required standard to be entered for an examination, you need to work through several past papers and have these marked by a tutor or assessor who is qualified and experienced in this field.

Results

If your finished work has 5 faults or fewer, you will be awarded a distinction.
If your finished work has between 6 and 14 faults, you will be awarded a pass.

Results are sent to the centre where you sit your examination.

Key in the following text, expanding abbreviations and making other amendments. This text will be used for Documents 1 and 4 in this unit. Save your work as **UNIT10PRELIMTASK**. Print a copy of this task and check it with the printout check at the back of the book before continuing with other documents in this unit.

EXECUTIVE SECRETARIES GROUP
NORTHERN AREA ANNUAL CONFERENCE AND EXHIBITION] ← *Centre and bold*
WHEATWOOD HOUSE, HARROGATE
Friday 4 December and Saturday 5 December 1998

For our second Annual Conference and Exhibition, we have taken the opp to visit Harrogate – a spa town in central northern England. The venue is situated approx 1 mile from the town centre on the Wetherby Road.

Accomodation is available at the Conference venue. (Further info and tariff can be obtained from The Conference Sec, ESG, 127-129 Vespergate Street, York, YO3 8PW.) We recomend that yr application for accomodation is recieved by the end of Sept as we beleive that Dec weekend breaks are likely to be in great demand in this attractive part of the country. (Reduced rates are offered for collegues from one org sharing a twin room.) The Conference venue is an 18th century country house with traditional architectural features and furnishings. You will appreacte the tasteful, modern accomodation block built in local matching stone which provides en-suite single and twin rooms with every poss facility to gntee a comfortable stay. The full range of business ~~and communications~~ services are available to visitors in the permanentley staffed Conference Office, where your correspondance and electronic communication needs can be ~~satisfied~~ *met*.

SENDITCO ← *(embolden headings)*

A leading inte(r)national distribution co which has recently introduced a new service – Importing Services. Forget the problems of foregn language barriers, time differences and exchangerates. You can arrange for the importing of documents, freight and parcels from your suppliers around the world. You can even track your consignment on the Web! ~~Their~~ *Senditco's* Air Charter service is available for really urgent goods and you can have confirmation of all deliveries to Europe by ~~means of~~ a telephone call.

Simply making

ROYAL MAIL

Responding to the challenge of the changing working environment. Special post boxes for franked mail and extended collection times in commercial areas help to ensure today's mail gets on it's way. Many supermarkets now sell postage stamps and some have post boxes; these services are being rapidly expanded.

QUI(c)KLINK *of Scotland, the northern counties, Wales and the south-west*

Garanteed overnight delivery service. Operating throughout the United Kingdom. Specialises' in remote locations such as the highlands, islands, moors, dales and vales. Provides a quick and reliable service for the veterinary and agricultural sector.

Recall this document stored as UNIT10PRELIMTASK and amend as shown. Adjust margins to give a line length of 16 cm. Change to double line-spacing (except where indicated) and retain full justification. Insert and delete page breaks so that the document prints on 4 pages. Save as UNIT10DOC1 and print one copy.

AND ADMINISTRATORS

EXECUTIVE SECRETARIES GROUP *underline this line*
NORTHERN AREA ANNUAL CONFERENCE AND EXHIBITION
WHEATWOOD HOUSE, HARROGATE
Friday 4 December and Saturday 5 December 1998

Inset by 25mm from left and right margins

2nd

For our ~~second~~ Annual Conference and Exhibition, we have taken the opportunity to visit Harrogate – a spa town in central northern England. ~~The venue~~ is situated approximately 1 mile from ~~the~~ town centre on the Wetherby Road.   W— H—

Harrogate

Accommodation is available at the Conference venue. (Further information and tariff can be obtained from The Conference Secretary, ESG, 127-129 Vespergate Street, York, YO3 8PW.) Reduced rates are offered for colleagues from one organisation sharing a twin room. We recommend that your application for accommodation is received by the end of September as we believe that December weekend breaks are likely to be in great demand in this attractive part of the country.

This sentence in all capitals

Single line-spacing

W— H—

~~The Conference venue~~ is an 18th century country house with traditional architectural features and furnishings. You will appreciate the tasteful, modern accommodation block built in local matching stone which provides en-suite single and twin rooms ~~with every possible facility to guarantee a comfortable stay~~. The full range of business services is available to ~~visitors~~ *guests* in the permanently staffed Conference Office, where your correspondence and electronic communication needs can be met.

Copy to A

B ◀ *Page 2 to start here.* **C** = 1st para on Page 2

SENDITCO

A leading international distribution company which has recently introduced a new service – Importing Services. Forget the problems of foreign language barriers, time differences and exchange rates. You can arrange for the importing of documents, freight and parcels from your suppliers around the world. You can even track your consignment on the Web! Senditco's Air Charter service is available for really urgent goods and you can have confirmation of all deliveries to Europe by simply making a telephone call.

ROYAL MAIL

Responding to the challenge of the changing working environment. Special post boxes for franked mail and extended collection times in commercial areas help to ensure today's mail gets on its way. Many supermarkets now sell postage stamps and some have post boxes; these services are being rapidly expanded.

Insert CONFERENCE 1998 as a header and ESAG/98/CONF/1 as a footer. Header and footer to appear on every page.

QUICKLINK UK

Guaranteed overnight delivery service.   Operating throughout the United Kingdom.
Specialises in remote locations such as the highlands, islands, moors, dales and vales of
Scotland, the northern counties, Wales and the south-west.   Provides a quick and reliable
service for the veterinary and agricultural sector.   Move to [B] on Page 1

✓ Exhibitors have been invited from the ~~full~~ whole spectrum of business
services. Demonstrations and presentations will take place
throughout both days. // Speakers from recruitment agencies,
software mfrs, ~~equipment distributors~~ & service providers
~~are~~ will be scheduled at pre-arranged times in the
Knaresborough Room so that delegates ~~and visitors~~ can
organise there own Conference ~~time~~ table.   Change typeface and/or pitch for this para

Details of some exhibitors are given on the ~~following~~ exhibition pages.
We anticipate that at least 30 ^ stands will be filled.   Move to [C] - top of Pg 2

✓ Further details + watch out for in next newsletter.

Page 3 to start here

DAZZLE PAPERS
The brand leader in presentation materials and equipment.
Get yr point across through OHP or EPS. ~~See~~ watch the latest
multi-media machine in action and see for yourself.

IMAGE SYSTEMS LTD
✓ ~~A label~~ The latest in office paper technology, giving optimum
print ~~quality~~ and prestige to all yr important documents.
Fully compatible with all types of printing equipment.

Page 4 to start here

MARKIT
A label for every purpose, and much more too! Printer,
diskette, copier, self-adhesive, filing, organiser and
wall/chart labels, stickers, markers and guides. Be
sure everything is in it's place.

MAGIC STRIPS
whether you want to ~~hide~~ correct yr mistakes, cover up
confidential or private info in a document, or label
yr files, folders and shelves, there's a tape product
to ~~do the~~ help you to job neatly and imperceptibly.

[A]   Please change Wheatwood House to
Marisco Wheatwood Hall throughout
the document

LETTER – Top + 2 please – One for Conference Sec, ESAG, one for our file. Indicate routing.

Our ref 98/CONF/VENUE

Mrs Mollie Pitman
Conference Office
Marisco Wheatwood Hall
Insert full address from Resource Sheet

Dear Mrs Pitman   *Check this title and amend if necessary*

NORTHERN ANNUAL CONFERENCE AND EXHIBITION

I am writing to confirm our telephone conversation of yesterday when I booked the Ripon Room and the Knaresborough Room for the above ESAG event, which is to take place on Fri and Sat, 4 and 5 Dec 1998.

I have informed all members and prospective exhibitors of the accommodation and facilities available at the Hall by including the following paragraph in all literature:

Insert here the 3rd paragraph of the document stored as UNIT10PRELIMTASK and change to italics.

As arranged, I would be pleased to receive 100 copies of yr leaflet, tariff and local area map. Please forward these direct to the Conference Secretary, ESAG, (*Insert full address from Document 1*). //The Group's officers wish to reserve 2 twin rooms for four nights from Wed 2 to Sat 5 Dec and, as agreed, require acess to both Conference Rooms from 9 am on Thursday to 2.00 pm on Sunday.

I enclose a copy of the Prime Results Business venue booking Catalogue which contains details of our venue booking and event organisation services. I hope to contact you shortly with a view to including the Halls' details in this publication.

Yrs scly

Michelle Carr-Holmes
Business Venues Administrator

Please key in as shown. Same as UNIT 10 DOC3 and print one copy with longest edge at top. Rule as shown.

ESAG NORTHERN AREA ANNUAL CONFERENCE AND EXHIBITION

CO NAME	TYPE OF BUSINESS	ADDRESS	CONTACT	TEL NO
SENDITCO INTERNATIONAL	International Distribution	140 Bolton Rd, MANCHESTER, M4 9LL	Mike Frost	0161-7349292
ROYAL MAIL	International Mail	PO House, St Paul's Close, LEEDS, LS1 7NJ	Steve Bulmer	01132-669991
QUICKLINK UK	UK delivery	Dale House, 13 Dale Rd, BRADFORD, BD8 9WH	Janet Good	01274-884343

Refer to Resource Sheet for remaining details. Follow layout given here

STAND ALLOCATION

EXHIBITOR	ROOM/STAND	FEE PAYABLE (£)
Magic Strips	Ripon A10	£560.25
Markit	Ripon A8-A9	£1,120.50
Dazzle Papers	Ripon A12-A14	£1,680.75

Refer to Resource Sheet for remaining info

Right-align this section

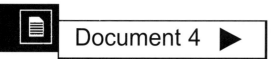

Recall the heading and first 3 paragraphs of the document stored as UNIT10PRELIM TASK and amend as shown. Display whole document in 2 columns (newspaper style). Save as UNIT10DOC4 and print one copy.

EXECUTIVE SECRETARIES GROUP
NORTHERN AREA ANNUAL CONFERENCE AND EXHIBITION
WHEATWOOD HOUSE, HARROGATE
Friday 4 December and Saturday 5 December 1998

For our second Annual Conference and Exhibition, we have taken the opportunity to visit Harrogate ~~a spa town in central northern England~~. The venue is situated approximately 1 mile from the town centre on the Wetherby Road.

Accommodation is available at the Conference venue. (Further information and tariff can be obtained from The Conference Secretary, ESG, 127-129 Vespergate Street, York, YO3 8PW.) Reduced rates are offered for colleagues from one organisation sharing a twin room. We recommend that your application for accommodation is received by the end of September as we believe that December weekend breaks are likely to be in great demand in this attractive part of the country.

Leave a space here in left column only, at least 35mm across from left margin and 35mm down but no more than 45mm across and 45mm down.
DO NOT RULE BOX

The Conference venue is an 18th century country house with traditional architectural features and furnishings. ~~You will appreciate the tasteful, modern accommodation block built in local matching stone which provides en-suite single and twin rooms with every possible facility to guarantee a comfortable stay.~~ The full range of business services is available to visitors in the permanently staffed Conference Office, where your correspondence and electronic communication needs can be met.

The following distribution cos will be in attendance:

SENDITCO   [A leading international distribution co which has recently introduced a new service — Importing Services.

ROYAL MAIL ← bold for these headings
Responding to the challenge of the changing working environment.

QUICKLINK UK
Gnteed overnight delivery service. Operating throughout the United Kingdom

Other exhibitors include: ← bold

Best (Secs) Recruitment
Dazzle Papers
ABC Indexing
Markit
Paralegal Services

Image Systems Ltd
Magic Strips
Major Minor Music
Prime Time Ltd

Display as one column and sort into alphabetical order

Retain abbreviation

PRIME RESULTS LTD
CONFERENCE VENUE BOOKING CHECKLIST

ESAG NORTHERN AREA ANNUAL CONFERENCE AND EXHIBITION
MARISCO WHEATWOOD HALL, Wetherby Road, HARROGATE, HG8 2TE

Type of Business	Company Name	Contact	Address	Tel No
International Distribution	SENDITCO £560.25 Ripon B20	Mike Frost	140 Bolton Road MANCHESTER M4 9LL	0161-7349292
International Mail	ROYAL MAIL Ripon B16-B19 £2,241-00	Steve Bulmer	PO House St Paul's Close LEEDS LS1 7NJ	01132-6669991
UK Delivery	QUICKLINK UK Ripon B10 £560.25	Janet Good	13 Dale Road BRADFORD BD8 9WH	01274-884343
Office tapes	MAGIC STRIPS Ripon A10 £560.25	Aslam Hussain	Abracadabra Mills HUDDERSFIELD HD2 2DS	01484-908767
Office stationery	MARKIT Ripon A8-A9 £1,120.50	Linda Rickaby	Empire House HALIFAX HX2 6HG	01422-334455
Office paper	DAZZLE PAPERS Ripon A12-A14 £1,680.75	Nick Blacker	120 Bright Street KEIGHLEY BD21 4SH	01535-545432
Presentation Packages	IMAGE SYSTEMS Ripon A3 £560.25	Ellen Birstall	EPS House Elm Way WAKEFIELD WF3 3WD	01924-212345

unit 11

▶ Document design

By the end of Unit 11 you should have learnt how to:

▶ produce a document containing an element of design
▶ apply borders and shading to enhance the appearance of the document
▶ add full-page borders.

Document presentation

Document presentation combines the effective use of text in various fonts and sizes with various visual effects, including:

▶ text boxes
▶ drawings
▶ graphics
▶ diagrams
▶ columns
▶ clip art
▶ borders.

The electronic age has brought desk top publishing (DTP) into the office. This means that even basic documents can be enhanced simply with a little know-how and flair. Word 97 allows you to combine many methods of document design within the same program.

DTP is still recognised as a profession in its own right and there are many courses which specialise in this subject to advanced levels. The purpose of this section of the book, however, is to provide you with sufficient knowledge and information to meet the standards of the RSA Document Presentation Stage III Part 2 examination. Once you have learnt the basic techniques, you will be able to apply them more creatively in other situations.

In the examination, make sure that you follow all the instructions given – do not allow your creative urges to run away with you. You can use Word 97's more advanced design features later to impress your boss or your friends.

Think carefully about the message you want to convey, your audience and your resources.

It is a good idea to draft out the layout of the page on a piece of rough paper first. Positioning the design elements beforehand will often provide you with a clearer outline of the end result you want to achieve. Include all headings/items. Arrange the layout in a logical manner using your own initiative, but according to any instructions given. You will get better with practice.

Check all instructions that specify certain sizes – eg font sizes, text boxes. Don't use too many different font types – the document will look cluttered and amateur.

Make good use of the paper size – don't squash everything together! The end result should look clear and presentable. Clever use of the 'white space' on the page – eg margins, space between paragraphs – can contribute to the overall presentation of the document.

Document presentation and layout

Some of the requirements of the RSA Document Presentation Stage III Part 2 examination include:

► recalling text that has been previously stored
► carrying out amendments to recalled text
► changing the font, typeface/character, point size, line spacing and alignment of text – within headers and footers as well as within the main text
► paginating documents so that no less than two lines of a paragraph appear at the top and bottom of each page – ie avoiding widows and orphans
► numbering pages correctly
► using drawing facilities to create text boxes, shapes and diagrams with or without shaded backgrounds
► importing graphics/clip art images into the document
► creating and inserting borders/dividers into the document
► inserting special characters – eg mathematical symbols, accents, fractions, bullet points, subscript and superscript
► presenting information in columns – this may apply to a specified section of the page only
► carrying out all ruling using the word processor and not by hand
► carrying out an aspect of modification as instructed (eg search and replace, case conversion, use of house style)
► abstracting information from another exercise or a resource/reference sheet
► using appropriate top, bottom, left and right margins – these must not be less than 13mm ($\frac{1}{2}$ in)
► using consistent spacing between and within similar items within a document.

 ## Add borders, lines and shading

You can add a wide range of lines, boxes or shaded backgrounds to enhance headings, paragraphs, portions of text, tables and pictures.

Mouse and menu method

► Select: The item – eg paragraph, heading – to which you want to add a border or shading
► Select: **Borders and Shading** from the **Format** menu.

The **Borders** dialogue box appears on screen.

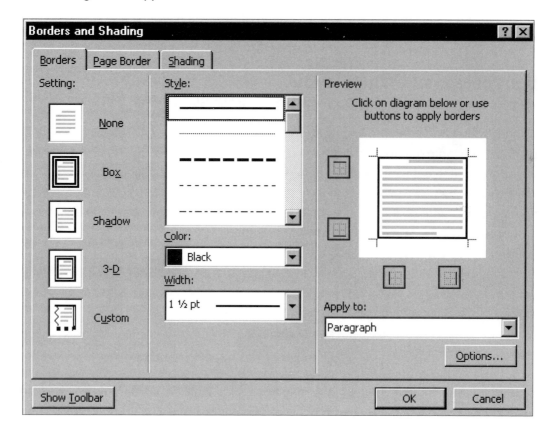

Figure 11.1 Borders dialogue box

To add a border or line(s):

▶ Click: The **Borders** tab
▶ Select: The required border display from the **Setting**, **Style**, **Color** and **Width** sections – you can view your choices in the **Preview** section
▶ Select: How far you want the border to extend in the **Apply to** box (eg **Paragraph**, **Table**, **Cell**)
▶ Click: **OK**

To adjust the distance between the border lines and the inside

Click: The **Options** button
Key in: The required internal margin specifications

To add shading:

Click: The **Shading** tab

The **Shading** dialogue box appears on screen.

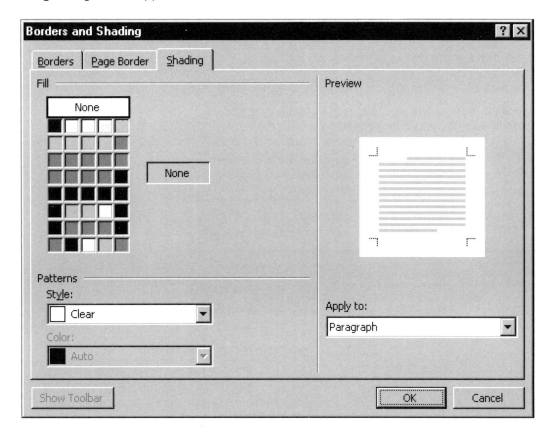

Figure 11.2 Shading dialogue box

▶ Select: The required shading from the **Fill**, **Style** and **Color** sections – you can view your choices in the **Preview** section

▶ Select: How far you want the shading to extend in the **Apply to** box (eg **Paragraph**, **Table**, **Cell**)

▶ Click: **OK**

Tool Bar method

▶ Select: The item – eg paragraph, heading – to which you want to add a border or shading

▶ Select: **Toolbars** from the **View** menu

▶ Select: **Tables and Borders**

The Tables and Borders Tool Bar appears on screen.

Figure 11.3 Tables and Borders Tool Bar

▶ Click: The [————— ▼] **Line Style** button to select a line style – eg dotted, straight, dashed

▶ Click: The [⬧ ▼] **Shading Color** button to select a fill colour

▶ Click: The [1 ½ ▼] **Line Weight** button to select a line thickness

▶ Click: The  **Borders** button to select a border or line position

▶ Click: The **Borders** button to select a border or line position

To adjust the width of the border or shading:

Drag the square left indent marker   and/or the right indent marker

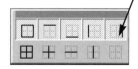

Remove borders or shading ▶

Borders

▶ Select: The bordered item

▶ Click: The **Borders** button on the Formatting Tool Bar

▶ Click: The **No Border** button on the drop-down grid

Shading

▶ Select: The shaded item

▶ Select: **Borders and Shading** from the **Format** menu

▶ Select: The **Shading** tab

▶ Click: **None** in the **Fill** section

Exercise 11A ▶

11.1 Starting with a new document on screen key in the following text, applying bold, borders and shading as indicated.

     ▶ Use Times New Roman, font size 12 for the document text

     ▶ Use Arial, font size 12 for the main heading and the sub headings.

Refer back to Unit 1 if you need to refresh your memory on bullets and their formatting. Save the document using the filename **EX11A**. Using the Print Preview facility, check your work with the printout at the back of the book. If you find any errors, correct them and print one copy.

CAUSE-AND-EFFECT DIAGRAM

USE AS A MANAGEMENT TOOL

Cause-and-effect diagrams are used to clarify thought processes, presenting a visual aid for the causes of given problems and the reasons surrounding certain situations. They can be used as tools for problem solving or for handling and presenting information. 'Brainstorming', either individually, or with others, and writing down the suggestions offered on paper usually generates the initial list of possible causes. If items on the list are grouped rationally, it is often possible to see similarities and patterns emerging in the diagram, conveying the idea that a collection of factors (causes) may lead to a particular effect.

KEY CATEGORIES

Interpretations of the appropriate key categories to use depend on the individual's perception of the main reasons for the status quo in an organisation as well as on the particular area and level being examined. The following key categories cover most situations and are a useful starting point for the cause-and-effect diagram to be applied:

- Methods
- Machines
- Materials
- Manpower (converted to the term 'People' by the gender-conscious)

What happens in the operating core of an organisation is fundamentally a question of people, working with various methods and machines, to turn materials into products and services.

Full-page borders ▶

You can apply a range of full-page decorative borders to enhance the appearance of your document.

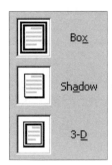
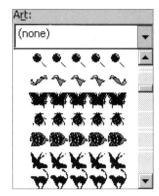

Figure 11.4 Simple and decorative page borders ·

▶ Select: **Borders and Shading** from the **Format** menu
▶ Select: The **Page Border** tab
▶ Select: The required border display from the **Setting**, **Style**, **Color**, **Width** or **Art** sections – you can view your choices in the **Preview** section
▶ Click: **OK**

To specify a particular page or section of the document for the border to appear in:

▶ Click: The option you want in the **Apply to** drop-down menu

To specify the exact position of the border on the page:

▶ Click: **Options**
▶ In the **Margin** section: Adjust the **Top**, **Bottom**, **Left** or **Right** margin settings
▶ In the **Measure from:** box: Choose where you want the border to be measured from – **Text** to measure from the page margins and **Edge of Paper** to measure from the edge of the page
▶ In the **Options** section: Choose whether to include the header and/or footer in the border – remove the tick to deselect ☐ or insert a tick to select ☑

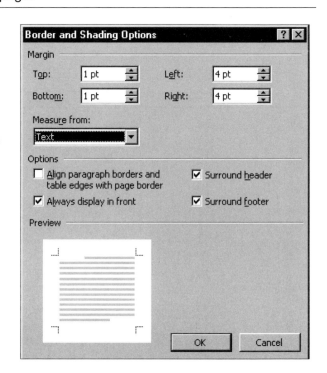

To position the border on selected side(s) of a page:

You can use the **Page Borders** facility to insert a ruled line at one side of the page only.

▶ Click: **Custom** in the **Setting** section
▶ Select: The display settings required as normal (select an option from the Art section if you want a graphical border)
▶ Under **Preview**, click: The diagram or use the border buttons to specify where you want the border to appear
▶ Click: **OK**

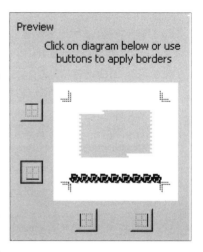

In this example the border will appear at the bottom of the page only.

 Exercise 11B ▶

11.2 Retrieve the file **EX11A**, unless it is already on your screen. Amend the document following the instructions given below. Save as **EX11B** and print one copy.

▶ Change the main heading only to Arial, font size 14
▶ Add the text below to the end of the document making it consistent with the original display
▶ Using Times New Roman, font size 9, insert a header **CAUSE-AND-EFFECT DIAGRAM** at the top right of the document and a footer **MANAGEMENT TOOL 3** at the bottom left of the document
▶ Insert a page break in a sensible place and number the pages at the bottom right of the page
▶ Add a full-page border:
   ▶ Settings: Shadow
   ▶ Color: Gray – 50%
   ▶ Width: 3 pt
   ▶ Click: The **Options** button Select: **Text** from the **Measure from** box
   ▶ Enter top, bottom, left and right margins of 12 pt
   ▶ Do not include the header and footer in the page border.

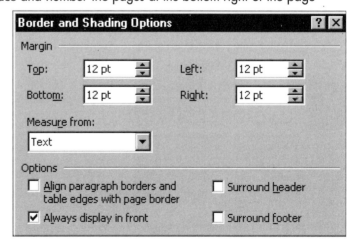

Note: The term **pt** is short for **point size** – point size is a measurement which may relate to the width of a line or border, the size of a font or the amount of margin space.

DRAWING THE DIAGRAM
The following stages are a suggested method of working:

a) enter the problem as an effect
b) add branches to main spine to represent a particular category/cause
c) list ideas about possible causes on lines linked to relevant main branch
d) add further analysis where appropriate to the preliminary ideas

A cause-and-effect diagram is not to be viewed as a magical solution to a problem. Rather, it records and presents information, and is an aid to structuring thought processes.

RELATIONSHIP DIAGRAMS

A cause-and-effect diagram doesn't show the inter-relationships between elements of a situation. A relationship diagram can be used to highlight the inter-relationship of causes which are often a feature of the actual problem. This consists of written words denoting factors and elements in a situation and lines showing the connections and relationships between them.

Alternatively, a cause-and-effect diagram could be extended to show the inter-relationship links between the factors identified under each category.

MULTIPLE CAUSE DIAGRAMS These combine elements from both types of diagram to portray connections between various causes.

In order for it to be effective, start with the event to be understood, then portray the contributing factors, then portray the factors which contributed to those factors, and so on. You need to be specific and think outward and backward as you go along. The diagram is a visual display of phrases, lines and arrows showing the direction of effects. The cause-and-effect diagram is thus extended to show the contributing factors.

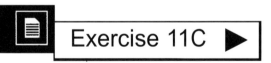

Exercise 11C ▶

11.3 Starting with a clear screen, key in the following document, following all the instructions. Save the document using the filename **EX11C** and print one copy.

▶ Use a document line length of 13cm ($5\frac{1}{4}$ in) and a justified right-hand margin throughout
▶ Use Perpetua, font size 11 for the document text
▶ Use Arial, font size 12, bold for the main and subheadings
▶ Add a border and shading to the main heading as shown

▶ Add shading only to all the subheadings and the clear line space below as shown in the first two examples shown below

▶ Add a full-page border – select an appropriate decorative border from the Art drop down menu.

THERAPEUTIC USE OF ESSENTIAL OILS

HAIR AND SCALP TREATMENT

Completely natural treatments for dry or greasy hair, and even dandruff, provide a welcome alternative for people who are allergic to strong perfumes and chemicals present in many standard preparations. Blends of essences, diluted in a vegetable oil, give off a wonderful scent too.

FACIAL CREAMS

General aromatherapy treatments can improve skin tone, stimulate circulation and aid toxin removal. Essences such as lavender and neroli are cytophylactic and have a rejuvenating effect on the skin. Other essences have an astringent cleansing effect and can be used in lotions to cleanse oily skin. Others are antiseptic and can be used to eradicate spots and other skin infections.

MASSAGE OILS

Oils can be blended to suit all sorts of individual problems, from emotional anxiety to muscular aches and pains. Essential oils are diluted in vegetable base oils, usually 2½% dilution for adults unless otherwise directed.

Use a 2-column layout for this section

AROMATIC BATHS
Bath oils are a vital aspect of aromatherapy both for health and beauty. The particular choice of oil will determine whether the bath is stimulating and refreshing or relaxing and sedating.

Essential oils are mixed with a vegetable base before being added to the bath water.

OIL BURNER, DIFFUSER Burners are a safe, natural ozone-friendly way of freshening a room or aiding sleep. Lavendar at night will reduce sleep and relaxation.

Eucalyptus will help to ease congestion during colds and flu infections. Other essences can help to promote a feeling of well-being and calm.

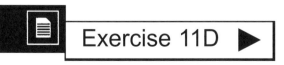

Exercise 11D ▶

11.4 Starting with a clear screen, key in the following document, following all the instructions given below. Save the document using the filename **EX11D** and print one copy.

- ▶ Use a document line length of 12.5cm (5in) and centre the text as shown
- ▶ Use Times New Roman, font size 12 unless otherwise indicated
- ▶ Add borders and/or shading where indicated
- ▶ Add a full-page border – select an appropriate decorative border from the Art drop-down menu
- ▶ Click: The **Options** button
- ▶ Enter top, bottom, left and right margins of **30 pt**
- ▶ Select: Text from the **Measure from** box

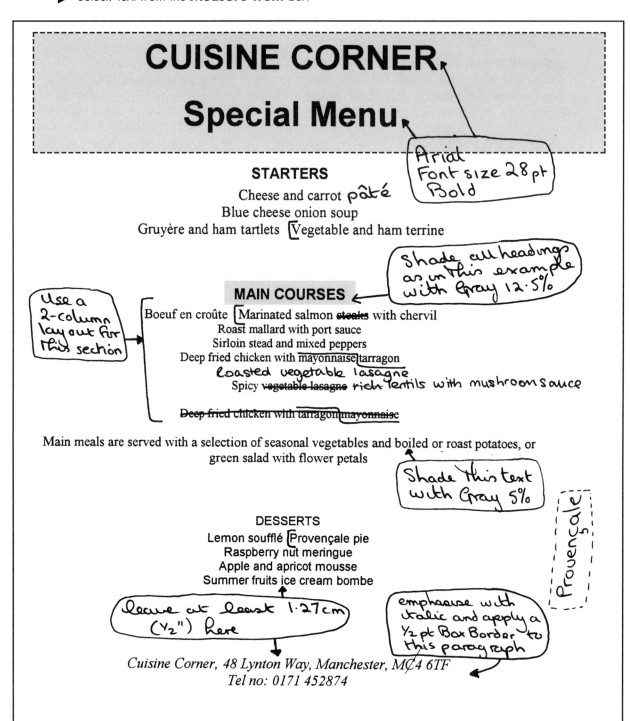

CUISINE CORNER

Special Menu

Arial Font size 28 pt Bold

STARTERS

Cheese and carrot pâté
Blue cheese onion soup
Gruyère and ham tartlets [Vegetable and ham terrine

Shade all headings as in this example with Grey 12.5%

MAIN COURSES

Use a 2-column layout for this section

Boeuf en croûte [Marinated salmon ~~steaks~~ with chervil
Roast mallard with port sauce
Sirloin stead and mixed peppers
Deep fried chicken with mayonnaise tarragon
Roasted vegetable lasagne
Spicy ~~vegetable lasagne~~ rich lentils with mushroom sauce

~~Deep fried chicken with tarragon mayonnaise~~

Main meals are served with a selection of seasonal vegetables and boiled or roast potatoes, or green salad with flower petals

Shade this text with Grey 5%

DESSERTS

Lemon soufflé [Provençale pie
Raspberry nut meringue
Apple and apricot mousse
Summer fruits ice cream bombe

Provençale

leave at least 1.27cm (½") here

emphasise with italic and apply a ½ pt Box Border to this paragraph

Cuisine Corner, 48 Lynton Way, Manchester, MC4 6TF
Tel no: 0171 452874

unit 12
▶ Drawing tools

By the end of Unit 12 you should have learnt how to:

▶ use Word 97's drawing tools to produce shapes, diagrams and dividers
▶ insert a text box into a document
▶ apply shading to text boxes and drawing shapes
▶ insert text into a drawing shape.

In the RSA Document Presentation Stage III Part 2 examination you will need to be able to produce a diagram for use within a document. Word 97 offers a range of drawing tools within the same software program. These allow you to combine text and drawings with relative ease.

Drawing tools

Word 97's drawing tools can be used in a variety of ways. You will need to familiarise yourself with the different functions of the drawing tools in order to analyse the best use for each tool in relation to the type of diagram or shape required. The best way to learn is to practise.

 ## Display (or hide) the Drawing Tool Bar ▶

Click: The **Drawing** button on the Standard Tool Bar
The **Drawing** Tool Bar appears on screen.

Figure 12.1 Drawing Tool Bar

Draw a basic shape ▶

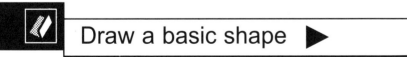

▶ Click: The required shape on the Drawing Tool Bar, ie the **Line, Arrow, Rectangle** or **Oval**
▶ Position the insertion pointer: Where you want to start drawing – the cursor changes to a + cross-hair pointer

► Hold down: The left mouse button; and
► Drag: The shape in the appropriate direction until it is the required size

To draw a perfect circle, square or straight line:

► Hold down: The **Shift** key whilst drawing the shape – the oval shape for a circle, and the rectangle shape for a square

Format or change a shape

Before you can edit a shape, you need to select it.

Select a shape ►

Click the mouse pointer: On the graphic – the cursor changes to a four-headed arrow ✢

The shape is selected when it appears with small 'handles' around it, eg: ▱⌁▱▱▱⌁▱

Select several shapes

► Click: The ⬚ **Select Objects** icon on the Drawing Tool Bar
► Move the arrowhead to: The shapes
► Hold down: The mouse button; *and*
► Drag the dotted outline around the group of objects that you want to select:

OR

► Hold down: The **Shift** key; *and*
► Select: Each shape in turn (still holding the **Shift** key down)
► Release: The **Shift** key when all the objects are selected.

Deselect a shape ►

Click the mouse pointer: In any area of white space.

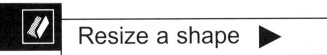

Resize a shape ▶

You can resize a shape by making it larger or smaller: stretching or shrinking it vertically, horizontally or both.

▶ ▶ Select: The shape to be edited

▶ ▶ Point to: The appropriate handle – a double-headed arrow is displayed ↔

▶ ▶ Click: The ↔ arrow or the ↕ arrow to alter the shape horizontally or vertically; *and*

▶ ▶ Drag the mouse: In the required direction to either increase or decrease the size

---

▶ ▶ Click: The ↗ arrow or the ↘ arrow to alter the shape both vertically and horizontally; *and*

▶ ▶ Drag the mouse: In the required direction to either increase or decrease the overall shape size

Note: To keep the same overall proportions, hold down the **Shift** key whilst resizing the shape.

Move a shape ▶

▶ Click: The shape to be moved/repositioned. The insertion point changes to a four-headed arrow

▶ Drag: The drawing object to its new position.

Shade, colour or pattern a shape ▶

▶ Click: The [🪣 ▾] **Fill Color** button, the [🖌 ▾] **Line Color** button, the [A̲ ▾] **Font Color** button, the [≡] **Line Style** button, the [⋮] **Dash Style** button or the **Arrow Style** button on the Drawing Tool Bar

▶ Select: From the menu choices offered.

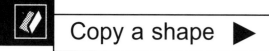

Copy a shape ▶

▶ Select: The shape to be copied
▶ Operate: The normal *copy* and *paste* commands; *and*
▶ Drag: The duplicate shape to the required position on the page.

Cut/delete a shape ▶

▶ Select: The shape to be cut/delete
▶ Operate: The normal cut/delete commands.

Group shapes together ▶

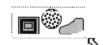

a selected group

▶ Select: All the shapes to be grouped
▶ Click: The [Draw ▾] **Draw** button on the Drawing Tool Bar
▶ Select: **Group** from the list of options offered
▶ *Note:* Any further changes will affect all the objects in the group, ie you may *colour, resize* or *move* them all together.

Ungroup previously grouped shapes ▶

▶ Select: The group
▶ Click: The [Draw ▾] **Draw** button on the Drawing Tool Bar
▶ Select: **Ungroup** from the list of options offered.

Send a shape in front
or behind another shape ▶

▶ Select: The shape to be repositioned
▶ Click: The [Draw ▾] **Draw** button on the Drawing Tool Bar
▶ Select: **Order**

► Choose: The appropriate command from the list of options offered – eg **Send to Back, Bring to Front**.

Send a shape in front or behind text

Send behind text

► Select: The shape to be repositioned
► Click: The [Draw ▾] **Draw** button on the Drawing Tool Bar
► Select: **Order**
► Choose: The appropriate command from the list of options offered – eg **Send Behind Text, Bring in Front of Text**

Flip, rotate or reshape a shape

shape flipped vertical

► Select: The shape to be repositioned
► Click: The [Draw ▾] **Draw** button on the Drawing Tool Bar
► Select: **Rotate or Flip**
► Choose: The appropriate command from the list of options offered.

Align shapes or distribute evenly

uneven alignment

shapes aligned at top

► Select: The shapes to be aligned
► Click: The [Draw ▾] **Draw** button on the Drawing Tool Bar
► Select: **Align or Distribute**
► Choose: The appropriate command from the list of options offered. When you chose the distribute evenly command, Word will distribute the shapes or graphics evenly between the first and last shape or graphic displayed on the page. You should therefore move the first and last shape or graphic to the appropriate start and end positions required.

Draw autoshapes ▶

You can edit autoshapes in exactly the same way as a standard shape

▶ Select: **Autoshapes** from the Drawing Tool Bar

The drop-down list contains several different types of shapes, including lines, basic shapes, arrows, flowchart elements, stars, banners and callouts. Many have a small yellow diamond-shaped adjustment handle that lets you change the most prominent feature of a shape, eg the size of the arrow point.

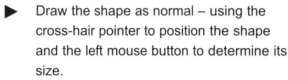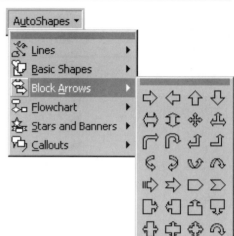

▶ Choose: A shape from the submenu of options

▶ Draw the shape as normal – using the cross-hair pointer to position the shape and the left mouse button to determine its size.

 ## Add shadow or 3-D to a shape ▶

▶ Select: The shape to be edited

▶ Click: The **Shadow button** or the **3-D** button on the Drawing Tool Bar

▶ Choose: From the menu of options offered.

 ## Add text to a shape ▶

You can add text to shapes and autoshapes.

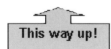

▶ Right-click: The shape

▶ Click: **Add Text** on the shortcut menu

▶ Key in: The text

Note: If you *move* the shape, the text will move with it. However, if you *rotate* or *flip* the shape, the text does *not* rotate or flip with it. You can change the *colour* of the text using the **Font Color** icon. You can rotate the text 90 degrees to the left or right by selecting **Text Direction** from the **Format** menu.

Wrap text around a shape

You can wrap text around an object of any size or shape. You can choose specific sides of the shape that you want the text to wrap around and also the distance between the shape and the text that surrounds it.

▶ Select: The shape
▶ Select: **Autoshape** from the **Format** menu
▶ Click: The **Wrapping** tab
▶ Select: The text wrapping option you require from the options shown.

 ## Snap to gridlines

This facility can be used if you want to align shapes, or draw shapes with set dimensions. Gridlines are not printed or displayed on the screen.

These shapes were drawn with identical grid proportions by using the snap to grid feature.

▶ Click: The Draw ▾ **Draw** button on the Drawing Tool Bar
▶ Select: ▦ **Grid**
▶ Click: The **Snap to grid** box to select the option – a tick will appear when the option is selected
▶ Click: The **Snap to grid** box again to deselect the option – the tick will disappear when the option is not selected

Note: The default spacing of gridlines is normally 0.25cm ($\frac{1}{8}$ in) – to alter the amount of space between both vertical and horizontal gridlines enter a new measurement in the horizontal or vertical spacing boxes.

To change the point at the left edge of the page where you want the gridlines to begin (normally defaulted to start at the 0cm point in the upper left-hand corner of the page) enter a new measurement in the horizontal or vertical **origin** boxes.

 ## Determine the exact size/position of a shape

▶ Right-click: The shape
▶ Select: **Format AutoShape** from the quick menu
▶ Click: The **Size** or **Position** tab as appropriate and enter the required settings.

▶ You can press the right mouse button to bring up the quick menu to format or edit shapes – this is sometimes quicker than using the Drawing Tool Bar
▶ You can use the **F4** key to repeat actions – this is useful, for example, when you want to repeat the paste command for multiple copies of the same shape.

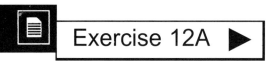

Exercise 12A ▶

12.1 Starting with a clear screen, display the Drawing Tool Bar on screen and practise using Word 97's drawing facilities. Have fun!

▶ Draw some basic shapes eg line, square, rectangle, circle, oval etc.
▶ Draw some Autoshapes eg scribble, freeform, block arrows, callouts, stars and banners.
▶ Resize the shapes you have drawn – try enlarging and reducing them.
▶ Add different fill colors, line color, line style, 3-D and shadow to the shapes.
▶ Move the shapes around the screen, then copy and delete some of them.
▶ Position a shape in front of another shape – use the send to front and send to back facilities.
▶ Key in a few words, move a shape in front of the text then use the send behind text facility.
▶ Rotate and flip some of your shapes – practise using the free rotate facility.
▶ Use the Align or Distribute command to align several shapes with each other.
▶ Group two or more shapes together, then ungroup them.
▶ Practise drawing shapes using the grid feature.
▶ Add text to a shape and change the font colour.

12.2 Close the file without saving or printing your work at this stage.

Exercise 12B ▶

12.3 Starting a new document, display the Drawing Tool Bar and turn on the **Snap to grid** facility with **Horizontal and Vertical spacing** set at 0.25cm ($\frac{1}{8}$ in). Follow the guidelines below to reproduce the drawing of a truck. It doesn't matter if your finished drawing is not exactly the same – this exercise is just for practice and for fun. Remember to use the **Send to Front/Back** facility to position the shapes.

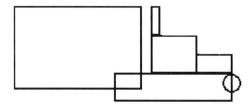

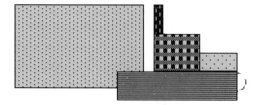

Step 1 Use the Rectangle and Oval icons to draw and position the shapes as shown above. You can adjust the sizes of the shapes as you go along. It doesn't matter if the shapes are not exactly the same size.

Step 2 Click each shape in turn and apply different colours, patterns and line styles using the Fill Color, Line Color and Line Style icons – you can choose different fill patterns if you want to.

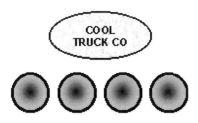

Step 3 Draw and fill an oval and add the text as shown above. Draw and fill/shade a circle. (The example given used Fill Effects, Gradient, Two colors, Shading styles, From center.) Copy the circle three times.

Step 4 Position the four circles and the oval as shown above. Select the Cloud Callout from the Autoshapes selection and use it to draw a puff of smoke as shown above (you may need to flip it horizontally, and use the small yellow adjustment handle to position it). Group all the shapes together.

Step 5 Flip the grouped drawing horizontally. Make it bigger – hold down the Shift key while you stretch the drawing to keep the same proportions. Key in and centre the heading at the top of the page in the usual way. Move the drawing to the top of the page and use the Send Behind Text facility. Draw a grey rectangle with no border lines underneath the truck – position it centrally by selecting both the truck and the rectangle and using the Align Center command.

12.4 Save and print a copy of your work using the filename **TRUCK**.

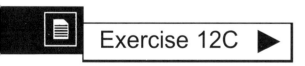

Exercise 12C ▶

12.5 Starting with a clear screen, try to reproduce the following diagrams. You do not have to draw them in the exact sizes or fill shown. Remember to use the Align command to line up the shapes and the Order command to position the shapes in front or behind each other. Save and print a copy of your work using the filename **DRAWINGS**.

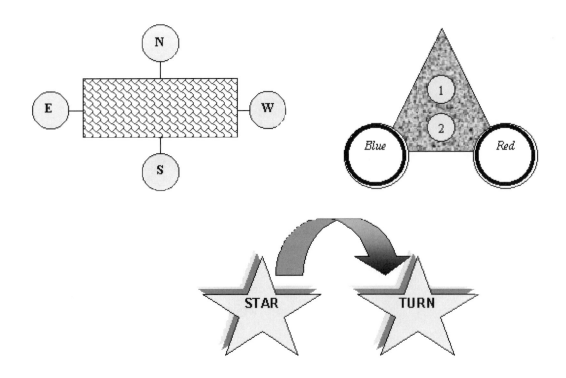

Insert a text box ▶

Text boxes are used as 'drawing objects' and act as containers for text that can be positioned anywhere on a page. Text boxes allow you to use new graphical effects to manipulate text in a more exciting way. A text box is useful for creating a *watermark* where text appears on top or behind existing text. For example, companies sometimes print 'Confidential' in light print across the pages of a document.

> This is an example of text entered into a text box. You can edit the size of the box to allow enough room for the text, and apply decorative finishes using the Drawing Toolbar.

Use the Drawing Tool Bar to apply 3-D effects, shadows, border styles, colours, fills and backgrounds to the text box. You can group text boxes together, change the alignment or distribution of them as a group, rotate and flip text boxes, and change the orientation of the text with the Text Direction command.

▶ Click: The **Text Box** icon on the Drawing Tool Bar (a cursor in the shape of a ⊹ appears on screen)

▶ Hold down: The left mouse button

▶ Drag: The box until it is an appropriate size for the text

Note: Text boxes do not automatically increase in size if you type in more text than the original box size will allow for – you must select the text box and make it larger to make room for the extra text.

▶ Position the insertion pointer: Inside the text box

▶ Key in: The text

Note: Text in a text box is formatted with the normal style – you can change the style of part or all of the text in a text box in the same way you would reformat text in the main document.

To adjust the space between the text box border and the text inside:

▶ Click: The text box to select it
▶ Right-click and select: **Format Text Box** from the quick menu
▶ Select: The Text Box tab
▶ Key in: A value in the **Internal Margin** boxes
▶ Click: **OK**

Standard internal margins   Internal margins adjusted

To change the orientation of the text in a text box:

▶ Click: The text box to select it
▶ Select: **Text Direction** from the Format menu
▶ Click: The orientation required – use the Preview box to view the layout
▶ Click: **OK**

Remember: You can press the right mouse button to bring up the quick menu to format or edit shapes and text boxes.

To format a text box:

▶ Click: The text box to select it
▶ Select: **Text box** from the Format menu
▶ Select: The appropriate tab shown on the Format Text Box dialogue box – **Color and lines**, **Size**, **Position**, **Wrapping**, **Text Box** – to alter the display or format of the text box

Exercise 12D ▶

12.6 Starting with a clear screen, reproduce the following diagram. You will find it easier if you use the Grid facility.

▶ Use grey-shaded text boxes for the rectangle shapes MACHINES, MANPOWER, MATERIAL and METHODS
▶ Use text boxes with No Line and No Fill for the text entries *Computers broke down, Staff off sick, Instructions missing, Procedure missed*
▶ Use a text box with No Line and Light Grey Fill for the caption Fig. 1 Cause-and-effect diagram
▶ Use a text box with a White Font Color for the text **EFFECT OR PROBLEM** and a Black Fill Color for the background to produce the **'reverse video'** effect.
▶ Group all the shapes together.

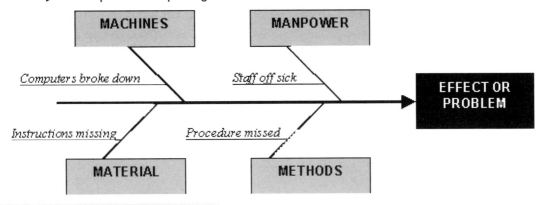

Fig. 1 Cause-and-effect diagram

12.7   Save your work using the filename **EFFECT**. Close the file without printing at this stage.

12.8   Open the file **EX11B** that you saved earlier in Unit 11. Position the cursor at the very end of the document, ie after the section headed **Multiple Cause Diagrams** on page 2.

12.9   Select **File** from the **Insert** menu. Select the file **EFFECT** and insert it into the document.

12.10 Position the diagram in a sensible place on page 2 of the document. Resave the file using the filename **EX12D**. Do not print at this stage.

 # Create dividers (rules) using drawing tools ▶

Dividers or rules are used to organise the miscellaneous elements in a document and separate one item from another. There are several different methods of inserting dividers into a document using Word 97.

A simple divider can be created using a grey shaded rectangle with or without border lines. You can copy and paste this throughout the document.

Another simple divider can be inserted using the Line tool from the Drawing Tool Bar. Format it with the Line Style, Arrow Style and Line Color tools.

Examples

You could create a more decorative divider by combining several different drawing shapes together. Group the shapes and paste the graphic divider as appropriate throughout the document.

Examples

 # Exercise 12D continued ▶

12.11 Refer to the instructions **Create dividers (rules) using drawing tools** above. Create a divider approximately 5cm (2in) wide using the Drawing Tool Bar. Insert the divider between the end of the text on page 2 and the diagram.

12.12 Resave the file using the same filename (**EX12D**). Use the Print Preview facility to check your layout against the printout check at the back of this book. If your layout is correct, print page 2 only by selecting **Print** from the **File** menu, then clicking **Pages** and entering **2** as the page range.

12.13 Exit the program if you have finished working or continue straight on to the next unit.

unit
13

▶ Clip art images and graphical dividers

By the end of Unit 13 you will have learnt how to:

▶ import and position a clip art image from the Clip Gallery
▶ use symbols for graphics
▶ import graphical dividers from the Microsoft Picture File

In the Document Presentation Stage III Part 2 examination, there will be an instruction to add an appropriate clip art image to the document. This unit will introduce you to the different methods of importing and formatting clip art. However, you should also familiarise yourself with the range of clip art stored on your computer as this will vary between systems.

Insert clip art from the Clip Gallery

You can insert a clip art image or a picture into your document from the Clip Gallery. After inserting it, you can convert the clip art image to a drawing object and then use options on the Drawing Tool Bar to edit different parts, eg change the fill or line colours.

 Insert a clip art image

▶ Position the insertion pointer: At the place where you want to insert the clip art image
▶ Select: **Picture** from the **Insert** menu
▶ Select: **Clip Art**
▶ Click: The **Clip Art** tab

Note: If a dialogue box appears with information about additional clips on CD-ROM, simply click OK.

▶ Click: A category at the left-hand side of the dialogue box
▶ Click: The image you want
▶ Click: The **Insert** button

The **Microsoft Clip Gallery** appears on screen.

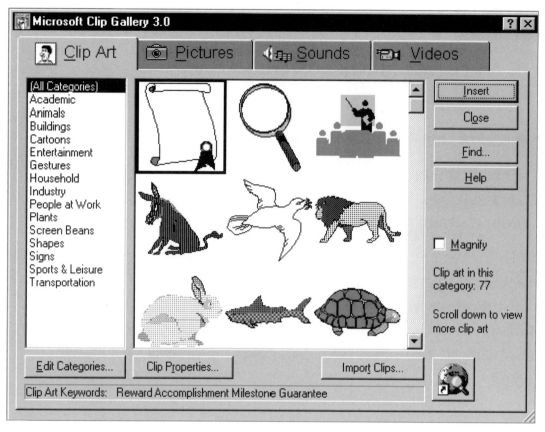

Figure 13.1 Microsoft Clip Gallery

Resize a clip art image ▶

▶ Select: The image (it is selected when small rectangular handles appear around it)

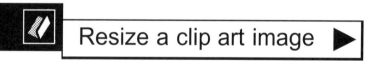
▶ Click: A handle arrow (eg ↗ ↕ ↔ ↘)

▶ Drag: The mouse in the direction required to increase or decrease the size

To keep the same overall proportions:

Hold down: The **Shift** key whilst resizing the image

Determine the exact size of a clip art image

▶ Select: The graphic image
▶ Select: **Picture** (or **Autoshape**) from the **Format** menu

The **Format Picture** dialogue box appears on screen.

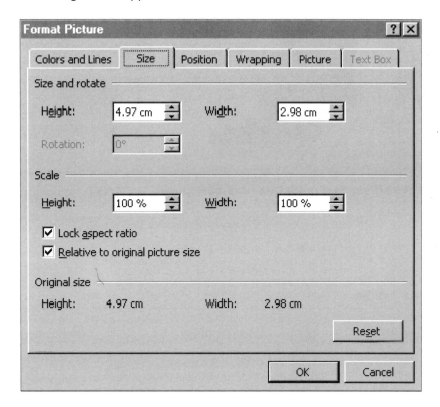

Figure 13.2 Format Picture dialogue box

▶ Click: The **Size** tab

The size of the image is shown both as an exact measurement (under **Size and rotate**) or as a percentage of the original size (under **Scale**). If the **Lock aspect ratio** check box is selected, the height and width settings will change automatically in relation to one another.

 Move/copy/paste/cut a clip art image

▶ Click: The image
▶ Drag: The image to its new position to *move* it, *or*
▶ Use: The normal *copy*, *paste* and *cut* commands as required.

Format a clip art image

You can format a clip art image using some of the Drawing Tools just as you would a drawing shape.

Examples

Apply Shadow

Send to Back

Apply a Fill Color to the background

When you insert a clip art image, the **Picture** Tool Bar appears on screen.

Figure 13.3 Picture Tool Bar

	Insert Picture from file		More Brightness		Text Wrapping
	Image Control		Less Brightness		Format Picture
	More Contrast		Crop		Set Transparent Color
	Less Contrast		Line Style		Reset Picture

You can use these tools to crop the image, add a border to it or adjust its brightness and contrast.

Note: If the Picture Tool Bar doesn't appear, right-click the picture, then click **Show Picture Tool Bar** on the quick menu.

 ## Wrap text around a clip art image

You can wrap text around a drawing object of any size and shape. You can specify particular sides of the graphic you want the text to wrap around and also the distance between the graphic and the text that surrounds it.

▶ Select: The image
▶ Select: **Picture** (or **Autoshape**) from the **Format** menu
▶ Click: The Wrapping tab

OR

► Click: The **Text Wrapping** button on the Picture Tool Bar
► Select: The text wrapping option you require from the options shown.

Position an image in relation to text or to the page ►

► Select: The object or image that you want to position
► Select: **Picture** (or **AutoShape, Text Box, Object**) from the **Format** menu
► Click: The **Position** tab
► Select: The required options for your horizontal and vertical anchors in the **From** boxes
► Enter: The distances from the anchors in the **Horizontal** and **Vertical** boxes

You can attach an object to a paragraph so that they move together in two ways:

1 To make sure that the selected object moves up or down with the paragraph it is anchored to, select the Move object with **text** check box.

2 To make sure that the selected object always appears on the same page as the paragraph it is anchored to, select the **Lock anchor** check box.

Note: The **Float over text** option allows you to place the object in the drawing layer where you can position it in front or behind text or other objects using the **Draw** command.

Exercise 13A ►

13.1 Open **EX3D** and save as **EX13A**.

13.2 Following the instructions **Insert a clip art image**, insert one of the clip art images from the **Screen Beans** category into your document.

13.3 Following the instructions in **Resize a clip art image**, decrease the size of the image, keeping the same overall proportions, until it is about 4cm high. Use the ruler at the left of the screen to help you estimate this measurement.

13.4 Wrap the text around the image:

► Click: The image to select it (unless it is already selected)
► Select: Picture from the Format menu
► Click: The Wrapping tab
► Select: Tight from the Wrapping style section and Left from the Wrap to section
► Click: OK

13.5 Move the image to the right-hand side of the first paragraph of the memo (look at the printout check at the back of this book if you need to check the position). The text should flow up to the left edge of the image.

13.6 Make a copy of the image and decrease the copy by about 50% keeping the same overall proportions. With the copy selected, choose **None** from the **Wrapping style**. (You may find it easier to use the **Wrapping** button on the Picture Tool Box which should now be displayed on the screen.)

13.7 With the Picture Tool Bar on screen, click the **Image Control** button and select **Watermark**.

13.8 Make four more copies of the watermark image and position these approximately 0.5cm apart. With the Drawing Tool Bar on screen, select all five watermark graphics using the Select Objects icon. Using the **Align or Distribute** command from the **Draw** menu, select **Align Top** and then **Distribute Horizontally**.

13.9 **Group** all five images together. Move the grouped picture to the centre of the paragraph that begins **As there well be five students...**

13.10 Resave the document. Check your work on screen (using the Print Preview facility) with the printout at the back of the book. If your layout is correct, print one copy of the document.

Exercise 13B ▶

13.11 Open the document **EX11C** and save as **EX13B**. Insert a clip art image from the **Plants** category into your document. Reduce the size of the image and position the picture in the middle of the white space at the bottom of the page.

13.12 Make one copy of the image. Decrease the size of the copy by about 50%. Make a second copy of the smaller image and arrange the trio as below (don't worry if you don't match the sizes exactly).

13.13 Use the **Shadow** tool on the Drawing Tool Bar to apply a shadow setting to each graphic.

13.14 Resave the document and print one copy.

Insert clip art images from other files ▶

▶ Position the insertion pointer: Where you want to insert the picture
▶ Select: **Picture** from the **Insert** menu
▶ Select: **From File**

The **Insert Picture** dialogue box is displayed on screen.

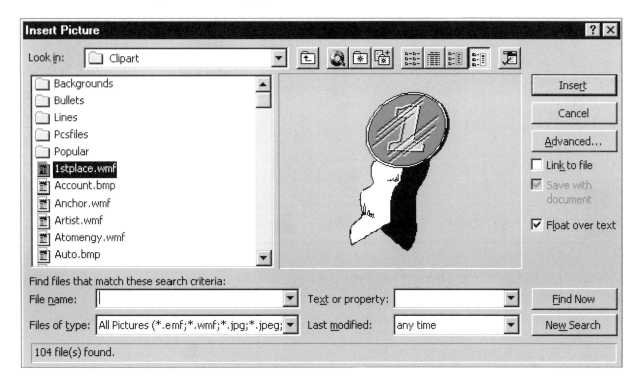

Figure 13.4 Insert Picture dialogue box

▶ Check: That the file that contains the picture you require is displayed in the **Look in** box, eg
    Clipart, Popular
▶ Click: The **Preview** button on the **Insert Picture** dialogue box so that you can view the choices
▶ Click: The picture that you want to insert

Note: To position the picture so that you can place it precisely on the page or in front of/behind text/other objects, make sure that the **Float over text** ☑ check box is ticked. (To insert the picture directly in the text at the insertion point clear the **Float over text** check box.)

Format the picture using the same methods as described earlier in the unit under **Insert clip art from the Clip Gallery**, eg adjust the size or position, text wrapping etc.

Note: You will need to check what clip art pictures are available on your particular computer – these may vary from the examples shown in this book. Choose appropriate alternatives if necessary.

 Insert an image into a text box ▶

You can predetermine the amount of space and the position which the picture takes up on the page by inserting it in a text box.

▶ Draw: A text box where you want the picture to appear on the page
▶ Click the insertion pointer: Inside the text box
▶ Insert: The picture as described above – the picture will fill the text box boundaries

Note: You can still increase or decrease the size of the picture afterwards – the text box boundaries will also increase or decrease accordingly.

You can format the text box and the picture using the usual methods.

 ## Use symbols as graphics ▶

▶ Select: **Symbol** from the **Insert** menu
▶ Select: The **Symbols** tab
▶ Select: A **Font** from the drop-down menu to display its character set in the grid below, eg Wingdings
▶ Click: The symbol that you want to insert into your document, eg
▶ Click: **Insert**
▶ Click: **Close**

To increase or decrease the size of the symbol:

▶ Select: The symbol as you would normal text
▶ Select: A point size from the **Font Size** menu on the Formatting Tool Bar

To display in reverse video

▶ Select: **White Font Color** and **Black Highlight** from the Formatting Tool Bar
▶ To move a symbol graphic around the page:

▶ Insert: The symbol into a text box

You can then format the text box and the symbol using the usual methods.

 ## Exercise 13C ▶

13.15 Open **EX11D** and save as **EX13C**. Carry out the following changes:

▶ Delete: The text: *Tel No:* at the bottom of the page
▶ Position the insertion pointer: Immediately before the *0171 452874* (telephone number)
▶ Select: Symbol from the Insert menu
▶ Select: The Wingdings font

▶ Click: The ☎ telephone symbol (on the top row)

▶ Click: Insert, Close

▶ Increase the telephone symbol size to 16 pt.

13.16 Draw two identical text boxes in the white space at either side of the **STARTERS** section – make these approximately 2.5cm high and 3.5cm wide. With both text boxes selected:

▶ Select: Text Box from the Format menu

▶ Click: The Size tab

▶ Enter: The Height and Width settings.

13.17 Insert a clip art image:

Note: Choose appropriate alternative images if the ones that are suggested at steps 13.17 and 13.18 are not available on your computer.

▶ Position the insertion pointer: Inside the text box at the left-hand side of the page

▶ Select: Picture from the Insert menu

▶ Select: From File

▶ Check: That the Microsoft Clipart folder is displayed in the Look in box

▶ Click: The Preview button on the Insert Picture dialogue box so that you can view the choices

▶ Insert the image Dinner1.wmf into the text box

▶ Repeat the above, but inserting the image **Dinner2.wmf** into the text box at the right-hand side of the page

▶ Remove the border lines from both text boxes.

13.18 Insert the image **Coffee.wmf** into the white space at the bottom of the page below the **Desserts** section. Do not use a text box this time – you will need to select **None** from the **Wrapping Style** section. Resize the image if necessary and position it centrally in the space available.

13.19 Resave your file. You do not need to print at this stage.

 ## Insert clip art borders

In Unit 11, you learnt how to apply a border around the page using the **Page Border** facility. As an alternative, Word 97 also offers you some decorative clip art border images.

Refer back to the instructions in **Insert clip art from other files**. Follow exactly the same procedures to insert borders that have been prestored as clip art image files.

After inserting the clip art border into your document:

▶ Select: **None** from the **Wrapping style** section

▶ Select: **Whole Page** from the **Zoom** button on the Standard Tool Bar so that you can see the full page

▶ Click: The clip art border and stretch it vertically and/or horizontally to the required position across the page

Examples

Document page   Clip art border inserted into a document Clip art border stretched across the page

In order to be able to edit the text later:

▶ Select: **Order** from the **Draw** menu on the Drawing Tool Bar
▶ Select: The **Send Behind Text** option to send the border behind the text

Note: If you want to set precise measurements for the border, you can select **Picture** from the **Format** menu to bring up the **Format Picture** dialogue box, then use the **Size** and **Position** tabs.

Insert clip art dividers ▶

Refer back to the instructions in **Insert pictures from other files**. Follow exactly the same procedures to insert dividers that have been prestored as clip art image files.

Examples

Note: You will need to check what clip art borders are available on your particular computer – these may vary from the examples shown here. Choose appropriate alternatives if necessary.

Format and edit clip art borders and dividers ▶

Format the border or divider using the same methods as described earlier in the unit under **Insert clip art from the Clip Gallery**, eg adjust the size or position, text wrapping etc.

13.20 With the document **EX13C** on screen, remove the page border:

▶ Select: Borders and Shading from the Format menu
▶ Select: The Page Border tab
▶ Click: None in the Setting section
▶ Click: OK.

13.21 Referring to the instructions in **Insert clip art dividers**:

▶ Insert: A clip art divider from the Clipart picture file, eg Divider3.wmf
▶ Position the divider: Between the STARTERS and MAIN COURSES section
▶ Copy: The divider
▶ Position the second divider: Between the MAIN COURSES section and the DESSERTS section
▶ Adjust: The line spacing to fit all the text on the page (if necessary).

Note: If for any reason you cannot access the Microsoft clip art file, create a divider using the drawing tools and insert as instructed above.

13.22 Referring to the instruction in **Insert clip art borders**:

▶ Insert: A clip art border from the Clipart picture file, eg Hmedeval.wmf
▶ In Whole Page view, stretch: The border across the page to the top, bottom, left and right margins and so that it is clear from all the text
▶ Select: Picture from the Format menu to bring up the Format Picture dialogue box
▶ Click: The Wrapping tab
▶ Select: Wrapping style: None
▶ Click: The Size tab
▶ Enter Height: 25 cm and Width: 17 cm in the Size and rotate section
▶ Click: The Position tab
▶ Enter: Horizontal: 2.5 cm, From: Page and Width: 1.5 cm, From: Page
▶ Click: OK
▶ Send the border behind the text.

Note: If for any reason you cannot access any suitable borders using the Microsoft clip art file, create a border using the Insert Page Border facility described in Unit 11.

13.23 Resave the document using the same filename (**EX13C**). Check your document layout with the printout at the back of the book. If your layout is correct, print one copy.

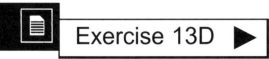 Exercise 13D ▶

13.24 Starting with a clear screen, key in the text on the following page. Follow all the manuscript instructions given and refer back to the instructions in this unit if necessary. Save and print a copy of your work using the filename **EX13D**. Check your printout with the printout at the back of the book. If you find any errors, correct them and print the document again, if necessary.

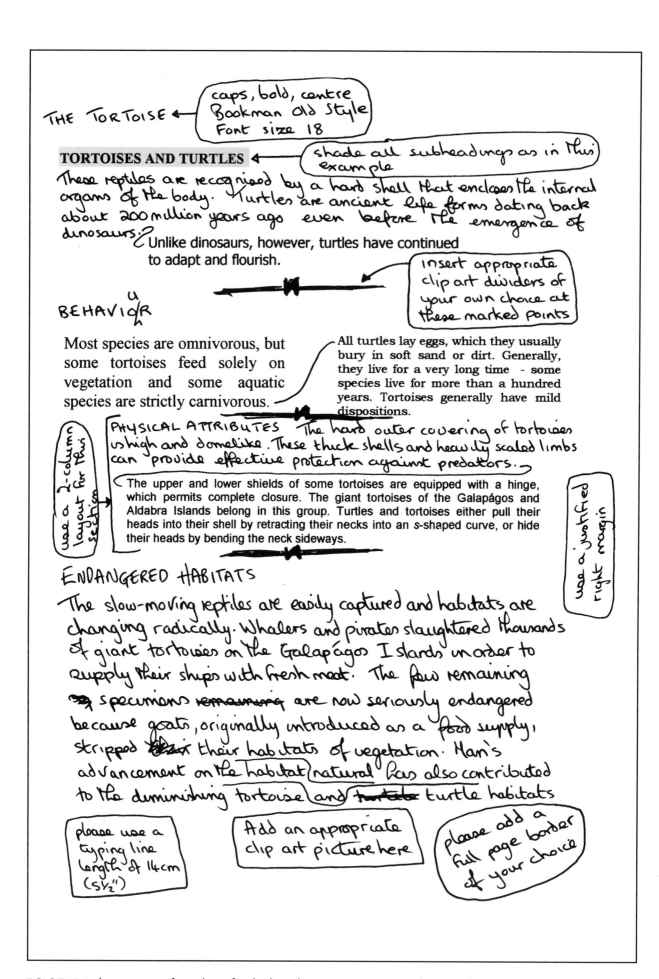

THE TORTOISE ← caps, bold, centre Bookman Old Style Font size 18

TORTOISES AND TURTLES ← shade all subheadings as in this example

These reptiles are recognised by a hard shell that encloses the internal organs of the body. Turtles are ancient life forms dating back about 200 million years ago even before the emergence of dinosaurs. Unlike dinosaurs, however, turtles have continued to adapt and flourish.

——— ✕ ——— ← insert appropriate clip art dividers of your own choice at these marked points

BEHAVIOUR

Most species are omnivorous, but some tortoises feed solely on vegetation and some aquatic species are strictly carnivorous.

All turtles lay eggs, which they usually bury in soft sand or dirt. Generally, they live for a very long time - some species live for more than a hundred years. Tortoises generally have mild dispositions.

use a 2-column layout for this section

PHYSICAL ATTRIBUTES The hard outer covering of tortoises is high and domelike. These thick shells and heavily scaled limbs can provide effective protection against predators.

The upper and lower shields of some tortoises are equipped with a hinge, which permits complete closure. The giant tortoises of the Galapágos and Aldabra Islands belong in this group. Turtles and tortoises either pull their heads into their shell by retracting their necks into an s-shaped curve, or hide their heads by bending the neck sideways.

use a justified right margin

——— ✕ ———

ENDANGERED HABITATS

The slow-moving reptiles are easily captured and habitats are changing radically. Whalers and pirates slaughtered thousands of giant tortoises on the Galapágos Islands in order to supply their ships with fresh meat. The few remaining specimens remaining are now seriously endangered because goats, originally introduced as a food supply, stripped their their habitats of vegetation. Man's advancement on the habitat natural has also contributed to the diminishing tortoise and turtle turtle habitats

please use a typing line length of 14cm (5½")

Add an appropriate clip art picture here

please add a full page border of your choice

13.25 Exit the program if you have finished working or continue straight on to the next unit.

unit 14

▶ Reformat a document to a three-column layout

By the end of Unit 14 you should have learnt how to:

▶ display documents in a specified house style indicated on a separate reference sheet

▶ produce specialist business documents such as an agenda and minutes

▶ reformat a document to a three-column layout

▶ apply triple line spacing.

Special business documents and house styles

As part of the Stage III examination – and often in the workplace – you will be required to produce specialist business documents which follow the layout of the organisation's house style. Examples of these may include technical documents, notices of meetings and agendas, minutes of meetings, etc. You may have been used to displaying your work to a particular layout, eg leaving a clear line space after headings. However, when following a specified house style you should follow the instructions or visual display given.

Although you will still be expected to follow written instructions, you will also be expected to interpret house style requirements from a separate resource or reference sheet. Examine the display shown on the resource/reference sheet very carefully. Note how the layout displays headings, margin alignment, space allocation, enumeration or bulleted points, column layout, text alignment, etc, and apply the house style format to the specified document.

Notice of a meeting and agenda

Notification of a meeting and the list of items to be discussed are often combined in one document. This is sent out to everyone who is entitled to attend a meeting approximately two weeks in advance of the date. The secretary of the organisation or committee is usually responsible for the preparation of the agenda in consultation with the chairperson, although nowadays many managers send out their own agendas for less formal in-house meetings.

Minutes of a meeting

The minutes of a meeting are issued to all members who were present at the meeting as an agreed record of the key topics of discussion. Minutes are often displayed in a three-column layout. The first column indicates the items discussed in numbered order. The second column provides a brief description of the key issues arising from each item and any action to be taken. The third column is used to record the name of the person who will take further action, usually by his or her initials.

Triple line spacing

▶ Select: The text you want to edit

▶ Select: **Paragraph** from the **Format** menu

▶ Select: **Multiple** from the **Line spacing** drop-down menu

▶ Enter: **3** in the **At** box

▶ Click: **OK**

	Single	Double	Triple
	Red	Red	Red
	Blue		
	Green	Blue	Blue
	Brown		
	Pink	Green	
	White		Green
	Yellow	Brown	

Line spacing: Single   Double   Triple

Exercise 14A ▶

14.1   Starting a new document, key in the following notice and agenda. Save the document using the filename **EX14A** and print one copy.

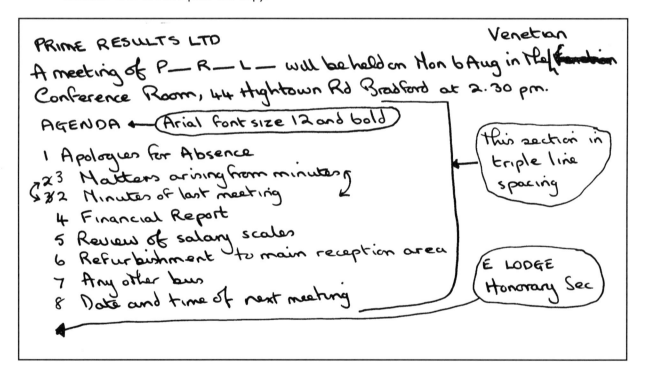

PRIME RESULTS LTD

A meeting of P—R—L— will be held on Mon 6 Aug in the ~~function~~ Venetian Conference Room, 44 Hightown Rd Bradford at 2.30 pm.

AGENDA ← (Arial font size 12 and bold)

1 Apologies for Absence
×3 2 Minutes of last meeting
×3 3 Matters arising from minutes
4 Financial Report
5 Review of salary scales
6 Refurbishment to main reception area
7 Any other bus
8 Date and time of next meeting

this section in triple line spacing

E LODGE Honorary Sec

Exercise 14B ▶

14.2   Starting a new document, key in the following minutes.

▶ Use Times New Roman, font size 12.

▶ Insert a two-column table after the PRESENT section with sufficient rows to take the numbered items.

▶ Make the first column approximately 1.5cm ($\frac{1}{2}$ in) wide leaving the second column to stretch to the right margin. Set a left-aligned tab in the second column for the indented items. (Remember to use Ctrl + T to wrap the text around the tab setting, and to press Ctrl + Tab to move to the next tab stop when in a table.)

▶ Enter the text as shown in the example below.

▶ Use the No Borders facility so that the table lines are not printed out.

▶ Save using the filename EX14B and print a copy of the document.

Note: Refer back to Unit 8 if you need to refresh your memory on using tables.

Example of the layout to be followed for Exercise 14B ▶

1	APOLOGIES FOR ABSENCE – Freda McBride, Hilary Wilkinson.
2	MINUTES of previous meeting were approved and signed.
3	MATTERS ARISING
	3.1 The work experience scheme for fifth-year students had been successful.
	3.2 The 'Employee Satisfaction In The Millennium' conference was fully booked and additional packs had been published in readiness.

MINUTES OF MEETING OF PRIME RESULTS LTD (Insert date from Ex 14A) AT 2.30 PM IN THE VENETIAN CONFERENCE ROOM

PRESENT   Aldred Graeme (Chair)
Hussain Zafar
Firth Brian
Benson Howard

(Turnstall Matthew
Potter Marie)

1   APOLOGIES FOR ABSENCE – Freda McBride, Hilary Wilkinson.

2   MINUTES of previous meeting were approved and signed.

3   MATTERS ARISING

(insert name of school from Ex 3C)

    3.1   The work experience scheme for - - - ._____. School's fifth-year students had been successful.

    3.2   The 'Employee Satisfaction In The Millennium' conference was fully booked and additional packs had been published in readiness.

(info)

4   FINANCIAL REPORT

The financial report showed good profits ~~to date~~ so far. Agreed that a summary ⊘ report should be prepared for Graeme Aldred to present to the Directors. (Action BF)

5 REVIEW OF SALARY SCALES
Agreed that there should be an urgent review of management ~~wage~~ *salary* scales and this should be reported to the next meeting. (Action MP)

6 REFURBISHMENT TO RECEPTION 6.1 A full report and estimate for work had been received by Graeme Aldred. It was agreed that works begin according to the lowest tender received. (Action GA)
6.2 *Agreed that a temp reception service area would need to be in place during the period of refurbishment. (Action MT)*

7 ANY OTHER BUSINESS
Marie Potter advised the meeting that Joan Braithwaite had taken retirement from S — G —— School. Future correspondence relating to work experience schemes should be temporarily sent to the School, % the School Administrator, until another contact name was identified.

8 DATE OF NEXT MEETING
To be notified

TIP: insert the % symbol from the (normal text) font using the Insert Symbols facility, or use superscript and subscript font.

Reformat a document to a three-column layout using tabulation ▶

The most appropriate method of reformatting a document to a three-column layout is to use the **Tables** facility. You can use the rows and columns to line up all the items as appropriate, then remove the table border lines. Refer back to Unit 8 if you need to refresh your memory on using this feature.

Note: If you convert text into columns using Word 97's **Columns** facility, the text flows freely from the first column to the last. This makes the **Columns** facility unsuitable when you want to position specific portions of text in specific columns.

To reformat a two-column layout to a three-column layout:

▶ Check that: The horizontal ruler is displayed on screen and that you are in **Page Layout View**
▶ Click: On the second column
▶ Select: **Select Column** from the **Table** menu ⟶

P11	Blue damask curtains. £45.00
P12	Green cotton curtains. £16.00
P13	Red velour curtains. £75.00

▶ Select: **Insert Columns** from the **Table** menu (a blank column is inserted)

► Select: The third column, then drag the text into the second column

P11		**Blue damask curtains. £45.00**
P12		**Green cotton curtains. £16.00**
P13		**Red velour curtains. £75.00**

P11	Blue damask curtains. £45.00	
P12	Green gingham curtains. £16.00	
P13	Red velour curtains. £75.00	

► Drag: The dividing column line between columns two and three to the left to the appropriate position on the horizontal ruler to decrease the width of the second column

P11	Blue damask curtains. £45.00	
P12	Green cotton curtains. £16.00	
P13	Red velour curtains. £75.00	

► Switch to: **Normal View** so that you can see the end of the third column
► Drag: The end column to the left so that it is aligned with the rest of the page

► Switch back to: **Page Layout View**
► Move: The appropriate text to the third column, *either:*
► use the mouse to drag the text across to its new position *or*
► cut the text and paste it to the appropriate position in the third column

P11	Blue damask curtains.	£45.00
P12	Green cotton curtains.	£16.00
P13	Red velour curtains. £75.00	

Note: You may need to press the Return key to insert line spaces into the third column.

► Adjust: The column dividers again if necessary
► Double-check that: All items and subitems of the three-column layout are in the right sequence and position, and numbered correctly if appropriate.

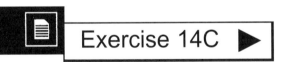

Exercise 14C ►

14.3 Read through the instructions **Reformat a document to a three-column layout using tabulation**. Recall the document stored as **EX14B**. Save the document using the filename **EX14C**. Amend it where indicated below and display it according to the house style shown on the **Reference Sheet** at the end of this unit (page 150), adding an **ACTION** column as shown. Print one copy.

Check the layout shown on the reference sheet at the end of this unit very carefully. Note the enumeration style; alignment of text; and general layout of each section of the display.

MINUTES OF MEETING OF PRIME RESULTS LTD ON MONDAY 6 AUGUST AT 2.30 PM IN THE VENETIAN CONFERENCE ROOM

PRESENT
Aldred Graeme (Chair)
Hussain Zafar (Finance Manager)
Firth Brian (Finance Director)
Benson Howard (Conference Organiser)
Turnstall Matthew (Buildings Manager)
Potter Marie (Personnel Manager)
Lodge Elsie (Honorary Sec)

sort into alphabetical order of surname

1 APOLOGIES FOR ABSENCE – Freda McBride, Hilary ~~Wilkinson~~ Walker.

2 MINUTES of previous meeting were approved and signed.

3 MATTERS ARISING

3.1 The work experience scheme for Silverdale Grammar School's fifth-year students had been successful.

3.2 The 'Employee Satisfaction In The Millennium' conference was fully booked and additional information packs had been published in readiness.

4 FINANCIAL REPORT

4.1 The financial report showed excellent ~~good~~ profits to date and a healthy bank balance. Agreed that a summary report should be prepared by Brian Firth for Graeme Aldred to present to the Directors. (Action BF)

5 REVIEW OF SALARY SCALES

5.1 Agreed that there should be an urgent review of management salary scales and this should be reported to the next meeting. (Action MP)

6 REFURBISHMENT TO MAIN RECEPTION AREA

6.1 A full report and estimate for work had been received by Graeme Aldred. It was agreed that works begin immed according to the lowest tender received. (Action GA)

6.2 Agreed that a temporary reception service area would need to be in place during the period of refurbishment. (Action MT)

7 ANY OTHER BUSINESS

7.1 Marie Potter advised the meeting that Joan Braithwaite had taken retirement from Silverdale Grammar School. Future correspondence relating to work experience schemes should be temporarily sent to the School, ℅ the School Administrator, until another contact name was identified.

8 DATE OF NEXT MEETING

~~To be notified~~. This was arranged for Mon 20 Aug at 1430 hours in the V—— C—— R——.

The meeting was closed at 4.45 pm.

Agreed that the review of all other salary scales would be deferred until after the current staff restructuring was completed in 2½ weeks

This is the second item under REVIEW OF SALARY SCALES

It was agreed that additional work to the foyer leading to the main reception should also be put in hand. (Action GA)

Make this the second item under REFURBISHMENT TO MAIN RECEPTION AREA

Howard Benson reported that he had entered into negotiations with a leading hotel chain suitable for future conference venues. It was agreed that a public relations exercise be undertaken to secure the contract. ~~XXXXX~~ (ACTION HB)

This is the first item under ANY OTHER BUSINESS

* Number second and subsequent pages only at bottom right of page, ie do not number first page
* Change 'Graeme' to 'Gordon' throughout the document
* Change 'agreed' to upper case throughout the document
* Split the Table in a sensible place for page 2 (Select: Split Table from the Table menu)

TIP: ▶ Read through the information section in this unit **Reformat a document to a three-column layout** very carefully.

▶ Check the layout shown in the Reference Sheet at the end of this unit very carefully – note the enumeration style, alignment of text, and general layout of each section of the display.

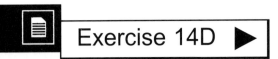

14.4 Recall the document **EX14B** again. Save as **EX14D**. Amend it where indicated and display it according to the **Reference Sheet** at the end of this unit (page 150), adding an **ACTION** column as shown. Print one copy.

MINUTES OF MEETING OF PRIME RESULTS LTD ON MONDAY 6 AUGUST AT 2.30 PM IN THE VENETIAN CONFERENCE ROOM

this heading – centred and bold

PRESENT   Aldred Graeme (Chair)
Hussain Zafar   (Finance Manager)
Firth Brian   (Finance Director)
Benson Howard   (Conference Organiser)
Turnstall Matthew   (Buildings Manager)
Potter Marie .   (Personnel Manager)
Lodge Elsie   (Honorary Sec)

sort into alphabetical order of surname

1   APOLOGIES FOR ABSENCE – Freda McBride, Hilary Wilkinson.

2   MINUTES of previous meeting were approved and signed.

3   MATTERS ARISING
    3.1   The work experience scheme for Silverdale Grammar School's fifth-year students had been successful.
    3.3   The 'Employee Satisfaction In The Millennium' conference was fully booked and additional information packs had been published in readiness.

demonstrated that the co had made outstanding

4   FINANCIAL REPORT
    4.1   The financial report ~~showed good~~ profits to date. Agreed that a summary report should be prepared ~~for~~ Graeme Aldred ~~to present~~ to the Directors. (Action BF)

by Brian Firth.   *will then submit this*

5   REVIEW OF SALARY SCALES
Agreed that there should be an urgent review of management salary scales and this should be reported to the next meeting. (Action MP)

6   REFURBISHMENT TO RECEPTION   *a number of*
    6.1   A full report and estimates for work had been received by Graeme Aldred. It was agreed that works begin according to the lowest tender received. (Action GA)
    6.3   Agreed that a temporary reception service area would need to be in place during the period of refurbishment. (Action MT)

7   ANY OTHER BUSINESS
Marie Potter advised the meeting that Joan Braithwaite had taken retirement from Silverdale Grammar School. Future correspondence relating to work experience schemes should be temporarily sent to the School, % the School Administrator, until another contact name was identified.

8   DATE OF NEXT MEETING
~~To be notified.~~ *This was arranged for Mon 27 Aug at 2.30pm in the V – C – R –. The meeting ended at 1630 hours*

use consistent enumeration and apply to each item

(this is the second item under FINANCIAL REPORT)

Invoices for the new computer systems were still outstanding. (Action BF)

The new staff canteen was now open again and it was agreed that a discount voucher for 12½% be issued to all staff for a one-week trial.

(Action EL

(make this the first item under MATTERS ARISING)

A request had been made by the trades unions for a series of meetings to examine the equal opportunities policy in relation to salary appointments. It was agreed that an initial meeting with Personnel would enable a framework to be drawn up on which to proceed. (ACTION MP)

(make this the second item of REVIEW OF SALARY SCALES)

Agreed that Hélène de Courcy be invited to the next meeting to comment on the new Public Relations strategy (Action EL)

(this is the first item under ANY OTHER BUSINESS)

* number all pages at bottom centre of page
* change 'Graeme' to 'Gordon' throughout the document
* change 'conference' to 'seminar' throughout the document
* format the text in column 2 only to a justified right margin

14.5 Exit the program if you have finished working or continue straight on to the next unit.

Note: The information below is not to be keyed in. It indicates the house style required for the documents.

Use capitalisation and three-column layout as in this specimen layout for minutes.

PRESENT

Mary Stevens	(Chair)	
Lee Sutcliffe	(Secretary)	
May Browne	(Treasurer)	
Sean Maynor	(Finance Director)	
Linda Welsh	(Marketing Manager)	

> **NOTE**
> Please ensure that initials are moved to the ACTION column as shown below, and align the initials directly opposite the relevant part of the text in the second column.

ACTION

1   MINUTES of the previous meeting were agreed and signed.

2   MATTERS ARISING
    2.1   The quarterly accounts had been submitted.
    2.2   Invoices for the kitchen decorations were still outstanding.   SM

3   MARKETING STRATEGY
    3.1   Agreed to set up a Marketing Strategy Group to oversee
          new developments.   LW

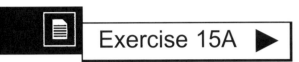

Exercise 15A ▶

15.1 Key in the following document using a consistent typeface and layout. Use a justified right margin and a typing line length of 14cm ($5\frac{1}{2}$ in). Use Times New Roman, font size 11 for the main body text. Display as indicated on the **Reference Sheet** and amend it as shown. Save and print a copy of your document – use the filename **EX15A**.

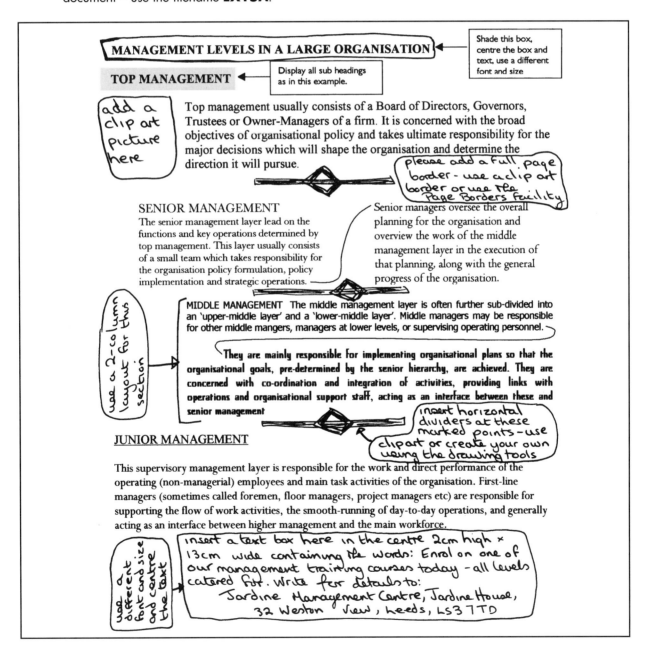

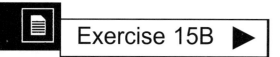
15.2 Key in the following document. Save and print a copy of your document – use the filename: **EX15B**.

NEW HOUSES FOR SALE

The following houses are new on the market. As part of our estate services we also offer:

Free mortgage advice;
Free valuations on your own property if you sell through us;
Competitive valuation and survey services on other properties;
Nationwide marketing through 150 branches;
No sale, no fee.

> Insert the text in this section in a 2-column table.

Contact our showroom staff: Brenda Forbes, Valerie Brooksbank, Kenneth Greenwood

Ref 453Y   3-bedroomed Victorian terraced house. Parlour, dining kitchen, hall. Central heating. Large gardens. £55,000

Ref 672R   4-bedroomed semi-detached. Parlour, dining room, kitchen and utility, hall. Central heating. Gardens and double garage. £85,000

Ref 895Y   3-bedroomed detached cottage. Parlour with dining area, kitchen and pantry, conservatory. Gardens, patio and pond. £65,000

Ref 993F   2-bedroomed town house. Parlour, kitchen, hall. Courtyard area and garage. Central heating. £48,000

Ref 428W   3-bedroomed detached. Parlour, dining room, kitchen and utility, study, playroom. Gardens, patio area and double garage. Central heating. £95,000

15.3 Retrieve the document **EX15B** unless it is already on your screen. Save it as **EX15C** and carry out the following amendments.

▶ Change the main heading to Arial, bold
▶ Display the document according to the Reference Sheet at the end of this unit reformatting it to a three-column layout as shown, and following all other reformatting indicated
▶ Sort the items into descending order of price
▶ Change Parlour to Lounge throughout the document.

15.4 Save your work. Check your document layout with the printout check at the back of this book. If it is correct print one copy.

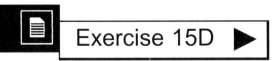

15.5 Key in the following document using a consistent typeface and heading layout.

▶ Insert a header SYMBOL DEVELOPMENT and a footer Journal 33 on each page using a point 8 font size for both.

▶ Number the pages at the foot of the page in the centre, starting with page 12

▶ Adjust the line length to 12.5cm (5in) and use ragged right-hand margins.

15.6 Save and print a copy of your document using the filename **EX15D**.

MATHEMATICAL SYMBOLS ← *centre and bold*

The term 'mathematical symbols' relates to the various signs and short forms that are used in mathematics to indicate entities, relations, or operations, eg $\pm, \sqrt{}, \geq$. The history of how mathematical symbols were originated and evolved is not entirely clear.

Background

inset this section by 13mm (½") at both left and right margins

The early Egyptians used symbols for addition and equality. The Greeks, Hindus and Arabs had symbols for equality and the unknown quantity.

However, from earliest times mathematical processes were cumbersome because proper symbols of operation were largely absent. The expressions for such processes were either written out in full or denoted by word short forms.

please insert here the diagram shown on the Reference Sheet at the end of this unit.

DECIMALS

keep the words primes, sekondes and terzes in italics

Simon Stevin, a Dutch mathematician, was responsible for developing the extension of the decimal position system below unity ~~is attributed~~. He called tenths, hundredths, and thousandths *primes, sekondes,* and *terzes* and used circled digits to denote the orders. A full stop was used to set off the decimal part of a number as early as the 15th century. The German astronomer Johannes Kepler used the comma to set off the decimal orders, and the Swiss mathematician Justus Byrgius used the decimal fraction in such forms as 3.2. Decimals are written differently in ~~a great many~~ different countries:

in the United States they are written in the form 1.$\overset{23}{\cancel{57}}$;

in Great Britain ~~1.23~~ 1·23;

in continental Europe 1,23;

in standard scientific notation, the number 0.000000123 would be written as 1.23×10^{-7}.

use bullet points for these four points

ADDITION AND SUBTRACTION SYMBOLS

The symbols for addition were not uniform. Some mathematicians indicated addition by using the short form *p*, some *e*, and the mathematician Niccolò Tartaglia commonly expressed the operation by Ø. Algebra mathematicians in Germany and England introduced   the sign +   , but first used it only to indicate excess.

Print the last 2 sections only in triple line spacing apart from the bulleted items which should be printed in single line spacing

15.7   Exit the program if you have finished working or continue straight on to the next unit.

Reference Sheet for use with Exercise 15C

The information below is not to be copied. It indicates the house style required for the documents.

- Free mortgage advice;

- Free valuations on your own property if you sell through us;

- Competitive valuation and survey services on other properties.

Please use bullet points as indicated and apply triple line spacing to this section only.

Contact our showroom staff: Brenda Forbes
Valerie Brooksbank
Kenneth Greenwood

Ref 453Y   3-bedroomed Victorian terraced house. Lounge, dining £55,000
kitchen, hall. Central heating. Large gardens.

Ref 672R   4-bedroomed semi-detached. Lounge, dining room, £85,000
kitchen and utility, hall. Central heating. Gardens and
double garage.

 Reference Sheet for use with Exercise 15D

This diagram does not have to be reproduced in the exact size and can be adjusted to fit the space available in your document. You may choose your own pattern or shading to fill the shapes and either circles, squares, rectangles or ovals can be used.

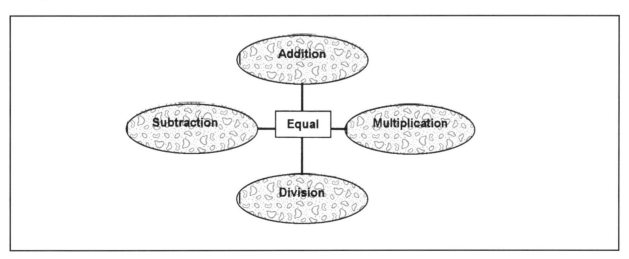

unit 16

▶ Examination Practice 3

By the end of Unit 16, you should have completed a mock examination for the RSA Document Presentation Stage III Part 2 award.

RSA Document Presentation Stage III Part 2

This examination assesses your ability to apply advanced word processing and production skills to meet presentation requirements. You will be assessed on your ability to produce from handwritten and typewritten drafts a variety of complex and/or specialist business documents, using recalled text and supplementary information, and to display them in an appropriate manner. Documents to be produced will include an element of design, columns, fonts, text boxes, diagrams and clip art. The award demonstrates competence to the level demanded by NVQ Level 3.

In addition to being assessed against standard word processing criteria (eg omissions and additions, typing/spelling/punctuation errors, abbreviations, transposition and misplacement etc) you will also be assessed on your presentation techniques. You should refer back to the section in Unit 11 headed **Document Presentation and Layout** to refresh your memory on some of the criteria you will be assessed against. However, it is recommended that you also check the RSA's published performance and assessment criteria for the examination for full details of the scheme.

The examination lasts for $1\frac{3}{4}$ hours and you must complete 4 documents using a word processor. Printing is done outside this time. The invigilator will give you instructions concerning the recalling of stored files.

Examination hints

When sitting your examination:

▶ you may use a manual prepared by the centre or the software manufacturer
▶ you must put your name, centre number and document number on each document
▶ check your work very carefully before printing – proofread and spellcheck
▶ assemble your printouts in the correct order at the end of the examination.

The list of assessment criteria for this examination is long and detailed. To be sure that you have reached the required standard to be entered for an examination, you need to work through several past papers and have these 'marked' by a tutor or assessor who is qualified and experienced in this field.

Results

If your finished work has 5 faults or fewer, you will be awarded distinction.
If your finished work has 14 faults or fewer, you will be awarded pass.

Results are sent to the centre where you sit your examination.
You are now ready to try a mock examination for Document Presentation Stage III Part 2. Take care and good luck!

Key in using a consistent typeface and layout. Display as indicated on the Reference Sheet. Save as EX16A and print a copy of the document on one side of a piece of A4 paper.

SPORTS MEDICINE

ISOTONIC AND ISOMETRIC EXERCISE

the ~~free~~ fuel for muscular activity

add a clip-art picture here

Isotonic exercise has beneficial effects on the cardiovascular system by increasing the amount of blood that the heart can pump and which ~~carry~~/carries oxygen to the muscles. It involves moving a muscle through a long distance against low resistance, as in running, swimming, or gymnastics.

Isometric exercise is best for developing large muscles and involves moving muscles through a short distance against a high resistance, as in pushing or pulling an immovable object. Rather than increasing the actual number of muscle fibres both types of exercise increase the thickness of the muscle fibres and their ability to store glycogen.

FIBRES

Types OF Injury

use a 2-column layout for this section

Most football and basketball injuries involve the knee, either through twisting or through application of lateral force.

Long-distance runners also suffer knee injuries, but this is more usually due to stress fracture, ie a weakening of the front of the shinbone through over-use, with pain and possible bone cracking as the result. Gymnasts are more likely to suffer ligament tears.

apply bold to all headings

ILLEGAL SUBSTANCES

1968   Tests for narcotic analgesics and stimulants, such as heroin or amphetamines, were first introduced at the Olympic Games.

1974 Anabolic steroids banned following the development of a suitable test.

There has been much controversy over the use of drugs and substances such as steroids that are used to enhance athletic performance, particularly in competitions. Anabolic steroids can also have harmful side effects such as liver damage.

A number of other international and national amateur athletic federations have not accepted the illegality of some drugs due to doubts about testing processes and banning of common drugs such as caffeine.

use a justified right hand margin

insert horizontal dividers at points marked ━━━━ either by importing a clip-art divider of your choice or by using the drawing tools

Recall the document stored as EX16A and amend as shown. Save as EX16B and print a copy on one side of a sheet of A4.

Insert a text box in the centre 1.3cm (½") high and 12.5cm (5") wide with the words: A branch of medicine that examines the effects of exercise on the human body and the diagnosis, treatment, and prevention of athletic injuries. (Centre the text and use a different font and size.)

SPORTS MEDICINE

centre this heading and use a larger font size

ISOTONIC AND ISOMETRIC EXERCISE

Isotonic exercise has beneficial effects on the cardiovascular system, by increasing the amount of blood that the heart can pump. ~~and~~ which carries oxygen to the muscles. It involves moving a muscle through a long distance against low resistance, as in running, swimming, or gymnastics. Isometric exercise is best for developing large muscles and involves moving muscles through a short distance against a high resistance, as in pushing or pulling an immovable object. ~~Rather than increasing the actual number of muscle fibres both types of exercise increase the thickness of the muscle fibres and their ability to store glycogen, the fuel for muscular activity.~~

please add a full page border of your own choice

TYPES OF SPORTS INJURY

Most football and basketball injuries involve the knee, either through twisting or through application of lateral force. Long-distance runners also suffer knee injuries, but this is ~~more~~ usually due to stress fracture, ie a weakening of the front of the shinbone through over-use, with pain and possible bone cracking as the result. Gymnasts are more likely to suffer ligament tears.

taken to improve strength and endurance.

• shade this box
• centre the text and use a different font and size

ILLEGAL SUBSTANCES

1968   Tests for narcotic analgesics and stimulants, such as heroin or amphetamines, were first introduced at the Olympic Games.

1974   Anabolic steroids banned following the development of a suitable test.

There has been much controversy over the use of drugs and substances such as steroids that are used to enhance athletic performance, particularly in competitions. Anabolic steroids can also have harmful side effects such as liver damage. A number of other international and national amateur athletic federations have not accepted the illegality of some drugs due to doubts about testing processes and banning of common drugs such as caffeine, or simply through lack of concern.

Although it is becoming increasingly popular, especially in America, sports medicine is still not fully recognised as a medical speciality.

Recall the document stored as EX15D and amend as shown. Use a consistent typeface and heading layout. Change the header to MATHEMATICAL SYMBOL DEVELOPMENT and the footer to Mathematical Journal 33 on each page and change them both to a point 9 font size. Number the pages at the Bot of the page, flush with the right margin, starting with page 15. Adjust the line length to 14cm and use a justified right margin. Save the document as EX16C and print one copy.

MATHEMATICAL SYMBOLS

The term 'mathematical symbols' relates to the various signs and short forms that are used in mathematics to indicate entities, relations, or operations, eg ±, √, ≥. The history of how mathematical symbols were originated and evolved is not entirely clear.

indent this section only by 13 mm (½") at left and right margins

BACKGROUND

remove indents at left and right margins and print this section only in triple line spacing

The early Egyptians used symbols for addition and equality. The Greeks, Hindus and Arabs had symbols for equality and the unknown quantity. However, from earliest times mathematical processes were cumbersome because proper symbols of operation were largely absent. The expressions for such processes were either written out in full or denoted by word short forms.

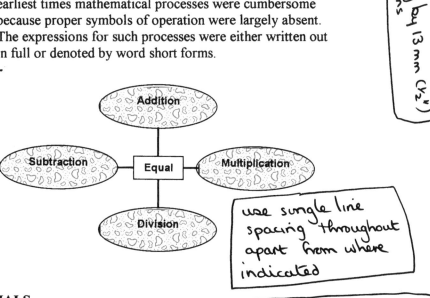

use single line spacing throughout apart from where indicated

DECIMALS

Simon Stevin, a Dutch mathematician, was ~~responsible for developing~~ *attributed with the development*

of

~~the~~ extension of the decimal position system below unity. He ~~called~~ *labeled*

tenths, hundredths, and ~~thousandths~~ *millionths* *primes, sekondes,* and *terzes* and ✓

period

used circled digits to denote the orders. A ~~full stop~~ was used to set off the decimal part of a number as early as the 15th century. The German

astronomer Johannes Kepler used the comma to set off the decimal

orders, ~~and~~ ⊤he Swiss mathematician Justus Byrgius used the decimal

fraction in such forms as 3.2. Decimals are written differently in different

countries:

use a different type of bullet point for these items

- in the United States they are written in the form 1.23;
- in Great Britain 1·23;
- in continental Europe 1,23;
- in standard scientific notation, the number 0.000000123 would be
  written as 1.23×10^{-7}.

ADDITION AND SUBTRACTION SYMBOLS

variable

The symbols for addition were ~~not uniform~~. Some mathematicians

indicated addition by using the short form p, some e, and the

mathematician Niccolò Tartaglia commonly expressed the operation by

plus

$\varnothing$. Algebra mathematicians in Germany and England introduced the sign,

+, but first used it only to indicate excess. *The Greek mathematician Diophantus indicated subtraction by the symbol ↗. The German and English algebraists were the 1st to use the present symbol — (minus sign). The addition and subtraction symbols + and − were first shown in 1489 by the German Johann Widman.*

DIOPHANTUS

Multiplication and Division Symbols

William Oughtred was the mathematician who first devised the ~~symbol~~ symbol ✗ for multiplication. The German mathematician Gottfried Wilhelm Leibniz 1st used a period to indicate multiplication and later employed the sign ∩ to denote multiplication and ∪ to denote division. Descartes developed the notation a^n for involution. The english mathematician John Wallis defined the negative exponent and first used the symbol ∞ for infinity.

print these in italics

OTHER SYMBOLS

The = symbol for equality was originated by the english mathematician Robert Recorde. The symbols =< for "equals greater than" and => for "equals less than" were the invention of another Englishman, Thomas Harriot. It was the French mathematician, François Viète, who introduce various symbols of aggregation. The calculus symbols of differentiation, dx, and integration, ∫, originated with the German born Leibniz. He was also responsible for the ~ symbol for similarity ~~that~~ is used in ~~geome~~ geometry. ✓

Please insert here the diagram on the Reference Sheet

please change short form(s) to abbreviation(s)

LEIBNIZ

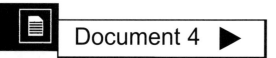
Key in the following document. Use a 2-column layout for the lower section which begins CHICKEN POx ... Save the document as EX16D part I. Print one copy and check it against the copy below.

CHILDREN'S INFECTIONS

Medical advice stresses the importance of getting your child(ren) immunised to avoid the risk of illnesses such as measles and whooping cough. These childhood illnesses can be very unpleasant and sometimes dangerous.

Doctors are able to provide full guidance and ensure that protection is available through safe immunisation.

At 2-3 and 4 months – one combined injection each month for diphtheria, tetanus, whooping cough and meningitis (may be separate injection); polio by mouth each month.
At 5 years – one combined injection for diphtheria and tetanus; polio (once by mouth).
At 13-15 months – one combined injection for measles, mumps and rubella.
At 10-13 years – Heaf test on forearm to check immunity to TB.

As a precaution against polio infection, unvaccinated adults in the same household should be vaccinated at the same time as their child(ren).

A doctor should always be consulted if there is: persistent earache, high fever or delirium, continued vomiting, severe eye inflammation, excessive pain or discomfort.

CHICKEN POX	The illness usually starts with spots on the trunk which become blistery then yellow and form scabs. (Incubation 10-25 days)
VIRAL HEPATITIS	Symptoms can resemble influenza with nausea, indigestion and pains under the ribs. As the yellow jaundice develops, fever and stomach symptoms lessen. (Incubation 2-6 weeks)
SCARLET FEVER	Starts with a sore throat and vomiting, with painful swollen glands in the neck. A rash of small slightly raised points appears against a bright red background. (Incubation 1-5 days)
MEASLES	Usually starts with a runny nose, bleary eyes and a hard cough. A rash starts behind the ears, spreading to the face and down the body. (Incubation 14 days)
GLANDULAR FEVER	The throat becomes increasingly painful and swollen with swollen glands in the sides of the neck and sometimes in the armpits and groin. A white patch covering the tonsils is a distinctive feature. (Incubation 6-8 weeks)

Retrieve the document EX16D part 1. Apply bold, centring and Arial font, size 14, to the main heading.
Display the document according to the Reference Sheet, reformatting it to a 3-column layout and following any other formatting.
Apart from the table section and the bulleted items, print the document in double line spacing. Sort the items of the table into ascending order of infection name in the first column. Number all the pages.
Save the document using the filename EX16D part 2 and print one copy.

There are often several crops of spots.

add this to the CHICKEN POX section

These are followed by yellow eyes, pale motions and dark orange or brown urine.

make this the second sentence in the VIRAL HEPATITIS section

Dark purplish spots develop into blotches.

make this the last sentence in the MEASLES section

The throat is vivid red and there may be a white deposit on the tonsils.

This is the first sentence of the SCARLET FEVER section

Information on this sheet is not to be copied. It indicates the house style required for the document.

Key in the dates at the left hand margin and indent the text as indicated.

1968	Tests for narcotic analgesics and stimulants, such as heroin or amphetamines, were first introduced at the Olympic Games.
1974	Anabolic steroids banned following the development of a suitable test.

This diagram does not have to be reproduced in the exact size and can be adjusted to fit the space available in your document. You may choose your own pattern or shading to fill the shapes. Do not apply any shading or lines to the text boxes containing the figures and symbols.

Reference Sheet for Document 4

Information on this sheet is not to be copied. It indicates the house style required for the document.

Doctors are able to provide full guidance and ensure that protection is available through safe immunisation.

- *AT 2-3 AND 4 MONTHS* – one combined injection each month for diphtheria, tetanus, whooping cough and meningitis (may be separate injection); polio by mouth each month.

- *AT 5 YEARS* – one combined injection for diphtheria and tetanus; polio (once by mouth).

> ➢ Use capitalisation, italic, and 3-column layout where indicated here.
> ➢ Please use bullet points indicated and inset by 2.54 cm (1") at the left margin. Display the list of bulleted items as shown.
> ➢ Align the text in the 3-column display as shown below.

A doctor should always be consulted if there is:

- persistent earache

- high fever or delirium

		INCUBATION
CHICKEN POX	The illness usually starts with spots on the trunk which become blistery then	10-25 days
GLANDULAR FEVER	Swollen glands in the sides of the neck and sometimes in the armpits and	6-8 weeks

Progress Review Checklist

Unit	Topic	Date completed	Comments
▶ 1	Document formatting revision (EX1A)		
	Page numbering from a given page		
	Changing appearance of headers and footers		
	Footnotes		
▶ 2	AutoCorrect		
	Apostrophes		
	Spelling in context		
	Abbreviations		
	Fractions		
	Accents		
	Symbols		
▶ 3	Memorandum and business letter layout		
	Printing on pre-printed forms and using templates		
	Multiple enclosures		
	Page numbering and continuation sheet(s)		
	Postdating documents		
	Confirming facts		
	Routing of copies		
▶ 4	Consolidation 1		
▶ 5	Examination Practice 1		
▶ 6	Pagination		
	House style		
	Locating and selecting information		
▶ 7	Formatting fonts		
	Using styles		
	Allocating horizontal space		
	Allocating vertical space		
	Allocating space using text box		
	Newspaper columns - whole document		
	Newspaper columns - section of document		
	Copying text from one document to another		
▶ 8	Using tabs for column work		
	Types of tab settings		
	Applying ruling (borders) to a table		
	Setting tabs inside a table		
	Changing paper size to landscape orientation		
	Complex table layouts		
▶ 9	Consolidation 2		

Unit	Topic	Date completed	Comments
▶ 10	Examination Practice 2		
▶ 11	Document presentation and layout		
	Adding and removing borders, lines and shading		
	Full-page borders		
▶ 12	Displaying the Drawing Tool Bar		
	Drawing shapes		
	Selecting and formatting drawing shapes		
	Inserting text into a drawing shape		
	Inserting a text box		
	Formatting a text box		
	Applying shading to drawing shapes and text boxes		
	Creating dividers using the drawing tools		
▶ 13	Inserting clip art images from the Microsoft Clip Gallery		
	Adjusting, moving, copying, formatting a clip art picture		
	Wrapping text around a clip art picture		
	Positioning a graphic object in relation to text or to the page		
	Inserting clip art images from other files		
	Inserting a picture into a text box		
	Using symbols as graphics		
	Inserting borders and dividers using clip art		
▶ 14	Special business documents and house styles		
	Examples of specialist business documents - agenda and minutes		
	Triple line spacing		
	Reformat a two-column document to a three-column layout using tabulation		
▶ 15	Consolidation 3		
▶ 16	Examination Practice 3		

Unit 1
Exercise 1A

SENSIBLE EATING

EATING FOR HEALTH

Most of us acknowledge nowadays that, to some extent, 'We are what we eat' and that we can only function to our full potential if we have a healthy body. Many common illnesses and health problems, including heart disease, are linked to our diet.

Every cell in our bodies needs nutrients to be able to perform its particular function. Nutrients are extracted from the foods we eat.

The main food groups are:

1   Proteins
2   Carbohydrates
3   Fats
4   Sugars
5   Alcohol

Many well-known phrases come to mind when giving advice on diet:

'VARIETY IS THE SPICE OF LIFE'

No single food or food group can provide the full range of nutrients required by the body. Different foods supply different combinations of nutrients. Eating a wide range of foods helps to make sure that we get all the nourishment we need to grow and stay healthy.

'KEEP IT IN PROPORTION'

In this country, most of us eat too much protein, fat and salt. The balance should be tipped more in favour of complex carbohydrates such as rice, pasta, bread, cereals, potatoes and yams. These should be the main part of any meal or snack: they are low in fat and sugar and give us lots of energy, vitamins, minerals and fibre. Provided we don't add too much fat or sugar when preparing dishes, we can all benefit from eating these starchy foods.

'EAT UP YOUR GREENS'

Vegetables, especially dark green leafy types, provide valuable vitamins, minerals and fibre. Poor storage, preparation and cooking practices deplete the vitamin content so it's best to buy and eat fresh – or grow your own! 'An apple a day, keeps the doctor away' could also be an appropriate saying here as fresh fruit is equally important – and not only apples!

1

Unit 1
Exercise 1A Continued

SENSIBLE EATING

'PICK UP A PINTA'

Dairy products such as cheese, milk and yoghurt are rich in calcium. Low fat versions contain just as much calcium, protein and vitamins but less of the animal fats we should avoid.

'BODY BUILDING'

Protein-rich foods such as meat, fish, beans, pulses, eggs and nuts also contain vitamins, minerals and fats. However, we tend to eat more of these types of food than we need and care needs to be taken because of the possible high fat content. Meat should be lean, skin should be removed from poultry, and fish should be poached or grilled rather than fried. Vegetarians learn to combine foods to ensure good quality proteins.

'A BIT OF WHAT YOU FANCY DOES YOU GOOD'

The types of food we tend to use as 'treats' are unfortunately not very good in terms of nutrition – often being high in fats, sugars and salt. However, in small amounts and eaten occasionally, they do not do us any harm. Alcohol and sugar are classed as foods but in fact contain no nutrients – just 'empty calories'. Malnutrition can result from excessive use of these especially if used instead of nourishing foods.

'MODERATION IN ALL THINGS'

Every cell in our bodies needs nutrients to be able to perform its particular function. Nutrients are extracted from the foods we eat.

Advertisements in the media make us believe that it is necessary to buy the manufacturers' latest food products to achieve a happy and healthy life for ourselves and our family. Immediate and convenient access to a wide range of attractively-packaged products is available to almost everyone. Obesity is increasing rapidly in this country although millions of pounds is spent by the government on health education and nutrition information. It seems that we can have 'too much of a good thing'!

2

Unit 1
Exercise1B

EATING FOR HEALTH

Most of us acknowledge nowadays that, to some extent, 'We are what we

eat' and that we can only function to our full potential if we have a healthy

body. Many common illnesses and health problems, including heart

disease, are linked to our diet.

Every cell in our bodies needs nutrients to be able to perform its particular
function. Nutrients are extracted from the foods we eat.

The main food groups are:

1. Proteins
2. Carbohydrates
3. Fats*
4. Sugars
5. Alcohol

Many well-known phrases come to mind when giving advice on diet:

'VARIETY IS THE SPICE OF LIFE'

No single food or food group can provide the full range of nutrients required
by the body. Different foods supply different combinations of nutrients.
Eating a wide range of foods helps to make sure that we get all the
nourishment we need to grow and stay healthy. Malnutrition can arise on
'crash' diets and when food variety is restricted, despite the fact that the
person may be overweight.

'KEEP IT IN PROPORTION'

In this country, most of us eat too much protein, fat and salt. The balance
should be tipped more in favour of complex carbohydrates such as rice,
pasta, bread, cereals, potatoes and yams. These should be the main part of
any meal or snack: they are low in fat and sugar and give us lots of energy,
vitamins, minerals and fibre. Provided we don't add too much fat or sugar
when preparing dishes, we can all benefit from eating these starchy foods.

* Fats contain more than double the number of calories than proteins and carbohydrates.

Your name

4

Unit 1
Exercise 1B Continued

'EAT UP YOUR GREENS'

Vegetables, especially dark green leafy types, provide valuable vitamins,
minerals and fibre. Poor storage, preparation and cooking practices deplete
the vitamin content so it's best to buy and eat fresh – or grow your own!
'An apple a day, keeps the doctor away' could also be an appropriate saying
here as fresh fruit is equally important – and not only apples!

'PICK UP A PINTA'

Dairy products such as cheese, milk and yoghurt are rich in calcium. Low
fat versions contain just as much calcium, protein and vitamins but less of
the animal fats we should avoid. It is becoming apparent that many people
are intolerant of animal milks. Calcium-enriched soya milk provides a good
alternative.

'BODY BUILDING'

Protein-rich foods such as meat, fish, beans, pulses, eggs and nuts also
contain vitamins, minerals and fats. However, we tend to eat more of these
types of food than we need and care needs to be taken because of the
possible high fat content. Meat should be lean, skin should be removed
from poultry, and fish should be poached or grilled rather than fried.
Vegetarians learn to combine foods to ensure good quality proteins.

'A BIT OF WHAT YOU FANCY DOES YOU GOOD'

The types of food we tend to use as 'treats' are unfortunately not very good
in terms of nutrition – often being high in fats, sugars and salt. However, in
small amounts and eaten occasionally, they do not do us any harm. Alcohol
and sugar are classed as foods but in fact contain no nutrients – just 'empty
calories'. Malnutrition can result from excessive use of these especially if
used instead of nourishing foods.

'MODERATION IN ALL THINGS'

Every cell in our bodies needs nutrients to be able to perform its particular
function. Nutrients are extracted from the foods we eat.

> Advertisements in the media make us believe that it is
> necessary to buy the manufacturers' latest food products to
> achieve a happy and healthy life for ourselves and our
> family. Immediate and convenient access to a wide range of
> attractively-packaged products is available to almost
> everyone. Obesity is increasing rapidly in this country
> although millions of pounds is spent by the government on
> health education and nutrition information. It seems that we
> can have 'too much of a good thing'!

Your name

5

Unit 1
Exercise 1C

SENSIBLE EATING

EATING FOR HEALTH

Most of us acknowledge nowadays that, to some extent, 'We are what we eat' and that we can only function to our full potential if we have a healthy body. Many common illnesses and health problems, including heart disease, are linked to our diet.

Every cell in our bodies needs nutrients to be able to perform its particular function. Nutrients are extracted from the foods we eat.

The main food groups are:

☐ Proteins
☐ Carbohydrates
☐ Fats
☐ Sugars
☐ Alcohol

Many well-known phrases come to mind when giving advice on diet:

'VARIETY IS THE SPICE OF LIFE'

No single food or food group can provide the full range of nutrients required by the body. Different foods supply different combinations of nutrients. Eating a wide range of foods helps to make sure that we get all the nourishment we need to grow and stay healthy. Malnutrition can arise on 'crash' diets and when food variety is restricted, despite the fact that the person may be overweight.

'KEEP IT IN PROPORTION'

In this country, most of us eat too much protein, fat and salt. The balance should be tipped more in favour of complex carbohydrates[1] such as rice, pasta, bread, cereals, potatoes and yams. These should be the main part of any meal or snack: they are low in fat[2] and sugar[3] and give us lots of energy, vitamins, minerals and fibre. Provided we don't add too much fat or sugar when preparing dishes, we can all benefit from eating these starchy foods.

[1] 3.75 kcal/g (calories per gram)
[2] 9.00 kcal/g
[3] 4.00 kcal/g – 'empty calories' – no nutrition

Your name   1

Unit 1
Exercise 1C Continued

SENSIBLE EATING

'EAT UP YOUR GREENS'

Vegetables, especially dark green leafy types, provide valuable vitamins, minerals and fibre. Poor storage, preparation and cooking practices deplete the vitamin content so it's best to buy and eat fresh – or grow your own!
'An apple a day, keeps the doctor away' could also be an appropriate saying here as fresh fruit is equally important – and not only apples!

'PICK UP A PINTA'

Dairy products such as cheese, milk and yoghurt are rich in calcium. Low fat versions contain just as much calcium, protein and vitamins but less of the animal fats we should avoid. It is becoming apparent that many people are intolerant of animal milks. Calcium-enriched soya milk provides a good alternative.

'BODY BUILDING'

Protein-rich foods such as meat, fish, beans, pulses, eggs and nuts also contain vitamins, minerals and fats. However, we tend to eat more of these types of food than we need and care needs to be taken because of the possible high fat content. Meat should be lean, skin should be removed from poultry, and fish should be poached or grilled rather than fried. Vegetarians learn to combine foods to ensure good quality proteins.

'A BIT OF WHAT YOU FANCY DOES YOU GOOD'

The types of food we tend to use as 'treats' are unfortunately not very good in terms of nutrition – often being high in fats, sugars and salt. However, in small amounts and eaten occasionally, they do not do us any harm. Alcohol and sugar are classed as foods but in fact contain no nutrients – just 'empty calories'. Malnutrition can result from excessive use of these especially if used instead of nourishing foods.

'MODERATION IN ALL THINGS'

Every cell in our bodies needs nutrients to be able to perform its particular function. Nutrients are extracted from the foods we eat.

Advertisements in the media make us believe that it is necessary to buy the manufacturers' latest food products to achieve a happy and healthy life for ourselves and our family. Immediate and convenient access to a wide range of attractively-packaged products is available to almost everyone. Obesity is increasing rapidly in this country although millions of pounds is spent by the government on health education and nutrition information. It seems that we can have 'too much of a good thing'!

Your name   2

Unit 2
Exercise 2A

We're leaving for our holiday today. The representatives said they're to meet us after we've landed at the local airport. Then they'll take us to the hotel where we're going to spend the first 5 days. There's to be a trip to local beaches and although we hadn't booked, the representative said there wouldn't be any problem in finding places as there'll be some guests who aren't able to take the trips.

The sun's heat when we land will surprise and delight us. We'll need to use good sun protection creams to protect the children's skin when they're playing on the island's beaches. The toddlers like to sit at the water's edge and squeal with anticipation as each wave's crest approaches them. The older children's plans are concerned more with the water in the swimming pool and they expect to join in the activities organised by the hotel's recreation team. We parents hope to be able to enjoy the island's cuisine, the hotel's poolside bar, and the chance to unwind for a few days.

The island's history shows that its culture has been influenced by many other civilisations. It's been invaded by neighbouring countries and its natural harbours have made it a valuable port of call for seafarers and merchants for centuries. This fact probably accounts for its cosmopolitan nature and it's this aspect of its atmosphere that attracts its many annual visitors. It's not unusual to see traces of European, African, and Asian cultures within the architecture or the cuisine of its famous restaurants. It's one of the most popular holiday destinations for many of the northern European nations.

Unit 2
Exercise 2B

COMPLEMENTARY THERAPIES

PAST REMEDIES FOR TODAY'S ILLS

Increasing interest is currently being shown in complementary therapies by the allopathic sector of medicine. Rigorous testing is required for western orthodox medicine to rely on the efficacy of therapies which use herbs, plants, essential oils, tinctures and so on. The scientific revolution of the early 19th century allowed chemists to isolate components in nature's products, and then to achieve success in developing synthetic drugs for the treatment of disease. This lead in turn to the pharmaceutical industry of today. The emphasis on logic and reasoning at that time tended to lead to a dismissal of the earlier experience of the interdependence of medicine (or rather therapy) and psychology.

Although the placebo effect has been considered responsible for the success of complementary therapies, some medical researchers acknowledge, and have proved, that this effect is definitely important and apparent in all branches of medicine.

ANCIENT CHRONICLES

Over 700 different substances are listed in Indian Vedic literature.[1] The Rig Veda classifies the use of these substances – for example, cinnamon, myrrh, coriander and sandalwood – for both therapeutic and liturgical purposes.

Chinese acupuncture combines work on the meridians with the use of herbs, and aromatics such as ginger and opium were recommended for use in the 'Yellow Emperor's Book of Internal Medicine'.[2] Egyptian papyrus manuscripts from the reign of Khufu, describe the use of 'fine oils and choice perfumes' by people who were experts in cosmetology.

---
[1] around 2,000 BC
[2] around 2,800 BC

Your name

1

Unit 2
Exercise 2B Continued

COMPLEMENTARY THERAPIES

Traces of scented unguents and oils such as cedar and myrrh which were employed in the embalming process, are still detectable today.

PASSING THE MESSAGE

The Egyptians' early practices and traditions were passed down through the centuries via the Phoenicians, Greeks and Romans to the Persians and Arabs.

Romans greatly appreciated aromatic substances and used perfumes categorised as:

- solid unguents (ladysmata)
- powdered perfumes (diaspasmata)
- scented oils (stymmata)

A famous and gifted Arabian physician and scholar, Avicenna (AD980-1037) wrote over 100 books and improved the art of distillation. However, it was discovered in 1975 that ancient inhabitants of the Indus valley had predated his work by 4,000 years. A perfectly preserved distillation unit is on permanent display in a local museum.

PERFUMES OF ARABIA

During the Middle Ages, Europeans began to have access to the 'perfumes of Arabia' and also to experiment with the native plants of Europe such as sage, rosemary and lavender. The 15th and 16th centuries saw the publication of many famous 'herbals' giving detailed information on herbs, and recommending their use for most ailments.

These books are still referred to today and products bearing one author's name – that of Nicholas Culpepper – are available for us to buy in the high street.

Your name

2

Unit 2
Exercise 2D

COMPLEMENTARY THERAPIES

PAST REMEDIES FOR TODAY'S ILLS

Increasing interest is currently being shown in complementary therapies by the allopathic sector of medicine. Rigorous testing is required for western orthodox medicine to believe in the efficacy of therapies which use herbs, plants, essential oils, tinctures and so on. The scientific revolution of the early 19th century allowed chemists to isolate components in nature's products, and then to achieve success in developing synthetic drugs for the treatment of disease. This lead in turn to the pharmaceutical industry of today. The emphasis on logic and reasoning at that time tended to lead to a dismissal of the earlier experience of the interdependence of medicine (or rather therapy) and psychology.

Although the placebo effect has been considered responsible for the success of complementary therapies, some medical researchers acknowledge, and have proved, that this effect is definitely important and apparent in all branches of medicine.

ANCIENT CHRONICLES

Over 700 different substances are listed in Indian Vedic literature.[1] The Rig Veda classifies the use of these substances, such as cinnamon, myrrh, coriander and sandalwood, for both therapeutic and liturgical purposes.

Chinese acupuncture combines work on the meridians with the use of herbs, and aromatics such as ginger and opium were recommended for use in the 'Yellow Emperor's Book of Internal Medicine'.[2] Egyptian papyrus manuscripts from the reign of Khufi, describe the use of 'fine oils and choice perfumes' by people who were experts in cosmetology. Traces of scented unguents and oils such as cedar and myrrh which were employed in the embalming process, are still detectable today.

PASSING THE MESSAGE

The Egyptians' early practices and traditions were passed down through the centuries via the Phoenicians, Greeks and Romans to the Persians and Arabs.

Romans greatly appreciated aromatic substances and used perfumes categorised as:

- solid unguents (ladysmata)
- powdered perfumes (diaspasmata)
- scented oils (stymmata)

A famous and gifted Arabian physician and scholar, Avicenna (AD980-1037) wrote over 100 books and improved the art of distillation. However, it was

[1] around 2,000 BC
[2] around 2,800 BC

Your name

1

Note: You may have inserted a page break at a different place in the text. Provided you have not left only one line of text on its own at the bottom or top of a page, an alternative position for the page break is acceptable. Your ordinals may have appeared as a superscripted *th*. This is acceptable.

COMPLEMENTARY THERAPIES

Ironically, just as the effectiveness of herbal medicines and aromatic therapies

began to be proved by scientific methods, the expanding synthetic drugs

industry led to a decline in the use of 'natural' remedies.

A French chemist, René-Maurice Gattefossé[3], discovered the exceptional

healing properties of the essential oil of lavender when he burnt his hand in the

laboratory. Recent research has brought complementary therapies such as

homoeopathy, acupuncture, reflexology and aromatherapy nearer to allopathic

medicine and the disciplines now often work together to great benefit.

[3] in 1928

Your name

3

COMPLEMENTARY THERAPIES

discovered in 1975 that ancient inhabitants of the Indus valley had predated his work by 4,000 years. A perfectly preserved distillation unit is on permanent display in a local museum.

PERFUMES OF ARABIA

During the middle ages, Europeans began to have access to the 'perfumes of Arabia' and also to experiment with the native plants of Europe such as sage, rosemary and lavender. The 15th and 16th centuries saw the publication of many famous 'herbals' giving detailed information on herbs, and recommending their use for most ailments.

Braunsweig's work in 1527, 'The Vertuose Boke of Distyllacyon of the Waters of all Maner of Herbes' gives us the following quotation which demonstrates the respect afforded to 'herbes' at that time:

"Lerne the hygh and mervelous vertue of herbes ... use the effectes with reverence, and give thankes to the maker celestyall."

These books are still referred to today and products bearing one author's name – that of Nicholas Culpepper – are available for us to buy in the high street.

FROM AGE TO AGE

The history of man's use of plants for medicine, perfume, food and cosmetics goes back to the earliest civilizations, from distillation in the Indus valley 3,000 years BC, through the Middle Ages where herbs were widely used in the household (An illustration from 'Das Kreuterbuch oder Herbarius' in 1534 shows herbs being placed in a linen chest to scent the linen and also probably to keep away moths!)

Some practices remain today. For example, in Tibetan temples, sprigs of juniper are burned for purification and frankincense is used during Roman Catholic masses. Religious and therapeutic factors have frequently been combined in this way.

Most medicines and drugs, whether synthetic or 'natural', can be toxic and it is therefore vital that correct procedures are followed in their use. One important consideration is to ensure that the botanical name for a plant is used rather than the common name. Examples of these, related to some of the plants mentioned in this document, are given below:

1 Rosemary – Rosmarin officinalis
2 Lavender – Lavandula angustifolia
3 Cinnamon – Cinnamon zeylanicum
4 Myrrh – Commaphora myrrha
5 Sandalwood – Santalum album
6 Cedar – Cedrus atlantica
7 Ginger – Zingiber officinale

Your name

2

PRIME RESULTS LTD

MEMORANDUM

FROM: Marie Potter
TO: Zafar Hussain
REF: MP/37Q
DATE: today's

Following your recent approval of the proposed work experience scheme for school students, I have arranged for a Year Eleven student from Silverdale Grammar School to spend a one-week placement with your staff in the Finance Department. The placement will begin on Monday, *date of fourth Monday of next month.*

I would be grateful if you could draw up a list of varied activities which the student will participate in and forward this directly to the school (a contact name and address is attached on a copy of their letter). Please include an element of work shadowing with a senior member of staff – I can recommend Jane Griffiths as she has done this kind of thing before.

You will also need to arrange for a mentor to look after the student for the week that he/she is visiting us. The mentor will be asked to complete a report at the end of the week reviewing the student's progress and achievements. This should be countersigned by yourself along with any further comments you may wish to make.

As there will be five students on placement with us I will arrange for them all to have an induction first thing on Monday morning – this will include a tour of the buildings and a meeting with the Health and Safety Officer.

If there is any aspect of the placement you would like to discuss with me, please do not hesitate to contact me on Extension 351.

Enc

PRIME RESULTS LTD

44 HIGHTOWN ROAD
BRADFORD
BD17 8HD

TEL NO: 01274 646542   FAX NO: 01274 646548

Your ref 372/TRM

today's date

URGENT

Ms Joan Braithwaite
Silverdale Grammar School
Silverdale Way
SHIPLEY
SH3 4TU

Dear Ms Braithwaite

WORK EXPERIENCE SCHEME

In response to your enquiry about work experience opportunities at this company for your Year Eleven students, I am delighted to advise you that we are able to offer a total of five one-week placements in different departments. The departments are marketing, personnel, sales, computer services and finance. Obviously we will rely on the school to match each individual's career aspirations to the appropriate job placement.

As one of the largest employers in the area we recognise the value of investing in young people who may well be our employees of the future. We sincerely hope that the placement will provide your students with a valuable insight into the needs of business.

I enclose a number of leaflets and information sheets which provide some background details about the organisation's activities and its various functions. I will also ask each Head of Department to contact you separately with an outline of the activities your students can expect to undertake in their week with us.

Students will be assigned a 'mentor' who will be responsible for their daily workload and personal welfare.

We will arrange an element of work shadowing with senior employees so that the students can develop an appreciation of some of the more complex activities in the department.

I trust these arrangements will be satisfactory and trust that you will contact me again shortly with a suggested start date.

Yours sincerely

Marie Potter
Personnel Manager

Encs

However, the main topic of the conference will be to introduce solutions to these problems, with a positive framework for stimulating business growth and financial stability through greater investment in human resources.

In addition to the leading European authorities in this area who will be speaking at the conference, there will be a number of workshops where you will be able to exchange information and network with other business managers who have a similar interest in the future of their workforce. There will also be an opportunity to discuss your company needs on an individual basis with our specialised Human Resource Consultancy Team.

I attach a conference catalogue giving full details of the day's events, along with a map showing how to get to the venue. A booking form is also enclosed with the pack. Overnight accommodation is available on request.

As places are limited, we would recommend early booking to avoid disappointment.

Yours faithfully

Howard Benson
Conference Organiser

Encs

2

PRIME RESULTS LTD

44 HIGHTOWN ROAD
BRADFORD
BD17 8HD

TEL NO: 01274 646542   FAX NO: 01274 646548

Our ref HB/TDL

Your ref 556/BG

today's date

CONFERENCE – EMPLOYEE SATISFACTION IN THE MILLENNIUM

Dale, Green & Winters Ltd
432 Newberry Industrial Estate
Newberry
LEEDS
LS3 9GB

Dear Sir or Madam

CONFERENCE – EMPLOYEE SATISFACTION IN THE MILLENNIUM

I would like to draw your attention to a special conference which we are holding on Wednesday, *third Wednesday of next month*. The conference will focus on employee satisfaction as a key corporate priority for business success.

A major European Research Study has shown that although competitive levels for customer service are more likely to be achieved with satisfied employees, there are some significant trends in worker dissatisfaction. British workers are shown to be among the most discontented, producing the lowest or second lowest favourable response in a significant number of questionnaire categories.

Statistics point to a pan-European decline in employee perceptions of the security of their employment, with UK employees feeling less secure in their jobs than employees anywhere else in Europe. British attitudes towards the organisation and the efficiency of their work are said to be among the least favourable in Europe and likely to have a profound effect on the employment contract. The full findings of this research, which includes references to over 500 companies, will be presented free of charge at the conference.

PRIME RESULTS LTD

MEMORANDUM

FROM: Howard Benson, Conference Organiser
TO: Hélène de Courcy, Public Relations Officer
REF: HB/342sw
DATE: today's

CONFERENCE – EMPLOYEE SATISFACTION IN THE MILLENNIUM

The campaign to publicise the above conference is underway. I enclose a sample copy of the standard letter which I have sent out to all the Human Resource Managers on our mailing database.

It has occurred to me that we may need additional copies of the conference information pack. Please can you arrange to have sufficient quantities printed as soon as possible. Can you also order some name badges from the same manufacturer we used previously. My secretary will be able to let you have their name and address from our conference correspondence file if you do not have all their details.

Also, can you check that the conference prices in any new publicity material are updated immediately. I will arrange for some new photographs and brief biographies of the speakers to be made available for the exhibition stands.

I have also made arrangements with Marie Potter, Personnel Manager, for someone to assist you on a temporary basis with the conference administration.

Enc

Copy: Marie Potter✓
       File

LOCAL TRENDS

EMPLOYMENT

General Comments

Recent economic trends give an encouraging picture although the Low Beck area suffered a major blow in the loss of over 350 jobs when Analogical Systems cut its workforce last month.

A new superstore opened in Pine Valley and it is anticipated that the immediate success of this venture will have a permanent impact on shopping patterns in the Valley. It should also attract shoppers from a wider area to experience the other amenities of the town and bring the prosperity necessary for the continued development of small business enterprises. (As a matter of interest, the store was opened by Herr Jürgen Freiwald, the 'Mayor' of Megèle, our twin town in Switzerland.)

Looking further afield and to broader issues, we can report that work is going ahead on a final bid for regeneration funds to be submitted to the Government Office[1] in 2 months' time. A possible decision is expected by the end of the year.

In conjunction with this bid, the Council is very much involved in the preparation of a Delivery Plan for a training and employment initiative designed to help the unemployed to obtain work and re-training relevant to local industrial and commercial needs.

---

[1] for Yorkshire and the Humber

LOCAL TRENDS

Sources

1 Average house price: Castle Building Society

2 Unemployed claimants: Office for National Statistics

3 Migration to and from borough: NHS Central Register

3

LOCAL TRENDS

Facts and Figures

A summary of the employment information is given below:

- In 1996, the total number of employees in the borough was estimated to be 84,550, over 4,250 more than in 1994.

- Despite the fact that numbers employed in manufacturing continued to drop – over 7,400 fewer in 1996 than in 1994 – the sector still definitely had an important role in the local economy accounting for a higher proportion of employees than at county, regional and national levels.

- Service sector employment rose by 8,300 between 1994 and 1996.

- Part-time employment fell after 1994; full-time employment rose by nearly 4,100.

- The average house price rose in 1994 to £61,567 but fell in 1996 to £58,755.

- The trend towards increased migration out of the borough changed to a positive balance of 30 migrating into the borough in 1995.

Every ward now has increased levels of unemployment compared with *(same month last year)*. The rising trend levelled out over the winter months.

Sector Changes

The number of Service Sector employees increased by $1/3$ over the last 3 years compared with $1/6$ over the last 15 years. There has been a contrasting decline of over 8,000 jobs in manufacturing ($1/5$ of the total) over the same 3 years. The construction industry, however, has suffered the largest decline – almost half ($5/12$) the number of employees compared to 3 years ago.

2

Employment Trends

EMPLOYMENT

General Comments

Recent economic trends give an encouraging picture although the Low Beck area suffered a major blow in the loss of over 350 jobs when Analogical Systems cut its workforce last month.

A new superstore opened in Pine Valley and it is anticipated that the immediate success of this venture will have a permanent impact on shopping patterns in the Valley. It should also attract shoppers from a wider area to experience the other amenities of the town and bring the prosperity necessary for the continued development of small business enterprises. (As a matter of interest, the store was opened by Herr Jurgen Freiwald, the 'Mayor' of Megele, our twin town in Switzerland.)

Looking further afield and to broader issues, we can report that work is going ahead on a final bid for regeneration funds to be submitted to the Government Office[1] in 2 months' time. A possible decision is expected by the end of the year.

In conjunction with this bid, the Council is very much involved in the preparation of a Delivery Plan for a training and employment initiative designed to help the unemployed to obtain work and re-training relevant to local industrial and commercial needs.

Sector Changes

The number of Service Sector employees increased by $^1/_3$ over the last 3 years compared with $^1/_6$ over the last 15 years. There has been a contrasting decline of over 8,000 jobs in manufacturing ($^1/_5$ of the total) over the same 3 years. The construction industry, however, has suffered the largest decline – almost half ($^5/_{12}$) the number of employees compared to 3 years ago.

GENDER ISSUES

The previously prevailing trend of decreased male and increased female employment was reversed during the past 2 years when the number of male employees rose at the rate of 5% compared with only 2% for female employees.

[1] for Yorkshire and the Humber

LOCAL TRENDS

6

Employment Trends

The following information is worthy of note:

1 Part-time employment in the Service Sector increased by 9%

2 The Service Sector accounts for 75% of all part-time employment

3 80% of part-time employees are women

4 35% of all full-time employment is in Manufacturing

5 Males make up 70% of all full-time employees

Facts and Figures[1]

A summary of the employment information is given below:

• In 1996, the total number of employees in the borough was estimated to be 84,550, over 4,250 more than in 1994.

• Despite the fact that numbers employed in manufacturing[2] continued to drop – over 7,400 fewer in 1996 than in 1994 – the sector still definitely had an important role in the local economy accounting for a higher proportion of employees than at county, regional and national levels.

• Service sector employment rose by 8,300 between 1994 and 1996.

• Part-time employment fell after 1994; full-time employment rose by nearly 4,100.

• The average house price rose in 1994 to £61,567 but fell in 1996 to £58,755.

• The trend towards increased migration out of the borough changed to a positive balance of 30 migrating into the borough in 1995.

Sources

1 Average house price: Castle Building Society

2 Unemployed claimants: Office for National Statistics

3 Migration to and from borough: NHS Central Register

[1] Analysis excludes the primary sector as reliable data is not available
[2] Following re-classification of industries, census figures prior to 1995 have been re-based

LOCAL TRENDS

7

PRIME RESULTS LTD

MEMORANDUM

To: Anne Müller

From: Paula Ferera

Ref: PF/Wall/464

Date: Date of typing

URGENT

The purchase of Squirrel View, Southlands Lane, Bitterton by Mrs Wall is going ahead subject to a satisfactory response from the mortgage lender, North East Building Society, and two minor queries arising from the documents received from the Vendors' solicitors.

The prospective purchaser of Mrs Wall's property at 35 Winter Grove is pressing for an early completion date, as the company by whom he is employed relocated to the area some months ago and unfortunately the resulting inconvenience and expense of travelling long distances, although temporary, is definitely causing severe difficulty.

I have assured Mrs Wall that we will do our best to expedite matters. To this end, in my absence, I would be grateful if you would acknowledge all communications from this client and from Stone & Co immediately they are received.

We require clarification on two matters from Stone & Co: with reference to the boundary fence on the north and east sides of the land, and the proximity of an electricity sub-station to the south. Please obtain the documents from Gemma and contact the Vendors' solicitors as a matter of urgency.

PRIME RESULTS LTD

44 HIGHTOWN ROAD
BRADFORD BD17 8HD

TEL NO: 01874 646548 FAX NO: 01874 646548

Our ref PF/Wall/464

Date of typing

Mrs D S Wall
35 Winter Grove
BITTERTON
Leicestershire
LE19 6PV

Dear Mrs Wall

PURCHASE OF SQUIRREL VIEW SOUTHLANDS LANE BITTERTON

Further to our telephone conversation, I am writing to inform you that I have now perused the documents which have been forwarded by the Vendors' solicitors and I am pleased to report that they appear to be satisfactory. One or two minor queries arose and my assistant, Anne Müller, is to request further information. As discussed, I enclose the list of fixtures, fittings and contents for your attention.

I have despatched an application for Local Search and would anticipate that the result should be received within two or three weeks. By that date, we should also have instructions from your mortgage lender.

I know that you are keen to proceed as quickly as possible and as soon as we have access to all the necessary information, I will contact you to make an appointment for us to go through all the documents together. I will then take your detailed instructions regarding exchange of Contracts and completion.

I will be on holiday for one week from *(next Monday's date)* but my secretary, Gemma White, will be able to answer any queries which you may have. Anne or Gemma will telephone you if necessary. Please do not hesitate to contact either of these two members of my staff if any problems arise in my absence.

Yours sincerely

Paula Ferera
LICENSED CONVEYANCER

Enc

THE HOUSE TRANSFER BOND

VITAL INFORMATION FOR YOUR PROTECTION

Most people remark after moving house that they will never repeat the exercise! The vast majority of house sales, purchases and removals go according to plan but, despite this fact, it is a very stressful time for everyone concerned.

THE BOND

The HOUSE TRANSFER BOND is an insurance scheme available for buyers and sellers. If something does go wrong, the legal costs still have to be paid and you can be left out of pocket with nothing to show for it. In order to help you, we automatically issue an insurance certificate to all our clients when they instruct us to act for them. This covers you for up to £75 in respect of our legal costs if the transaction falls through before exchange of contracts. However, by paying an additional premium of £30*, the amount of cover can be increased to £400** – usually sufficient to cover all legal costs incurred.

We'll take care of your bills. No complicated claim forms are necessary. All we ask is that you pay the additional premium within 10 days of giving us your instructions to act for you.

---

* £55 if you have instructed us in a sale and a purchase
** £750 if sale and purchase involved

1

YOUR COVER

The cover applies to buyers if the seller withdraws.

The cover applies to sellers if the buyer withdraws for any reason except:

1 an unreasonable delay on your part

2 following an adverse survey on your property

3 because of a defect in your property.

WHAT COULD GO WRONG?

You arrive at your new home to find the floor flooded because the vendor disconnected the dishwasher and damaged the plumbing.

The vendors cannot (or will not) move out.

The vendors' removal firm did not turn up and they are still in the house so you can't move in.

Legal problems mean the completion is delayed and you have nowhere to stay in the meantime.

WHAT DO YOU DO THEN?

Simply telephone us on 0800-9786543. We are open 7 days a week, 24 hours a day.

Our experts will solve your problems: booking hotels, locating reliable tradesmen, recovering your car, organising transport.

The HOUSE TRANSFER BOND is the solution to your problems. Make sure you're covered.

2

Investing in the community

Jeremiah's concerns regarding the workforce at his Union Road mill in the middle of the last century made him a pioneer amongst employers of the time, many of whom were less than desirable characters. In fact, he was probably the first industrialist to deserve the IiP award!

The village he built stands proud today as a symbol of community life. Every weekend you will see the Central Hall and the Church, which he designed with such care, hosting social activities of all kinds and providing a focus for the local community.

Educational involvement takes the form of national and local links with the aim of promoting the skills, understanding and attitudes necessary for industry today and in the future.

Our priorities include:

    Curriculum materials
    Education management training
    Preparation for IiP standards
    School governor courses for our employees
    Student placements
    Teacher placements
    Teacher support packs

2

Unit 6
Exercise 6A

Investing in the community

JEREMIAH'S HERITAGE

Building on the philosophy of the founder of our company, the tradition of philanthropy continues to play an important part in the culture of the modern-day organisation. Jeremiah Turnbull's ideals are still converted into practical support for the local community and environment wherever the organisation operates in the world.

Over the past 150 years, the development of the company has been linked to:

    Community welfare
    Education
    Environment
    Health
    Housing
    Technology
    The Arts
    Training

In the competitive and professional environment of today, corporate giving needs to be well structured and based on efforts and themes with real impact. It is vital that we never lose sight of the fact that it is our employees who create the wealth, and that we act on behalf of our shareholders.

At least 1.5% of our pre-tax profit is distributed in cash, in time or in kind to organisations, communities or projects which reflect our aims and which are proven to be professionally managed. In 1997 £6 million was contributed in cash.

1

Unit 6
Exercise 6B

JEREMIAH'S HERITAGE

Building on the philosophy of the founder of our company, the tradition of philanthropy continues to play an important part in the culture of the modern-day organisation. Jeremiah Turnbull's ideals are still converted into practical support for the local community and environment wherever the organisation operates in the world.

Over the past 150 years, the development of the company has been linked to:

Community welfare
Education
Environment
Health
Housing
Technology
The Arts
Training

In the competitive and professional environment of today, corporate giving needs to be well structured and based on efforts and themes with real impact. It is vital that we never lose sight of the fact that it is our employees who create the wealth, and that we act on behalf of our shareholders.

At least 1.5% of our pre-tax profit is distributed in cash, in time or in kind to organisations, communities or projects which reflect our aims and which are proven to be professionally managed. In 1997 £6 million was contributed in cash.

1

Investing in the community

Unit 6
Exercise A Continued

Investing in the community

Jeremiah Turnbull would be proud of the fact that local support continues only a few miles from his original mill in the Dean Basin. The aim is to bring the water of the estuary and river to a state where it is once again clean enough to sustain fish. Already it is possible to see some encouraging signs such as the return of bird life.

Jeremiah Turnbull's ideals are still converted into practical support for the local community and environment wherever the organisation operates in the world.

3

Jeremiah Turnbull would be proud of the fact that local support continues only a few miles from his original mill in the Dean Basin. The aim is to bring the water of the estuary and river to a state where it is once again clean enough to sustain fish. Already it is possible to see some encouraging signs such as the return of bird life.

In addition to reassurance regarding the wise distribution of profits, our stakeholders also expect to be kept informed about our environmental policies and performance.

National organisations such as The Green Trust and The Stewardship Foundation benefit from our involvement on a partnership basis. Our support enables school lectures and field trips to be offered free of charge or at very reduced rates (Investors in People again!). We are also working towards the establishment of standards to ensure consumers have the right to choose products from sustainable sources.

The Green Trust gives 250 school lectures, 25 field trips, and 10 weeks of residential courses in a typical year.

Jeremiah Turnbull's ideals are still converted into practical support for the local community and environment wherever the organisation operates in the world.

3

Jeremiah's concerns regarding the workforce at his Union Road mill in the middle of the last century made him a pioneer amongst employers of the time, many of whom were less than desirable characters. In fact, he was probably the first industrialist to deserve the Investors in People award!

The village he built stands proud today as a symbol of community life. Every weekend you will see the Central Hall and the Church, which he designed with such care, hosting social activities of all kinds and providing a focus for the local community.

Educational involvement takes the form of national and local links with the aim of promoting the skills, understanding and attitudes necessary for industry today and in the future.

Our priorities include:

   Curriculum materials
   Education management training
   Preparation for Investors in People standards
   School governor courses for our employees
   Student placements
   Teacher placements
   Teacher support packs

Six of our sites are offering support in the form of workshops in conjunction with the Understanding British Industry programme:

   Bury
   Leamington Spa
   Milton Keynes
   Newcastle
   Nottingham
   Sheffield

Business simulations help students to experience company decision-making skills and management processes. We are involved in SELECT, PRISM and PROJECT ENTERPRISE projects throughout the country.

2

Employment Trends

EMPLOYMENT

General Comments

Recent economic trends give an encouraging picture although the Low Beck area suffered a major blow in the loss of over 350 jobs when Analogical Systems cut its workforce last month.

A new superstore opened in Pine Valley and it is anticipated that the immediate success of this venture will have a permanent impact on shopping patterns in the Valley. It should also attract shoppers from a wider area to experience the other amenities of the town and bring the prosperity necessary for the continued development of small business enterprises. *(As a matter of interest, the store was opened by Herr Jürgen Freiwald, the 'Mayor' of Megèle, our twin town in Switzerland.)*

Looking further afield and to broader issues, we can report that work is going ahead on a final bid for regeneration funds to be submitted to the Government Office' in 2 months' time. A possible decision is expected by the end of the year.

In conjunction with this bid, the Council is very much involved in the preparation of a Delivery Plan for a training and employment initiative designed to help the unemployed to obtain work and re-training relevant to local industrial and commercial needs.

Sector Changes

The number of Service Sector employees increased by $1/3$ over the last 3 years compared with $1/6$ over the last 15 years. There has been a contrasting decline of over 8,000 jobs in manufacturing ($1/3$ of the total) over the same 3 years. The construction industry, however, has suffered the largest decline – almost half ($5/12$) the number of employees compared with 3 years ago.

Gender Issues

The previously prevailing trend of decreased male and increased female employment was reversed during the past 2 years when the number of male employees rose at the rate of 5% compared to only 2% for female employees.

' for Yorkshire and the Humber

LOCAL TRENDS

6

PRIME RESULTS LTD

44 HIGHTOWN ROAD
BRADFORD
BD17 8HD

TEL NO: 01274646542
FAX NO: 01274 646548

Our ref: JB-D/YOU/Marketing/Ext 5056

Date of typing

Mrs C Pickard
Small Business Publications Ltd
First Floor, Wharfe Building
BRADFORD
BD2 4TH

Dear Mrs Pickard

'PRIME TIME' Staff Magazine

With reference to our telephone conversation earlier this week, I enclose 2 copies of previous 'PRIME TIME' publications. The magazine is distributed to all our employees quarterly. I enclose draft copy of an article entitled 'Jeremiah's Heritage'. We would like to incorporate photographs of Jeremiah Turnbull, Union Garden Village and schoolchildren enjoying residential courses partly funded by the company. I hope to discuss final details with you at our next meeting.

Our new management team wishes to update the design and content of the magazine to appeal to the increasingly younger and more technologically-minded staff profile. Your design for the new-style magazine should incorporate the new company logo as a footer on each page.

I enclose hard copy of the logo which I understand you will be able to scan into your computer. We look forward to seeing your designer's ideas at our meeting on Thursday 24 *(next month)*. However, please contact me if you need further information in the meantime.

Yours faithfully
PRIME RESULTS LTD

Jennie Burton-Denby
MARKETING DIRECTOR

Enclosures: 2 copies of 'PRIME TIME'
              Draft copy of article
              Company logo

THE INTERNATIONAL MILLENNIUM CHALLENGE

Conference to be held on Saturday and Sunday
(dates for last weekend of next month inserted)

in the
Central Civic Hall
SHEFFIELD

10.00 am to 5.00 pm each day

Delegates:

Representatives of Department for International Development
International Banks
International Aid Agencies
Private Sector
Voluntary Organisations
Environmental Organisations
Scientific Organisations

The Challenge:

Sustainable development of the planet
Eliminating poverty and establishing economic well-being
World health and human development
Partnerships
International trade and agriculture

The Debate:

A lively, well-informed debate is expected. Listen to the experts. Find out what is already being done. Consider the future options. Decide on the best strategies. Learn what you can do.

TICKETS AVAILABLE FROM THE DEPARTMENT OF POLITICS, TOTLEY HALL, SHEFFIELD

Remember: your document may have a different appearance to this as the choice of font, font size and text emphasis was yours.

Employment Trends

The following information is worthy of note:

1   Part-time employment in the Service Sector increased by 9%

2   The Service Sector accounts for 75% of all part-time employment

3   80% of part-time employees are women

4   35% of all full-time employment is in Manufacturing

5   Males make up 70% of all full-time employees

Facts and Figures[1]

A summary of the employment information is given below:

- In 1996, the total number of employees in the borough was estimated to be 84,550, over 4,250 more than in 1994.

- Despite the fact that numbers employed in manufacturing[2] continued to drop – over 7,400 fewer in 1996 than in 1994 – the sector still definitely had an important role in the local economy accounting for a higher proportion of employees than at county, regional and national levels.

- Service sector employment rose by 8,300 between 1994 and 1996.

- Part-time employment fell after 1994; full-time employment rose by nearly 4,100.

- The average house price rose in 1994 to £61,567 but fell in 1996 to £58,755.

- The trend towards increased migration out of the borough changed to a positive balance of 30 migrating into the borough in 1995.

Sources

1   Average house price: Castle Building Society

2   Unemployed claimants: Office for National Statistics

3   Migration to and from borough: NHS Central Register

[1] Analysis excludes the primary sector as reliable data is not available
[2] Following re-classification of industries, census figures prior to 1995 have been re-based

LOCAL TRENDS

7

CERTIFICATE IN PUBLIC SERVICES

Course Structure:

Core and option units combined in 8 units of study

Course Content:

Core: Public services in society, Working in a public service organisation

Options: Emergency procedures, Community groups, Social biology, Health studies, Physical recreation, Navigation skills

Assessment:

In-course and final assignments, minimum of Pass grade required in all units

Career progression:

The Certificate is the first step towards a career in the public services. Successful completion provides access to a range of advanced courses. Career opportunities exist in the health and social services, the emergency services, the armed forces and the prison service.

Methods of learning:

An experienced team of lecturers provides a balanced programme of lectures and hands-on activities. Work placement is a large feature of the programme and you will be expected to carry out research projects and work-based assignments. Specialist speakers from the services will be used where appropriate and there is a wide range of opportunities for supervised – and supervising – recreation and leisure pursuits within the local community.

Entry Requirements:

Good general education: at least 2 good GCSE passes

Good physical fitness

Relevant previous experience (subject to satisfactory evidence and interview)

Contact:

Lee Darnley, Course Co-ordinator, Department of Recreation and Leisure Studies, Nethertown College, Tel: 01234-6784562

THE ART OF CONVERSATION

The literal meaning of the word conversation indicates an activity where individuals 'turn or change together' in the sense of responding, co-operating and being interactive. Most of us learn to converse through experience. However, in the modern age when there seems to be so much emphasis on transmitting a message, we seem to have lost the art of listening. Without this basic skill, we cannot hope to enjoy satisfactory conversations.

If a person joins in a conversation with the aim of scoring points or applying pressure, then the listening aspect, and usually the enjoyment, is lost. Each person needs to feel that they can express their ideas and explain their thoughts and needs without having another person 'step on their toes'.

Conversation is our way of getting to know another person and finding out what is going on in their mind. Each of us lives to some extent in our own world which has been built up from the circumstances and influences which have shaped our lives. It is easy to assume that we

know what another person feels or thinks, but unless we listen we will never really find out. We will be making assumptions based on our own ideas and experiences and not the other person's.

We rely on open conversations to establish good relationships. As well as listening to others and being open to their opinions, we need to be open ourselves and explain what is on our minds. If we do this, then guesses and assumptions will not cause confusion and misunderstanding.

Despite the old adage 'Sticks and stones may break my bones but words can't hurt me.', words can harm us considerably, and can affect our self-esteem to a great extent. Negative emotions can build up if we are constantly criticised. Even the first few words of a conversation can create a permanent barrier between the people involved which may never be overcome.

HOLIDAY SPECIALS – SUMMER OFFERS (FROM MANCHESTER AIRPORT)

RESORT	DEPARTURE DATE	ACCOMMODATION TYPE	NUMBER OF NIGHTS	PRICE
Turkey – Alanya	3 July	2AA/SC	7	£229.00
Malta – Valleta	4 July	3A/HB	7	£339.00
Tenerife – Playa de Las Americas	10 July	2A/BB	14	£329.00
Majorca – Palma Nova	12 July	2A/HB	14	£389.00
Costa Blanca – Benidorm	16 July	3A/SC	14	£299.00
Portugal – Villamoura	21 July	2A/BB	7	£249.00
Ibiza – San Antonio	30 July	3A/RO	14	£329.00
Costa del Sol – Marbella	2 August	2A/RO	7	£239.00
Cyprus – Paphos	12 August	2A/SC	14	£369.00
Gran Canaria – Puerto Rico	14 August	2A/HB	14	£349.00

OFFER DETAILS

ACCOMMODATION	ADDITIONAL COSTS	CONDITIONS OF BOOKING
HB = Half Board SC = Self Catering BB = Bed and Breakfast RO = Room Only	Insurance @ £38 per person for 14 days' cover. Insurance @ £22 per person for 7 days' cover. £6 per person booking fee for telephone bookings. Credit card surcharge of 1%.	All prices are subject to availability. Prices are per person and based on 2 full fare passengers sharing. The company reserves the right to withdraw this offer without notice.

CERTIFICATE IN RETAIL STUDIES

Course Structure:
Core and option units combined in 8 units of study

Course Content:
Core: Retailing and Wholesaling, Customer Service
Options: Food hygiene, First Aid, Information Technology

Assessment:
In-course and final assignments, minimum of Pass grade required in all units

Career Progression:
The Certificate is the first step towards a career in the retailing industry – one of the fastest growing sectors of the economy. In the local area, demand for qualified staff has increased recently.

A new superstore opened in Pine Valley and it is anticipated that the immediate success of this venture will have a permanent impact on shopping patterns in the Valley, also attracting shoppers from a wider area to experience the other amenities of the town and bringing the prosperity necessary for the continued development of small business enterprises. *(As a matter of interest, the store was opened by Herr Jürgen Freiwald, the 'Mayor' of Megële, our twin town in Switzerland.)*

Methods of learning:
An experienced team of lecturers provides a balanced programme of lectures and hands-on activities. Work placement is a large feature of the programme and you will be expected to carry out research projects and work-based assignments.

Entry Requirements:
Good general education: at least 2 good GCSE passes
Good physical fitness
Relevant previous experience (subject to satisfactory evidence and interview)

Contact:
Julie Brookes, Course Co-ordinator, Department of Consumer Studies, Netherton College, Tel: 01234-6748261

THE CALDERDALE JUBILEE HANDICAP STAKES (CLASS C)

HORSE NUMBER	JOCKEY	HORSE AND TRAINER DETAILS	LANE NUMBER	RATING
201	S Ashworth	JON'S DREAM 5-10-0 (C Wills)	4	94
202	D Roberts	FLYING SARAH 7-9-10 (R Force)	2	93
203	Carl Peters	CAPATROL 4-9-7 (R Bass)	7	99
204	D Paige	LEE-VIT-OUT 8-9-7 (B Jake)	5	96
205	Jim Hunter	KATHALIAN 6-9-7 (P Caroma)	1	89
206	V Lowry	MY GOOD WILL 4-9-5 (P Terre)	3	92
207	Martin Vell	BEN 'M' 7-9-10 (C Mawdsley)	9	90
208	Will Smithies	CARLORAC 4-9-0 (D Range)	11	88
209	M Briggs	DEL BOY 7-9-10 (C McKenzie)	6	95
210	C Davies	JAUNTY JESS 4-8-6 (J Riley)	10	91
211	Darren Bounce	JACKIE SPRAT 5-8-3 (C Boot)	8	98

TIC TAC

HORSE	ODDS	RACE
CAPATROL	9-2	Value to the winner = £5,500.00. Left-handed, U-shaped, undulating course of 1m 4f
JACKIE SPRAT	11-2	10yds with a 4f run-in. 5f course is fast and mostly downhill. Going: good (good to
DEL BOY	6-1	soft in places).

GARDENING TELE-DIAGNOSTIC LINES – NEW SERVICE LINES

LINE TYPE	TOPIC	AVAILABILITY DATE	CALL DURATION	TELEPHONE NUMBER
FRUIT	Plum, pear and cherry problems	4 June	2.0 minutes	0645 68 5081
FRUIT	Raspberry and blackberry problems	4 June	3.0 minutes	0645 68 5082
FRUIT	Strawberry problems	4 June	2.5 minutes	0645 68 5083
VEGETABLES	Carrot/parsnip problems	6 June	1.0 minutes	0645 68 5221
VEGETABLES	Courgette problems	6 June	1.5 minutes	0645 68 5222
VEGETABLES	Potato problems	7 June	12.0 minutes	0645 68 5223
PEST CONTROL	Greenfly, whitefly and blackfly problems	7 June	7.0 minutes	0645 68 5342
PEST CONTROL	Leaf spots and leaf scorch problems	7 June	5.0 minutes	0645 68 5343
LEGAL	Lawn mower servicing	9 June	10.0 minutes	0645 68 5442
LEGAL	Mail order rights	10 June	3.5 minutes	0645 68 5443
LEGAL	Returning goods to garden centres	10 June	2.0 minutes	0645 68 5444
LEGAL	Overgrowing weeds from neighbour's garden	11 June	5.0 minutes	0645 68 5445

NEW SERVICE FEATURE – ALL LINE TYPES

WHAT	REQUIRED ACTION	HOW
We have added a special feature to all our Tele-diagnostic Lines. Callers will be able to pause, slow down, speed up, rewind and repeat particular sections of the message. To access this special facility callers must have a touch-pad telephone.	Slow the message down	Press 1
	Speed the message up	Press 2
	Pause the message	Press 3
	Restart the message	Press 5
	Rewind the message by 30 seconds	Press 7

ORAL COMMUNICATIONS

Conversation is our way of getting to know another person and finding out what is going on in their mind. Each of us lives to some extent in our own world which has been built up from the circumstances and influences which have shaped our lives. It is easy to assume that we know what another person feels or thinks, but unless we listen we will never really find out. We will be making assumptions based on our own ideas and experiences and not the other person's.

We rely on open conversations to establish good relationships. As well as listening to others and being open to their opinions, we need to be open ourselves and explain what is on our minds. If we do this, then guesses and assumptions will not cause confusion and misunderstanding.

Despite the old adage 'Sticks and stones may break my bones but words can't hurt me.', words can harm us considerably, and can affect our self-esteem to a great extent. Negative emotions can build up if we are constantly criticised. Even the first few words of a conversation can create a permanent barrier between the people involved which may never be overcome.

The resulting hurt or anger can lead to withdrawal or attack, none of which leads to a helpful outcome. It is therefore important that we learn to create the right conditions for things to go well.

AC/Course Notes 3/J Welsh

15

ORAL COMMUNICATIONS

THE ART OF CONVERSATION

The literal meaning of the word conversation indicates an activity where individuals 'turn or change together' in the sense of responding, co-operating and being interactive.

Most of us learn to converse through experience. However, in the modern age when there seems to be so much emphasis on transmitting a message, we seem to have lost the fundamental art of listening. Without this basic skill, we cannot hope to enjoy satisfactory conversations.

If a person joins in a conversation with the aim of scoring points or applying pressure, then the listening aspect, and usually the enjoyment, is lost. At least one participant in such a conversation does not particularly want to hear what the other has to say. Each person needs to feel that they can express their ideas and explain their thoughts and needs without having another person 'step on their toes'.

AC/Course Notes 3/J Welsh

14

Unit 9
Exercise 9A Continued

ORAL COMMUNICATIONS

We all know how it feels to be threatened or patronised. Other people almost certainly feel exactly the same so what's needed is a way of ensuring that each participant can treat the others with respect. From time to time we all need to say things which other people might not want to hear. If we try to anticipate the feelings which the other person may have, we can attempt to put across the point in a way which leaves each participant feeling that their feelings and opinions are respected, even if they do not agree on the subject under discussion.

We can prepare for a productive conversation by considering at the outset what the other person hopes to achieve. Is s/he wanting some help in sorting out his or her own thoughts; is s/he anxious and needing reassurance; is s/he aiming to get an agreement on an issue; is s/he wanting to get to know you better, or is s/he simply wanting a chat for company. If we know the purpose of the conversation, we can try to make sure that it succeeds.

AC/Course Notes 3/J Welsh

16

Unit 9
Exercise 9A Continued

ORAL COMMUNICATIONS

During a conversation, one person is often explaining something while the other person is trying to understand. The roles change throughout a conversation. Each can help the other by really listening, by paraphrasing what the other person said to receive confirmation of understanding, and by asking questions (but not too many!) to help the other person to give a clear explanation.

The literal meaning of the word conversation indicates an activity where individuals 'turn or change together' in the sense of responding, co-operating and being interactive.

- Is the art of conversation really lost?
- If so, what factors have contributed to this loss?
- What strategies can we use in our own conversations?
- How can we help others to master the art of conversation?

AC/Course Notes 3/J Welsh

17

TOTLEY HALL COLLEGE, SHEFFIELD

SECTION	COURSE	CO-ORDINATOR	MODULE	TOPIC	TUTOR
Politics	World Politics	L D Forrester	1(1)	The Pacific Rim	H K Kamara
Politics	European Studies	H Fürstenberger	2(1)	The New Europe	H Fürstenberger
Economics	World Economies	J Mandanos	4(1)	The Middle East	H Razahan
Economics	World Economies	J Mandanos	4(2)	The Far East	H K Kamara
Economics	World Economies	J Mandanos	4(3)	The New Europe	Elsa Granby
Humanities	Social Psychology	O J Cananga	3(3)	Oral Communications	J Welsh
Humanities	Social Psychology	O J Cananga	3(1)	Barriers to Communication	O J Cananga

COURSE TUITION FEES

SECTION	MODULE(S)	SESSION(S)	FEE (£)
Economics	1, 2, 3, 4	Semester 1 – October to January	550.00
Humanities	3, 4, 5, 7, 9	Semesters 1 and 2 – October to January, February to June	450.50
Politics	1, 2, 6, 10	Semester 1 – October to January	1,050.00

THE INTERNATIONAL MILLENNIUM CHALLENGE

Conference to be held on Saturday and Sunday
(dates inserted)

in the
Central Civic Hall
SHEFFIELD

10.00 am to 5.00 pm each day

DELEGATES:

- Environmental Organisations
- International Aid Agencies
- Private Sector
- Representatives of Department for International Development
- Scientific Organisations
- Voluntary Organisations

THE DEBATE:

A lively, well-informed debate is expected. Listen to the experts. Find out what is already being done. Consider the future options. Decide on the best strategies. Learn what you can do.

A representative from the Department for International Links and Development will be present to give information on the recent Government White Paper. A brief overview of the current global situation and policy proposals will be presented.

The conference will be of interest to students, educators, environmentalists, and many others.

THE CHALLENGE:

- Eliminating poverty and establishing economic well-being
- International trade and agriculture
- Sustainable development of the planet
- World health and human development

TICKETS AVAILABLE FROM THE DEPARTMENT OF POLITICS, TOTLEY HALL, SHEFFIELD

EXECUTIVE SECRETARIES GROUP
NORTHERN AREA ANNUAL CONFERENCE AND EXHIBITION
WHEATWOOD HOUSE, HARROGATE
Friday 4 December and Saturday 5 December 1998

For our second Annual Conference and Exhibition, we have taken the opportunity to visit Harrogate – a spa town in central northern England. The venue is situated approximately 1 mile from the town centre on the Wetherby Road.

Accommodation is available at the Conference venue. (Further information and tariff can be obtained from The Conference Secretary, ESG, 127-129 Vespergate Street, York, YO3 8PW.) Reduced rates are offered for colleagues from one organisation sharing a twin room. We recommend that your application for accommodation is received by the end of September as we believe that December weekend breaks are likely to be in great demand in this attractive part of the country.

The Conference venue is an 18th century country house with traditional architectural features and furnishings. You will appreciate the tasteful, modern accommodation block built in local matching stone which provides en-suite single and twin rooms with every possible facility to guarantee a comfortable stay. The full range of business services is available to visitors in the permanently staffed Conference Office, where your correspondence and electronic communication needs can be met.

SENDITCO

A leading international distribution company which has recently introduced a new service – Importing Services. Forget the problems of foreign language barriers, time differences and exchange rates. You can arrange for the importing of documents, freight and parcels from your suppliers around the world. You can even track your consignment on the Web! Senditco's Air Charter service is available for really urgent goods and you can have confirmation of all deliveries to Europe by simply making a telephone call.

ROYAL MAIL

Responding to the challenge of the changing working environment. Special post boxes for franked mail and extended collection times in commercial areas help to ensure today's mail gets on its way. Many supermarkets now sell postage stamps and some have post boxes; these services are being rapidly expanded.

QUICKLINK

Guaranteed overnight delivery service. Operating throughout the United Kingdom. Specialises in remote locations such as the highlands, islands, moors, dales and vales of Scotland, the northern counties, Wales and the south-west. Provides a quick and reliable service for the veterinary and agricultural sector.

CONFERENCE 1998

EXECUTIVE SECRETARIES AND ADMINISTRATORS GROUP
NORTHERN AREA ANNUAL CONFERENCE AND EXHIBITION
MARISCO WHEATWOOD HALL, HARROGATE
Friday 4 December and Saturday 5 December 1998

For our 2nd Annual Conference and Exhibition, we have taken the opportunity to visit Harrogate – a spa town in central northern England. Marisco Wheatwood Hall is situated approximately 1 mile from Harrogate town centre on the Wetherby Road.

Accommodation is available at the Conference venue. (Further information and tariff can be obtained from The Conference Secretary, ESAG, 127-129 Vespergate Street, York, YO3 8PW.) Reduced rates are offered for colleagues from one organisation sharing a twin room.

WE RECOMMEND THAT YOUR APPLICATION FOR ACCOMMODATION IS RECEIVED BY THE END OF SEPTEMBER AS WE BELIEVE THAT DECEMBER WEEKEND BREAKS ARE LIKELY TO BE IN GREAT DEMAND IN THIS ATTRACTIVE PART OF THE COUNTRY.

Marisco Wheatwood Hall is an 18th century country house with traditional architectural features and furnishings. You will appreciate the tasteful, modern accommodation block built in matching local stone which provides en-suite single and twin rooms. The full range of business services is available to guests in the permanently staffed Conference Office, where your correspondence and electronic communication needs can be met.

Exhibitors have been invited from the full spectrum of business services. Demonstrations and presentations will take place throughout both days.

Speakers from recruitment agencies, software manufacturers and service providers will be scheduled at pre-arranged times in the Knaresborough Room so that delegates can organise their own Conference timetable.

ESAG/98/CONF/1

1

CONFERENCE 1998

IMAGE SYSTEMS LTD

The brand leader in presentation materials and equipment. Get your point across through OHP or EPS. Watch the latest multi-media machine in action and see for yourself.

DAZZLE PAPERS

The latest in office paper technology, giving optimum print quality and prestige to all your important documents. Fully compatible with all types of printing equipment.

3

ESAG/98/CONF/1

CONFERENCE 1998

Details of some exhibitors are given on the following pages. We anticipate that at least 30 exhibition stands will be filled. Watch out for further details in next newsletter.

SENDITCO INTERNATIONAL

A leading international distribution company which has recently introduced a new service – Importing Services. Forget the problems of foreign language barriers, time differences and exchange rates. You can arrange for the importing of documents, freight and parcels from your suppliers around the world. You can even track your consignment on the Web! Senditco's Air Charter service is available for really urgent goods and you can have confirmation of all deliveries to Europe by simply making a telephone call!

ROYAL MAIL

Responding to the challenge of the changing working environment. Special post boxes for franked mail and extended collection times in commercial areas help to ensure today's mail gets on its way. Many supermarkets now sell postage stamps and some have post boxes; these services are being rapidly expanded.

QUICKLINK UK

Guaranteed overnight delivery service. Operating throughout the United Kingdom. Specialises in remote locations such as the highlands, islands, moors, dales and vales of Scotland, the northern counties, Wales and the south-west. Provides a quick and reliable service for the veterinary and agricultural sector.

2

ESAG/98/CONF/1

PRIME RESULTS LTD

44 HIGHTOWN ROAD
BRADFORD
BD17 8HD

TEL NO: 01274646542 FAX NO: 01274 646548

Our ref 98/CONF/VENUE

Date of typing

Mrs Mollie Pitman
Conference Office
Marisco Wheatwood Hall
Wetherby Road
HARROGATE
HG8 2TE

Dear Mrs Pitman

ESAG NORTHERN AREA ANNUAL CONFERENCE AND EXHIBITION

I am writing to confirm our telephone conversation of yesterday when I booked the Ripon Room and the Knaresborough Room for the above ESAG event, which is to take place on Friday and Saturday, 4 and 5 December 1998.

I have informed all members and prospective exhibitors of the accommodation and facilities available at the Hall by including the following paragraph in all literature:

The Conference venue is an 18th century country house with traditional architectural features and furnishings. You will appreciate the tasteful, modern accommodation block built in local matching stone which provides en-suite single and twin rooms with every possible facility to guarantee a comfortable stay. The full range of business services is available to visitors in the permanently-staffed Conference Office, where your correspondence and electronic communication needs can be met.

As arranged, I would be pleased to receive 100 copies of your leaflet, tariff and local area map. Please forward these direct to the Conference Secretary, ESAG, 127-129 Vespergate Street, York, YO3 8PW.

The Group's officers wish to reserve 2 twin rooms for 4 nights from Wednesday 2 to Saturday 5 December and, as agreed, require access to both Conference Rooms from 9.00 am on Thursday to 2.00 pm on Sunday.

1

CONFERENCE 1998

MARKIT

A label for every purpose, and much more too! Printer, diskette, copier, self-adhesive, filing, organiser and wall chart labels, stickers, markers and guides. Be sure everything is in its place.

MAGIC STRIPS

Whether you want to correct your mistakes, cover up private or confidential information in a document, or label your files, folders and shelves, there's a tape product to help you to do the job neatly and imperceptibly.

Marisco Wheatwood Hall is an 18th century country house with traditional architectural features and furnishings. You will appreciate the tasteful, modern accommodation block built in matching local stone which provides en-suite single and twin rooms. The full range of business services is available to guests in the permanently-staffed Conference Office, where your correspondence and electronic communication needs can be met.

ESAG/98/CONF/1

4

ESAG NORTHERN AREA ANNUAL CONFERENCE AND EXHIBITION

COMPANY NAME	TYPE OF BUSINESS	ADDRESS	CONTACT	TEL NO
SENDITCO	International Distribution	140 Bolton Road, MANCHESTER, M4 9LL	Mike Frost	0161-7349292
ROYAL MAIL	International Mail	PO House, St Paul's Close, LEEDS, LS1 7NJ	Steve Bulmer	0113-2666999
QUICKLINK UK	UK Delivery	13 Dale Road, BRADFORD, BD8 9WH	Janet Good	01274-884343
MAGIC STRIPS	Office tapes	Abracadabra Mills, HUDDERSFIELD, HD2 2DS	Aslam Hussain	01484-908767
MARKIT	Office stationery	Empire House, HALIFAX, HX2 6HG	Linda Rickaby	01422-334455
DAZZLE PAPERS	Office paper	120 Bright Street, KEIGHLEY, BD21 4SH	Nick Blacker	01535-545432
IMAGE SYSTEMS	Presentation packages	EPS House, Elm Way, WAKEFIELD, WF3 3WD	Ellen Birstall	01924-212345

STAND ALLOCATION

EXHIBITOR	ROOM/STAND	FEE PAYABLE (£)
Magic Strips	Ripon A10	£560.25
Markit	Ripon A8-A9	£1,120.50
Dazzle Papers	Ripon A12-A14	£1,680.75
Image Systems Ltd	Ripon A3	£560.25
Quicklink UK	Ripon B10	£560.25
Royal Mail	Ripon B16-B19	£2,241.00
Senditco International	Ripon B20	£560.25

I enclose a copy of the Prime Results Business Venue Catalogue which contains details of our venue booking and event organisation services. I hope to contact you shortly with a view to including the Hall's details in this publication.

Yours sincerely

Michelle Carr-Holmes
Business Venues Administrator

Enc

Copy to Conference Secretary, ESAG
File

2

Did you remember to indicate routing by ticking or highlighting the copies?
If you reduced the pitch or margins for your letter, it may fit on one page. This is acceptable provided the pitch is not so small that the text is difficult to read.
You may have used a ragged right margin. If no instruction is given, you may use the right allignment of your choice.

CAUSE-AND-EFFECT DIAGRAM

CAUSE-AND-EFFECT DIAGRAM

USE AS A MANAGEMENT TOOL

Cause-and-effect diagrams are used to clarify thought processes, presenting a visual aid for the causes of given problems and the reasons surrounding certain situations. They can be used as tools for problem solving or for handling and presenting information. 'Brainstorming', either individually, or with others, and writing down the suggestions offered on paper usually generates the initial list of possible causes. If items on the list are grouped rationally, it is often possible to see similarities and patterns emerging in the diagram, conveying the idea that a collection of factors (causes) may lead to a particular effect.

KEY CATEGORIES

Interpretations on the appropriate key categories to use depend on the the individual's perception of the reasons for the status quo in an organisation as well as on the particular area and level being examined. The following key categories cover most situations and are a useful starting point for the cause-and-effect diagram to be applied:

* Methods
* Machines
* Materials
* Manpower (converted to the term 'People' by the gender-conscious)

What happens in the operating core of an organisation is fundamentally a question of people, working with various methods and machines, to turn materials into products and services.

DRAWING THE DIAGRAM

The following stages are a suggested method of working:

a) enter the problem as an effect
b) add branches to main spine to represent a particular category/cause
c) list ideas about possible causes on lines linked to relevant main branch
d) add further analysis where appropriate to the preliminary ideas

A cause-and-effect diagram is not to be viewed as a magical solution to a problem. Rather, it records and presents information, and is an aid to structuring thought processes.

MANAGEMENT TOOL 3

1

EXECUTIVE SECRETARIES
GROUP
NORTHERN AREA ANNUAL
CONFERENCE AND
EXHIBITION
WHEATWOOD HOUSE,
HARROGATE
**Friday 4 December and Saturday 5
December 1998**

For our second Annual Conference and Exhibition, we have taken the opportunity to visit Harrogate. The venue is situated approximately 1 mile from the town centre on the Wetherby Road.

The Conference venue is an 18th century country house with traditional architectural features and furnishings. The full range of business services is available to visitors in the permanently staffed Conference Office, where your correspondence and electronic communication needs can be met.

Accommodation is available at the Conference venue. (Further information and tariff can be obtained from The Conference Secretary, ESAG, 127-129 Vespergate Street, York, YO3 8PW.) Reduced rates are offered for colleagues from one organisation sharing a twin room. We recommend that your application for accommodation is received by the end of September as we believe that December weekend breaks are likely to be in great demand in this attractive part of the country.

The following distribution companies will be in attendance:

SENDITCO

A leading international distribution company which has recently introduced a new service – Importing Services.

ROYAL MAIL

Responding to the challenge of the changing working environment.

QUICKLINK UK

Guaranteed overnight delivery service. Operating throughout the United Kingdom.

Other exhibitors include:

ABC Indexing
Best Secs Recruitment
Dazzle Papers
Image Systems Ltd
Magic Strips
Major Minor Music
Markit
Paralegal Services
Prime Time Ltd

THERAPEUTIC USE OF ESSENTIAL OILS

HAIR AND SCALP TREATMENT

Completely natural treatments for dry or greasy hair, and even dandruff, provide a welcome alternative for people who are allergic to strong perfumes and chemicals present in many standard preparations. Blends of essences, diluted in a vegetable oil, give off a wonderful scent too.

FACIAL CREAMS

General aromatherapy treatments can improve skin tone, stimulate circulation and aid toxin removal. Essences such as lavender and neroli are cytophylactic and have a rejuvenating effect on the skin. Other essences have an astringent cleansing effect and can be used in lotions to cleanse oily skin. Others are antiseptic and can be used to eradicate spots and other skin infections.

MASSAGE OILS

Oils can be blended to suit all sorts of individual problems, from emotional anxiety to muscular aches and pains. Essential oils are diluted in vegetable base oils, usually 2½% dilution for adults unless otherwise directed.

AROMATIC BATHS

Bath oils are a vital aspect of aromatherapy both for health and beauty. The particular choice of oil will determine whether the bath is stimulating and refreshing or relaxing and sedating. Essential oils are mixed with a vegetable base before being added to the bath water.

OIL BURNER, DIFFUSER

Burners are a safe, natural, ozone-friendly way of freshening a room or aiding sleep. Lavender at night will induce sleep and relaxation. Eucalyptus will help to ease congestion during colds and flu infections. Other essences can help to promote a feeling of well-being and calm.

CAUSE-AND-EFFECT DIAGRAM

RELATIONSHIP DIAGRAMS

A cause-and-effect diagram doesn't show the inter-relationships between elements of a situation. A relationship diagram can be used to highlight the inter-relationship of causes which are often a feature of the actual problem. This consists of written words denoting factors and elements in a situation and lines showing the connections and relationships between them. Alternatively, a cause-and-effect diagram could be extended to show the inter-relationship links between the factors identified under each category.

MULTIPLE CAUSE DIAGRAMS

These combine elements from both types of diagram to portray connections between various causes. In order for it to be effective, start with the event to be understood, then portray the contributing factors, then portray the factors which contributed to those factors, and so on. You need to be specific and think outward and backward as you go along. The diagram is a visual display of phrases, lines and arrows showing the direction of effects. The cause-and-effect diagram is thus extended to show the contributing factors.

MANAGEMENT TOOL 3

2

Unit 11
Exercise 11D

CUISINE CORNER
Special Menu

STARTERS
Cheese and carrot pâté
Blue cheese onion soup
Gruyère and ham tartlets
Vegetable and ham terrine

MAIN COURSES
Boeuf en croûte
Marinated salmon with chervil
King Henry lamb
Roast mallard with port sauce
Sirloin steak and mixed peppers
Deep fried chicken with tarragon mayonnaise
Roasted vegetable lasagne
Spicy lentils with mushroom sauce

Main meals are served with a selection of seasonal vegetables and boiled or roast potatoes, or green salad with flower petals

DESSERTS
Lemon soufflé
Provençale pie
Raspberry nut meringue
Apple and apricot mousse
Summer fruits ice cream bombe

Cuisine Corner, 48 Lynton Way, Manchester, M4 6TF
Tel no: 0171 452874

Unit 12
Exercise 12D

CAUSE-AND-EFFECT DIAGRAM

RELATIONSHIP DIAGRAMS

A cause-and-effect diagram doesn't show the inter-relationships between elements of a situation. A relationship diagram can be used to highlight the inter-relationship of causes which are often a feature of the actual problem. This consists of written words denoting factors and elements in a situation and lines showing the connections and relationships between them. Alternatively, a cause-and-effect diagram could be extended to show the inter-relationship links between the factors identified under each category.

MULTIPLE CAUSE DIAGRAMS

These combine elements from both types of diagram to portray connections between various causes. In order for it to be effective, start with the event to be understood, then portray the contributing factors, then portray the factors which contributed to those factors, and so on. You need to be specific and think outward and backward as you go along. The diagram is a visual display of phrases, lines and arrows showing the direction of effects. The cause-and-effect diagram is thus extended to show the contributing factors.

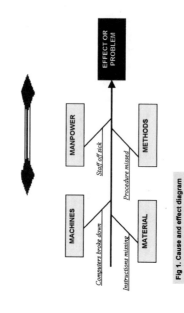

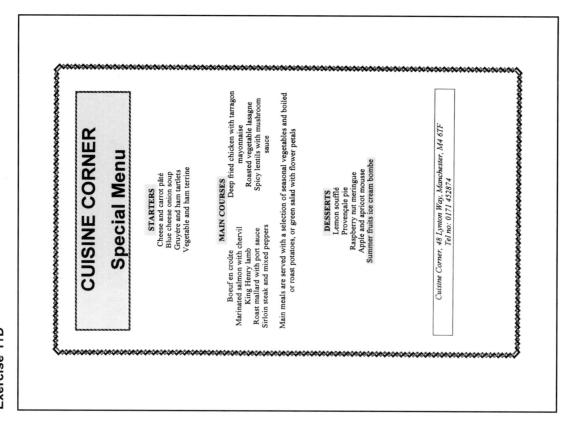

Fig 1. Cause and effect diagram

MANAGEMENT TOOL 3

2

PRIME RESULTS LTD

MEMORANDUM

FROM: Marie Potter
TO: Zafar Hussain
REF: MP/37Q
DATE: today's

Following your recent approval of the proposed work experience scheme for school students, I have arranged for a fifth-year student from Silverdale Grammar School to spend a one-week placement with your staff in the Finance Department. The placement will begin on Monday, *date of fourth Monday of next month.*

I would be grateful if you could draw up a list of varied activities which the student will participate in and forward this directly to the school (a contact name and address is attached on a copy of their letter). Please include an element of work shadowing with a senior member of staff – I can recommend Jane Griffiths as she has done this kind of thing before.

You will also need to arrange for a mentor to look after the student for the week that he/she is visiting us. The mentor will be asked to complete a report at the end of the week reviewing the student's progress and achievements. This should be countersigned by yourself along with any further comments you may wish to make.

As there will be five students on placement with us I will arrange for them all to have an induction first thing on Monday morning – this will include a tour of the buildings and a meeting with the Health and Safety Officer.

If there is any aspect of the placement you would like to discuss with me, please do not hesitate to contact me on Extension 351.

Enc

THERAPEUTIC USE OF ESSENTIAL OILS

HAIR AND SCALP TREATMENT

Completely natural treatments for dry or greasy hair, and even dandruff, provide a welcome alternative for people who are allergic to strong perfumes and chemicals present in many standard preparations. Blends of essences, diluted in a vegetable oil, give off a wonderful scent too.

FACIAL CREAMS

General aromatherapy treatments can improve skin tone, stimulate circulation and aid toxin removal. Essences such as lavender and neroli are cytophylactic and have a rejuvenating effect on the skin. Other essences have an astringent cleansing effect and can be used in lotions to cleanse oily skin. Others are antiseptic and can be used to eradicate spots and other skin infections.

MASSAGE OILS

Oils can be blended to suit all sorts of individual problems, from emotional anxiety to muscular aches and pains. Essential oils are diluted in vegetable base oils, usually 2½% dilution for adults unless otherwise directed.

AROMATIC BATHS

Bath oils are a vital aspect of aromatherapy both for health and beauty. The particular choice of oil will determine whether the bath is stimulating and refreshing or relaxing and sedating. Essential oils are mixed with a vegetable base before being added to the bath water.

OIL BURNER, DIFFUSER

Burners are a safe, natural, ozone-friendly way of freshening a room or aiding sleep. Lavendar at night will induce sleep and relaxation. Eucalyptus will help to ease congestion during colds and flu infections. Other essences can help to promote a feeling of well-being and calm.

THE TORTOISE

TORTOISES AND TURTLES

These reptiles are recognised by a hard shell that encloses the internal organs of the body. Turtles are ancient life forms dating back about 200 million years ago even before the emergence of dinosaurs. Unlike dinosaurs, however, turtles have continued to adapt and flourish.

BEHAVIOUR

Most species are omnivorous, but some tortoises feed solely on vegetation and some aquatic species are strictly carnivorous. All turtles lay eggs, which they usually bury in soft sand or dirt. Generally, they live for a very long time - some species live for more than 100 years. Tortoises generally have mild dispositions.

PHYSICAL ATTRIBUTES

The hard outer covering of tortoises is high and domelike. These thick shells and heavily scaled limbs can provide effective protection against predators. The upper and lower shields of some tortoises are equipped with a hinge, which permits complete closure.

The giant tortoises of the Galapágos and Aldabra Islands belong in this group. Turtles and tortoises either pull their heads into their shell by retracting their necks into an s-shaped curve, or hide their heads by bending the neck sideways.

ENDANGERED HABITATS

The slow-moving reptiles are easily captured and habitats are changing radically. Whalers and pirates slaughtered thousands of giant tortoises on the Galapagos Islands in order to supply their ships with fresh meat. The few remaining specimens are now seriously endangered because goats, originally introduced as a food supply, stripped their habitats of vegetation. Man's advancement on the natural habitat has also contributed to the diminishing turtle and tortoise habitats.

CUISINE CORNER
Special Menu

STARTERS
Cheese and carrot pâté
Blue cheese onion soup
Gruyère and ham tartlets
Vegetable and ham terrine

MAIN COURSES
Boeuf en croûte
Marinated salmon with chervil
Roast mallard with port sauce
Sirloin steak and mixed peppers

Deep fried chicken with tarragon mayonnaise
Roasted vegetable lasagne
Spicy rich lentils with mushroom sauce

Main meals are served with a selection of seasonal vegetables and boiled or roast potatoes, or green salad with flower petals

DESSERTS
Lemon soufflé
Provençale pie
Raspberry nut meringue
Apple and apricot mousse
Summer fruits ice cream bombe

Cuisine Corner, 48 Lynton Way, Manchester, M4 6TF
☎ 0171 452874

MINUTES OF MEETING OF PRIME RESULTS LTD ON MONDAY 6 AUGUST AT 2.30 PM IN THE VENETIAN CONFERENCE ROOM

PRESENT   Aldred Graeme (Chair)
Hussain Zafar
Firth Brian
Benson Howard
Turnstall Matthew
Potter Marie

1   APOLOGIES FOR ABSENCE – Freda McBride, Hilary Wilkinson.

2   MINUTES of previous meeting were approved and signed

3   MATTERS ARISING
3.1   The work experience scheme for Silverdale Grammar School's fifth-year students had been successful.
3.2   The 'Employee Satisfaction In The Millennium' conference was fully booked and additional information packs had been published in readiness.

4   FINANCIAL REPORT
The financial report showed good profits to date. Agreed that a summary report should be prepared for Graeme Aldred to present to the Directors. (Action BF)

5   REVIEW OF SALARY SCALES
Agreed that there should be an urgent review of management salary scales and this should be reported to the next meeting. (Action MP)

6   REFURBISHMENT TO RECEPTION
6.1   A full report and estimate for work had been received by Graeme Aldred. It was agreed that works begin according to the lowest tender received. (Action GA)
6.2   Agreed that a temporary reception service area would need to be in place during the period of refurbishment. (Action MT)

7   ANY OTHER BUSINESS
Marie Potter advised the meeting that Joan Braithwaite had taken retirement from Silverdale Grammar School. Future correspondence relating to work experience schemes should be temporarily sent to the School, % the School Administrator, until another contact name was identified.

8   DATE OF NEXT MEETING
To be notified.

PRIME RESULTS LTD

A meeting of Prime Results Ltd will be held on Monday 6 August in the Venetian Conference Room, 44 Hightown Road Bradford at 2.30 pm.

AGENDA

1   Apologies for absence

2   Minutes of last meeting

3   Matters arising from minutes

4   Financial Report

5   Review of salary scales

6   Refurbishment to main reception area

7   Any other business

8   Date and time of next meeting

E LODGE
Honorary Secretary

MINUTES OF MEETING OF PRIME RESULTS LTD ON MONDAY 6 AUGUST AT
2.30 PM IN THE VENETIAN CONFERENCE ROOM

PRESENT

Aldred Gordon	(Chair)
Benson Howard	(Conference Organiser)
Firth Brian	(Finance Director)
Hussain Zafar	(Finance Manager)
Lodge Elsie	(Honorary Secretary)
Potter Marie	(Personnel Manager)
Turnstall Matthew	(Buildings Manager)

ACTION

1 APOLOGIES FOR ABSENCE – Freda McBride, Hilary
Walker.

2 MINUTES of previous meeting were approved and signed.

3 MATTERS ARISING
3.1 The work experience scheme for Silverdale Grammar
School's fifth-year students had been successful.
3.2 The 'Employee Satisfaction In The Millennium'
conference was fully booked and additional information
packs had been published in readiness.

4 FINANCIAL REPORT
4.1 The financial report showed excellent profits to date and
a healthy bank balance. AGREED that a summary report
should be prepared by Brian Firth for Gordon Aldred to   BF
present to the Directors.

5 REVIEW OF SALARY SCALES
5.1 AGREED that there should be an urgent review of
management salary scales and this should be reported to
the next meeting.
5.2 AGREED that the review of all other salary scales would   MP
be deferred until after the current staff restructuring was
completed in 2½ weeks.

6 REFURBISHMENT TO MAIN RECEPTION AREA
6.1 A full report and estimate for work had been received by
Gordon Aldred. It was AGREED that works begin
immediately according to the lowest tender received.   GA
6.2 It was AGREED that additional work to the foyer leading   GA
to the main reception should also be put in hand.
6.3 AGREED that a temporary reception service area would   MT
need to be in place during the period of refurbishment.

7 ANY OTHER BUSINESS
7.1 Howard Benson reported that he had entered into
negotiations with a leading hotel chain suitable for future
conference venues. It was AGREED that a public
relations exercise be undertaken to secure the contract.   HB
7.2 Marie Potter advised the meeting that Joan Braithwaite
had taken retirement from Silverdale Grammar School.
Future correspondence relating to work experience
schemes should be temporarily sent to the School, ℅ the
School Administrator, until another contact name was
identified.

8 DATE OF NEXT MEETING
**This was arranged for Monday 20 August at 2.30 pm in
the Venetian Conference Room.**

The meeting was closed at 4.45 pm.

2

6   REFURBISHMENT TO RECEPTION

6.1   A full report and a number of estimates for work had been received by Gordon Aldred. It was agreed that works begin according to the lowest tender received.   **GA**

6.2   Agreed that a temporary reception service area would need to be in place during the period of refurbishment.   **MT**

7   ANY OTHER BUSINESS

7.1   Agreed that Hélène de Courcy be invited to the next meeting to comment on the new Public Relations Strategy.   **EL**

7.2   Marie Potter advised the meeting that Joan Braithwaite had taken retirement from Silverdale Grammar School. Future correspondence relating to work experience schemes should be temporarily sent to the School, □ the School Administrator, until another contact name was identified.

8   DATE OF NEXT MEETING
This was arranged for Monday 27 August at 2.30 pm in the Venetian Seminar Room.

The meeting ended at 4.30 pm.

2

MINUTES OF MEETING OF PRIME RESULTS LTD ON MONDAY 6 AUGUST AT 2.30 PM IN THE VENETIAN SEMINAR ROOM

PRESENT

Aldred Gordon	(Chair)
Benson Howard	(Seminar Organiser)
Firth Brian	(Finance Director)
Hussain Zafar	(Finance Manager)
Lodge Elsie	(Honorary Secretary)
Potter Marie	(Personnel Manager)
Turnstall Matthew	(Buildings Manager)

                                ACTION

1   APOLOGIES FOR ABSENCE – Freda McBride, Hilary Wilkinson.

2   MINUTES of previous meeting were approved and signed.

3   MATTERS ARISING

3.1   The new staff canteen was now open and it was agreed that a discount voucher for 12½% be issued to all staff for a one-week trial.

3.2   The work experience scheme for Silverdale Grammar School's fifth-year students had been successful.   **EL**

3.3   The 'Employee Satisfaction In The Millenium' seminar was fully booked and additional information packs had been published in readiness.

4   FINANCIAL REPORT

4.1   The financial report demonstrated that the company had made outstanding profits to date. Agreed that a summary report should be prepared by Brian Firth. Gordon Aldred will then submit this to the Directors.   **BF**

4.2   Invoices for the new computer systems were still outstanding.   **BF**

5   REVIEW OF SALARY SCALES

5.1   Agreed that there should be an urgent review of management salary scales and this should be reported to the next meeting.   **MP**

5.2   A request had been made by the trades unions for a series of meetings to examine the equal opportunities policy in relation to salary appointments. It was agreed that an initial meeting with Personnel would enable a framework to be drawn up on which to proceed.   **MP**

1

Unit 15
Exercise 15C

NEW HOUSES FOR SALE

The following houses are new on the market. As part of our estate services we also offer:

- Free mortgage advice;

- Free valuations on your own property if you sell through us;

- Competitive valuation and survey services on other properties;

- No sale, no fee.

Contact our showroom staff: Brenda Forbes
                              Valerie Brooksbank
                              Kenneth Greenwood

Ref 428W	3 bedroomed detached. Lounge, dining room, kitchen and utility, study, playroom. Gardens, patio area and double garage. Central heating.	£95,000
Ref 672R	4-bedroomed semi-detached. Lounge, dining room, kitchen and utility, hall. Central heating. Gardens and double garage.	£85,000
Ref 895Y	3 bedroomed detached cottage. Lounge with dining area, kitchen and pantry, conservatory. Gardens, patio and pond.	£65,000
Ref 453Y	3-bedroomed Victorian terraced house. Lounge, dining kitchen, hall. Central heating. Large gardens.	£55,000
Ref 993F	2 bedroomed town house. Lounge, kitchen, hall. Courtyard area and garage. Central heating.	£48,000

Unit 15
Exercise 15A

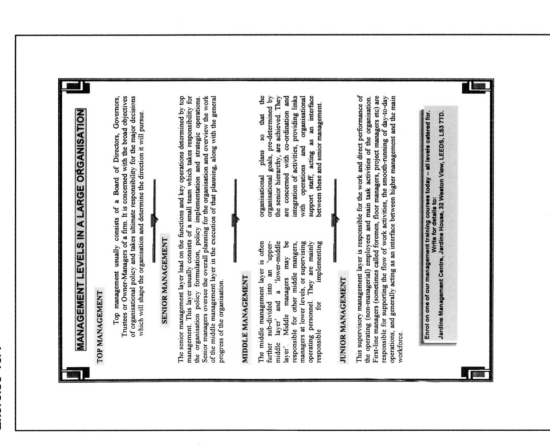

MANAGEMENT LEVELS IN A LARGE ORGANISATION

TOP MANAGEMENT

Top management usually consists of a Board of Directors, Governors, Trustees or Owner-Managers of a firm. It is concerned with the broad objectives of organisational policy and takes ultimate responsibility for the major decisions which will shape the organisation and determine the direction it will pursue.

SENIOR MANAGEMENT

The senior management layer lead on the functions and key operations determined by top management. This layer usually consists of a small team which takes responsibility for the organisation policy formulation, policy implementation and strategic operations. Senior managers oversee the overall planning for the organisation and overview the work of the middle management layer in the execution of that planning, along with the general progress of the organisation.

MIDDLE MANAGEMENT

The middle management layer is often further sub-divided into an 'upper-middle layer' and a 'lower-middle layer'. Middle managers may be responsible for other middle mangers, managers at lower levels, or supervising operating personnel. They are mainly responsible for implementing organisational plans so that the organisational goals, pre-determined by the senior hierarchy, are achieved. They are concerned with co-ordination and integration of activities, providing links with operations and organisational support staff, acting as an interface between these and senior management.

JUNIOR MANAGEMENT

This supervisory management layer is responsible for the work and direct performance of the operating (non-managerial) employees and main task activities of the organisation. First-line managers (sometimes called foremen, floor managers, project managers etc) are responsible for supporting the flow of work activities, the smooth-running of day-to-day operations, and generally acting as an interface between higher management and the main workforce.

> Enrol on one of our management training courses today – all levels catered for.
> Write for details to:
> Jardine Management Centre, Jardine House, 32 Weston View, LEEDS, LS3 7TD.

Note: Your display may not be exactly identical to the above, but check that the content is accurate and you have included the key features.

SYMBOL DEVELOPMENT

astronomer Johannes Kepler used the comma to set off the decimal orders, and the Swiss mathematician Justus Byrgius used the decimal fraction in such forms as 3.2. Decimals are written differently in different countries:

- in the United States they are written in the form 1.23;
- in Great Britain 1·23;
- in continental Europe 1,23;
- in standard scientific notation, the number 0.000000123 would be written as 1.23×10^{-7}.

ADDITION AND SUBTRACTION SYMBOLS

The symbols for addition were not uniform. Some mathematicians indicated addition by using the short form p, some e, and the mathematician Niccolò Tartaglia commonly expressed the operation by ⇔. Algebra mathematicians in Germany and England introduced the sign +, but first used it only to indicate excess.

SYMBOL DEVELOPMENT

MATHEMATICAL SYMBOLS

The term 'mathematical symbols' relates to the various signs and short forms that are used in mathematics to indicate entities, relations, or operations, eg ±, √, ≥. The history of how mathematical symbols were originated and evolved is not entirely clear.

BACKGROUND

The early Egyptians used symbols for addition and equality. The Greeks, Hindus and Arabs had symbols for equality and the unknown quantity. However, from earliest times mathematical processes were cumbersome because proper symbols of operation were largely absent. The expressions for such processes were either written out in full or denoted by word short forms.

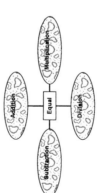

DECIMALS

Simon Stevin, a Dutch mathematician, was responsible for developing the extension of the decimal position system below unity. He called tenths, hundredths, and thousandths *primes*, *sekondes*, and *terzes* and used circled digits to denote the orders. A full stop was used to set off the decimal part of a number as early as the 15th century. The German

SPORTS MEDICINE

A branch of medicine that examines the effects of exercise on the human body and the diagnosis, treatment, and prevention of athletic injuries.

ISOTONIC AND ISOMETRIC EXERCISE

Isotonic exercise has beneficial effects on the cardiovascular system, which carries oxygen to the muscles, by increasing the amount of blood that the heart can pump. It involves moving a muscle through a long distance against low resistance, as in running, swimming, or gymnastics.

Isometric exercise is best for developing large muscles and involves moving muscles through a short distance against a high resistance, as in pushing or pulling an immovable object.

TYPES OF SPORTS INJURY

Most football and basketball injuries involve the knee, either through twisting or through application of lateral force. Long-distance runners also suffer knee injuries, but this is usually due to stress fracture, ie a weakening of the front of the shinbone through over-use, with pain and possible bone cracking as the result. Gymnasts are more likely to suffer ligament tears.

ILLEGAL SUBSTANCES

1968 Tests for narcotic analgesics and stimulants, such as heroin or amphetamines, were first introduced at the Olympic Games.

1974 Anabolic steroids banned following the development of a suitable test.

There has been much controversy over the use of drugs and substances such as steroids that are used to enhance athletic performance, particularly in competitions. Anabolic steroids, taken to improve strength and endurance, can also have harmful side effects such as liver damage. A number of other international and national amateur athletic federations have not accepted the illegality of some drugs due to doubts about testing processes, banning of common drugs such as caffeine, or simply through lack of concern.

Although it is becoming increasingly popular, especially in America, sports medicine is still not fully recognised as a medical specialty.

SPORTS MEDICINE

ISOTONIC AND ISOMETRIC EXERCISE

Isotonic exercise has beneficial effects on the cardiovascular system by increasing the amount of blood that the heart can pump and which carries oxygen to the muscles. It involves moving a muscle through a long distance against low resistance, as in running, swimming, or gymnastics.

Isometric exercise is best for developing large muscles and involves moving muscles through a short distance against a high resistance, as in pushing or pulling an immovable object. Rather than increasing the actual number of muscle fibres both types of exercise increase the thickness of the muscle fibres and their ability to store glycogen, the fuel for muscular activity.

TYPES OF INJURY

Most football and basketball injuries involve the knee, either through twisting or through application of lateral force. Long-distance runners also suffer knee injuries, ie a more usually due to stress fracture, ie a weakening of the front of the shinbone through over-use, with pain and possible bone cracking as the result. Gymnasts are more likely to suffer ligament tears.

ILLEGAL SUBSTANCES

1968 Tests for narcotic analgesics and stimulants, such as heroin or amphetamines, were first introduced at the Olympic Games.

1974 Anabolic steroids banned following the development of a suitable test.

There has been much controversy over the use of drugs and substances such as steroids that are used to enhance athletic performance, particularly in competitions. Anabolic steroids can also have harmful side effects such as liver damage. A number of other international and national amateur athletic federations have not accepted the illegality of some drugs due to doubts about testing processes and banning of common drugs such as caffeine.

Unit 16
Document 2

MATHEMATICAL SYMBOLS

The term 'mathematical symbols' relates to the various signs and abbreviations that are used in mathematics to indicate entities, relations, or operations, eg $\pm$, $\sqrt{}$, $\geq$. The history of how mathematical symbols were originated and evolved is not entirely clear.

BACKGROUND

The early Egyptians used symbols for addition and equality. The Greeks, Hindus, and Arabs had symbols for equality and the unknown quantity. However, from earliest times mathematical processes were cumbersome because proper symbols of operation were largely absent. The expressions for such processes were either written out in full or denoted by word abbreviations.

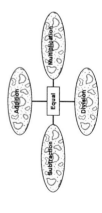

DECIMALS

Simon Stevin, a Dutch mathematician, was attributed with the development of the extension of the decimal position system below unity. He labelled tenths, hundredths, and thousandths *primes*, *sekondes*, and *terzes* and used circled digits to denote the orders. A period was used to set off the decimal part of a number as early as the 15th century. The German astronomer Johannes Kepler used the comma to set off the decimal orders. The Swiss mathematician Justus Byrgius used the decimal fraction in such forms as 3.2.

15

Unit 16
Document 3 Continued

Decimals are written differently in different countries:

- in continental Europe 1,23;
- in Great Britain 1·23;
- in the United States they are written in the form 1.23;
- in standard scientific notation, the number 0.000000123 would be written as 1.23×10^{-7}.

ADDITION AND SUBTRACTION SYMBOLS

The symbols for addition were variable. Some mathematicians indicated addition by using the abbreviation p, some ϵ, and the mathematician Niccolò Tartaglia commonly expressed the operation by $\Leftrightarrow$. Algebra mathematicians in England and Germany introduced the plus sign, $+$, but first used it only to indicate excess. The Greek mathematician Diophantus indicated subtraction by the symbol $\cap$. The German and English algebraists were the first to use the present symbol $-$ (minus sign). The addition and subtraction symbols $+$ and $-$ were first shown in 1489 by the German Johann Widman.

MULTIPLICATION AND DIVISION SYMBOLS

William Oughtred was the English mathematician who first devised the symbol $\times$ for multiplication. The German mathematician Gottfried Wilhelm Leibniz first used a period to indicate multiplication and later employed the sign 3 to denote multiplication and 4 to denote division. Descartes developed the notation a^n for involution. The English mathematician John Wallis defined the negative exponent and first used the symbol $\equiv$ for infinity.

OTHER SYMBOLS

The $=$ symbol for equality was originated by the English mathematician Robert Recorde. The symbols $=<$ for "equals greater than" and $=>$ for "equals less than" were the invention of another Englishman, Thomas Harriot. It was the French mathematician, François Viète, who introduced various symbols of aggregation. The calculus symbols of differentiation, dx, and integration, $\circ$, originated with the German born Leibniz. He was also responsible for the $\sim$ symbol for similarity that is used in geometry.

16

CHILDREN'S INFECTIONS

Medical advice stresses the importance of getting your child(ren) immunised to avoid the risk of illnesses such as measles and whooping cough. These childhood illnesses can be very unpleasant and sometimes dangerous.

Doctors are able to provide full guidance and ensure that protection is available through safe immunisation.

- *AT 2-3 AND 4 MONTHS* – one combined injection each month for diphtheria, tetanus, whooping cough and meningitis (may be separate injection); polio by mouth each month.

- *AT 5 YEARS* – one combined injection for diphtheria and tetanus; polio (once by mouth).

- *AT 13-15 MONTHS* – one combined injection for measles, mumps and rubella.

- *AT 10-13 YEARS* – Heaf test on forearm to check immunity to TB.

As a precaution against polio infection, unvaccinated adults in the same household should be vaccinated at the same time as their child(ren).

A doctor should always be consulted if there is:

- persistent earache
- high fever or delirium
- continued vomiting
- severe eye inflammation
- excessive pain or discomfort.

1

		INCUBATION
CHICKEN POX	The illness usually starts with spots on the trunk which become blistery then yellow and form scabs. There are often several crops of spots.	10-25 days
GLANDULAR FEVER	The throat becomes increasingly painful and swollen with swollen glands in the sides of the neck and sometimes in the armpits and groin. A white patch covering the tonsils is a distinctive feature.	6-8 weeks
MEASLES	Usually starts with a runny nose, bleary eyes and a hard cough. A rash starts behind the ears, spreading to the face and down the body. Dark purplish spots develop into blotches.	14 days
SCARLET FEVER	The throat is a vivid red and there may be a white deposit on the tonsils. Starts with a sore throat and vomiting, with painful swollen glands in the neck. A rash of small slightly raised points appears against a bright red background.	1-5 days
VIRAL HEPATITIS	Symptoms can resemble influenza with nausea, indigestion and pains under the ribs. These are followed by yellow eyes, pale motions and dark orange or brown urine. As the yellow jaundice develops, fever and stomach symptoms lessen.	2-6 weeks

2

Glossary

Action	Keyboard	Mouse	Menu
Accents (combination keys)	Select: **International characters** from the **Help** index to see the combinations Hold down/Press keys: As shown *See also*: Symbols		
Alignment of text	*See*: Ragged right margins. Centre text, Justified right margin		
Allocate a rectangular space using a text box	Select: **View**, **Tool Bars**, **Drawing** Click: ▣ on the Drawing Tool Bar Click: Anywhere in the document Select: **Text Box** from the **Format** menu Click: **Size** Key in: The required dimensions in the **Size and rotate** section Click: **Line** Select: **No line** Click: **Wrapping** Select: **Square** Click: **OK** Drag: Text box to required position		
Allocate clear lines	Press: ↵ once for each line required, plus one		
Allocate horizontal space from left or right margin		Select: The text to be positioned at side of space or position cursor just before first character Drag: The left or right indent marker to the required position on the ruler	
Allocate vertical space across the full typing line			**Format**, **Paragraphs**, **Spacing**, **Before** Key in: The required measurement
Allocate vertical space			**Format**, **Paragraphs**, **Spacing**, **Before** Key in: The required measurement
AutoCorrect			**Tools**, **AutoCorrect**
AutoFormat	Press: **Alt + Ctrl + K**		**Format**, **AutoFormat**
Blocked capitals	Press: **Caps Lock** key		
Bold text	Press: **Ctrl + B**	Click: **B** on the Formatting Tool Bar	**Format**, **Font**
Borders and Lines		Select: The area to which you want to add a border Click: ▣ on the Formatting Tool Bar	Select: The area to which you want to add a border **Format**, **Borders and Shading**, **Borders** Select: From the **Setting**, **Style**, **Color** and **Width** sections as appropriate Select: The area of text to apply the border to in the **Apply To** box, *or* Select: **View**, **Toolbars**, **Tables and Borders** to use the Tool Bar method
Borders		Click: ▣ on the Formatting Tool Bar	**Format**, **Borders and Shading**, **Borders**
(to remove)		Click: ▣ on the Formatting Tool Bar	Repeat the above menu commands but select the None option

Action 👆	Keyboard ⌨	Mouse 🖱	Menu 📄
Bulleted lists		Click: ☰ on the Formatting Tool Bar	**Format, Bullets and Numbering** Select: **Bulleted** Click: The required style
Capitalise letters	Press: **Ctrl + Shift + A**		**Format, Change Case, Uppercase**
Case of letters (to change)	Press: **Shift + F3**		**Format, Change Case**
Centre text	Press: **Ctrl + E**	Click: ☰ on the Formatting Tool Bar	**Format, Paragraph, Indents and Spacing, Alignment, Centred**
Close a file (clear screen)	Press: **Ctrl + W**		**File, Close**
Change case	Select: The text to be changed Press: **Shift + F3** until the required format is displayed		**Format, Change case** Select: The required case Click: **OK**
Clip Art *(from the Microsoft Clip Gallery)*			**Insert, Picture, Clip Art** Select: The required image from the categories shown Click: **Insert**
Clip Art *(from other files)*			**Insert, Picture, From File** Select: The correct drive or folder that contains the file you want in the Look in section Select: The required image from the selected file Click: **Insert**
Copying text from one document to another	Select: **Window** Select: The source document Select: The text to be copied Copy: The text in the normal way Select: **Window** Select: The destination document Position the cursor: In the required position Paste: The text in the normal way		
Copy a block of text Highlight text to be copied	Press: **Ctrl + C**	Click: 📋 on the Standard Tool Bar *or* Press: Right mouse button and Select: **Copy**	**Edit, Copy**
Position cursor where text is to be copied to	Press: **Ctrl + V**	Click: 📋 on the Standard Tool Bar *or* Press: Right mouse button and Select: **Paste**	**Edit, Paste**
Cursor movement Move cursor to required position	Use arrow keys: → ↑ ← ↓	Click: The left mouse button in the required position	
Move to top of document	Press: **Ctrl + Home**		
Move to end of document	Press: **Ctrl + End**		
Move left word by word	Press: **Ctrl + ←**		
Move right word by word	Press: **Ctrl + →**		
Move to end of line	Press: **End**		
Move to start of line	Press: **Home**		
Move to top/bottom of paragraph	Press: **Ctrl + ↑** *or* **Ctrl + ↓**		
Move up/down one screen	Press: **PgUp** *or* **PgDn**		
Cut text	*See*: Delete/cut a block of text		
Date insertion	Press: **Alt + Shift + D**		**Insert, Date and Time**
Delete/cut a block of text	Select: Text to be deleted Press: ← (**Del**)	Select: Text to be deleted/cut: Click: ✂ on the Formatting	Select: Text to be deleted/cut: Select: **Edit, Cut** *or*

Action ☞	Keyboard ⌨	Mouse 🖱	Menu 📄
	or Select: Text to be deleted; Press **Ctrl + X**	Tool Bar	Press: Right mouse button; select: **Cut**
Delete/cut a character	Move cursor to correct character; Press: **Del** *or* Move cursor to right of incorrect character; Press:← (**Del**)		
Delete/cut a word	Select: To end of word	Select: Word to be deleted/cut:	Select: Word to be deleted/cut:
	Press: ← (**Del**) *or* Select: Word to be deleted: Press: **Ctrl + X**	Click: ✂ on the Formatting Tool Bar	Select: **Edit**, **Cut** *or* Press: Right mouse button; select: **Cut**
Drawing Tool Bar *(to display)*		Click: 🔷 on the Standard Tool Bar	**View**, **Toolbars**, **Drawing**
Enumeration	Key in: The enumeration, eg **A)**	Click: 🔢 on the Formatting Tool Bar	**Format**, **Bullets and**
Exit the program	Press: **Alt + F4**	Click: Control button at right of Title Bar	**File**, **Exit**
Enumeration	Key in: The enumeration e.g. A) Press: The **Tab** key Key in: The rest of the text Repeat for each enumerated paragraph	Click: 🔢 on the Formatting Tool Bar	**Format**, **Bullets and Numbering Numbered** Click: On the required style
Find text	Press: **Ctrl + F**		**Edit**, **Find**
Font colour *(to change)*		Click: 🅰 on the Formatting Tool Bar	**Format**, **Font** Select: A colour from the Color drop-down menu
Font size	Press: **Ctrl + Shift + P** Choose: Desired size	Click: 10 ▾ on the Formatting Tool Bar Choose: Desired size	**Format**, **Font** Choose: Desired size
Next larger point size Next smaller point size	Press: **Ctrl +]** Press: **Ctrl + [**		
Font typeface style	Press: **Ctrl + Shift + F** Choose: Desired font	Click: [font] on the Formatting Tool Bar Choose: Desired font	**Format**, **Font** Choose: Desired font
Footnote separator *(to remove)*			**View**, **Normal** **View**, **Footnotes** Select: **All footnotes** Select: **Footnote separator** Highlight and delete: **Line**
Footnotes *(to insert)*	Press: **Alt + Ctrl + F**		Insert, Footnote Select: **Options** Click: **OK** Enter: The footnote text
Format Painter *(to copy formats)*	Position the cursor: In the text with the required format Press: **Ctrl + Shift + C** Select text to be formatted: Press: **Ctrl + Shift + V**	Position the cursor: In the text with the required format: Click: 🖌 on the Formatting Tool Bar To copy to one word: Click: The word To copy to a block of text: Select: The text Click: The left mouse button	

Action	Keyboard	Mouse	Menu
Formatting *(to review)*	Press: Shift + F1 Click: The text to be reviewed		Select: The text to be reviewed Check: The displayed formats on the Formatting Tool Bar Press: **Shift + F1** to reverse
Fractions *(using superscript and subscript)*	Press: **Ctrl + Shift + +** (plus sign) Key in: The numerator Press: **Ctrl + Spacebar** Key in: **/** (solidus) Press: **Ctrl + =** Key in: The denominator Press: **Ctrl + Spacebar**		**Format, Font, Effects, Superscript, OK** Key in: The numerator **Format, Font, Effects, Superscript, OK** Key in: **/** (solidus) **Format, Font, Effects, Subscript, OK** Key in: The denominator **Format, Font, Effects, Subscript, OK**
Full page borders *(to add)*			**Format, Borders and Shading, Page Border** Select: From the **Setting, Style, Color, Width** and **Art** sections as appropriate Select: The area of page to apply the border to in the **Apply To** box
Go to (a specified page)	Press: **Ctrl + G** *or* **F5**		**Edit, Go To …**
Grammar tool	Press: **F7**	Click: [ABC✓] on the Standard Tool Bar	**Tools, Spelling and Grammar**
Headers and Footers			Select: **View, Header and Footer** Key in: The header text and/or footer text
To delete:	Select: The actual text or page number Press: ← (**Del**)		
Headers and footers *(to change text formatting)*			**View, Header and Footer** **Format, Font** Select: The required format Click: **OK** Click: **Close**
Help function **and Office Assistant**	Press: **F1** (for Contents) Press: **Shift + F1** (for **What's This?** – context-sensitive help)	Click: [?] on the Formatting Tool Bar for the **Office Assistant**	**Help**
Highlight/shade text		Click: [✎] on the Formatting Tool Bar	**Format, Borders and Shading, Shading**
Indent function Indent at left to next tab stop	Press: **Ctrl + M**	Click: [⫷] on the Formatting Tool Bar	**Format, Paragraph, Indents and Spacing**
Indent at left to previous tab stop	Press: **Ctrl + Shift + M**		
Action	**Keyboard**	**Mouse**	**Menu**
Indent as a hanging paragraph	Press: **Ctrl + T**		
Unindent and return to standard margin	Press: **Ctrl + Q**	Click: [⫷] on the Formatting Tool Bar	

Action	Keyboard	Mouse	Menu
		Using ruler first-line indent ▽ left indent ⬒ first-line and left indent ⬓ right indent △	
Insert special character/symbols	To change the selection to symbol font: Press: **Ctrl + Shift + Q**		To insert a symbol: Position cursor: Where you want the character/symbol to appear: Select: **Insert**, **Symbol**
Insert text	Simply key in the missing character(s) at the appropriate place – the existing text will 'move over' to make room for the new text. If **OVR** is displayed (overtyping), Press: **Ins(ert)** key to remove		
Italics	Press: **Ctrl + I**	Click: *I* on the Formatting Tool Bar	**Format, Font**
Justified right margin	Press: **Ctrl + J**	Click: ▤ on the Formatting Tool Bar	**Format, Paragraph, Indents and Spacing, Alignment, Justified**
Landscape orientation			**File, Page Setup, Paper Size** Click: **Landscape**
Line break (to insert)	Press: **Shift + ↵**		
Line length – to change	Select text. Display horizontal ruler. Move margin markers to required position on ruler		
Line spacing *(to set triple line spacing)*			Select: **Multiple** from the **Line Spacing** drop-down menu Enter: **3** in the **At** box
Line spacing – to set	Press: **Ctrl + 1** (single) Press: **Ctrl + 2** (double) Press: **Ctrl + 0** (to add or delete a line space)		**Format, Paragraph, Indents and Spacing, Line Spacing**
Mailmerge – add record		**Switch to Data Form** Click: **Add New** Key in: The record Click: **Add New** *or* **Switch to View Source** Click: **Add New** Record Key in: The record	
Mailmerge – amend fields		**Switch to View Source** Click: 🖳 on the Database Tool Bar	
Mailmerge – create data source	Select: **Tools, Mail Merge, Get Data** in Section 2, **Create Data Source**		
Mailmerge – create main document	Select: **Tools, Mail Merge, Create** in Section 1, **Form Letters, Active Window**		
Mailmerge – delete record		Select: **Switch to Data Form** Select: **Find Record** Click: **Delete** *or* Select: **Switch to View Source** Select: The required record Select: **Delete**	
Mailmerge – enter records		**Switch to Data Form** Key in: The record Select: **Add New**	

Action	Keyboard	Mouse	Menu
Mailmerge – find record		**Switch to Data Form** Click: **Find** Click: [icon] Key in: The data Select: **In Field** Click: **Find First** *or* **Switch to Data Form** Click: **View Source**	
Mailmerge – insert merge codes		**Switch to Main Doc** Click: **Insert Merge Field** Select: The required filename	
Mailmerge – open data source		Select: **Tools, Mail Merge** Click: **Get Data** in Section 2 Select: **Open Data Source**	
Mailmerge – print merged file		Click: [icon]	
Mailmerge – select records		Select: **Query Options** in the **Mail Merge Helper** dialogue box Select: The required field Key in: The required options	
Mailmerge – sort data source		**Switch to View Source** Place the cursor: In the appropriate column Click: [icon] or [icon]	
Mailmerge – switch between Data Source and Main Document		Click: [icon] Select: **Edit** in Section 1 or 2 *OR* Click: [icon] or [icon] on the Database Tool Bar	**Window, Main Doc** **Window, Datafile**
Mailmerge – view merged file		**Switch to Main Doc** Click: [icon]	
Margins (to change)	Use the mouse pointer to drag the left and/or right margin boundaries to the appropriate place on the horizontal ruler. Press: The **Alt** key at the same time [icon] to view the measurements on screen		**File, Page Setup, Margins**
Move around document	*See*: Cursor movement		
Move a block of text Select: Text to be moved	Press: **F2** *or* **Ctrl + X**	Click: [icon] on the Standard Tool Bar	**Edit, Cut**
Position cursor where text is to be moved to	Press: **Ctrl + V** *or* ⏎	Click: [icon] on the Standard Tool Bar *drag and drop moving:* Select: Text to be moved Click: Left mouse button in middle of text and keep held down Drag: Selection to required location Release: Mouse button	**Edit, Paste** *or* Press: Right mouse button; Select: **Cut** Press: Right mouse button; Select: **Paste**
Newspaper columns *(to change column width)*		Position cursor in section to be changed: Drag: Column markers to required position on ruler	
Newspaper columns *(for section of document)*			Select: The text to be formatted into columns Operate the commands as for **Newspaper columns** *(for whole document)*
Newspaper columns *(for whole document)*		Click: [icon] on the Standard Tool Bar Drag: across grid to select number of columns	**View, Page Layout, Edit, Select All** **Format, Columns**

Action	Keyboard	Mouse	Menu
			Select: The columns required in the **Presets** section Click: **OK**
Newspaper columns *(insert column break)*			Position the cursor: Where the new column is to start **Insert, Break, Column break**
Newspaper column *(inserting vertical lines between)*			Position the cursor: In the section to be changed **Format, Columns, Line between**
Newspaper columns *(to remove column formatting)*		Position the cursor: In the section to be changed Click: ▦ on the Standard Tool Bar Drag: Across the grid to select one column	**View, Page Layout, Edit, Select All** Format, Columns Select: One column in the **Presets** section Click: **OK**
Open an existing file	Press: **Ctrl + O**	Click: 📂 on the Standard Tool Bar	**File, Open**
Open a new file	Press: **Ctrl + N**	Click: ▯ on the Standard Tool Bar	**File, New**
Page break (to insert)	Press: **Ctrl + ⏎**		**Insert, Break, Page break**
Page numbering	Press: **Alt + Shift + P**		**Insert, Page Numbers**
Page numbering from a given page			**Insert, Page numbers** Select: **Position and alignment** Select: **Format** Select: **Start at** Key in: The page number for the first page
Page Setup			**File, Page Setup** Choose from **Margins, Paper Size, Paper Source and Layout**
Paragraphs – splitting/joining	Make a new paragraph (i.e. split a paragraph into two): Move cursor to first letter of new paragraph: Press ⏎ twice Join two consecutive paragraphs into one: Move cursor to first letter of new paragraph: Press ← (**Del**) twice (backspace delete key) Press: **Space Bar** (to insert a space after full stop)		
Print out hard copy	Press: **Ctrl + P**	Click: 🖨 on the Standard Tool Bar	**File, Print**
Print Preview	Press: **Ctrl + F2**	Click: 🔍 on the Standard Tool Bar	**File, Print Preview** Select: **Zoom** or **Full Page**
Ragged right margin	Press: **Ctrl + L**	Click: ▤ on the Formatting Tool Bar	**Format, Paragraph, Indents and Spacing, Alignment, Left**
Remove text emphasis First, select the emphasised text to be changed back to normal text	Press: **Ctrl + Space Bar** *or* Press: **Ctrl + Shift + Z**	Click: Appropriate emphasis button on the Formatting Tool Bar (to deselect)	**Format, Paragraph, Indents and Spacing**
Repeat typing or actions (redo)	Press: **F4** to repeat previous action *or* Press: **Ctrl + Y**	Click: ↪ on the Formatting Tool Bar To redo (repeat) sets of actions, drag down the **Redo** drop-down list: Select: The group of actions you wish to repeat	**Edit, Repeat Typing**
Replace text	Press: **Ctrl + H**		**Edit, Replace**
Replace text – typeover	1 Select: The incorrect text and then type in the correct entry – Word will fit the replacement text exactly into the original space		

Action ☞	Keyboard ⌨	Mouse 🖰	Menu 📄
	2 Move cursor: To incorrect entry: Press: The **Ins** key (typeover on) and overtype with correct entry Press: The **Ins** key again (typeover off) to stop overtyping of text		
Restore deleted text	Press: **Ctrl + Z**	Click: ↰ on the Formatting Tool Bar	**Edit, Undo Typing**
Ruler – to display			**View, Ruler**
Save work to disk Save a file for the first time	Press: **F12**		**File, Save As**, **Enter Filename** Select: Correct Directory/Drive; Click: **OK**
Save an active file which has been saved previously	Press: **Ctrl + S** *or* Press: **Shift + F12**	Click: 💾 on the Standard Tool Bar	**File, Save**
Save all open files			**File, Save All**
Scroll bars **(to view)**			**Tools, Options, View** Select: Horizontal Scroll Bar and Vertical Scroll Bar options
Search for text	*See* Find text		
Select text One character (or more) One word To end of line Start of line A full line A paragraph Whole document Any block of text	Press: **Shift + → or ←** Press: **Shift + Ctrl + →** *or* **←** Press: **Shift + End** Press: **Shift + Home** Press: **Shift + End** *or* **Home** — Press: **Ctrl + A** —	Click and drag: Pointer across text Double-click: On word Click and drag: Pointer right or down Click and drag: Pointer left or up Click: In selection border Double-click: In selection border Triple-click: In selection border Position pointer: At start of text and Hold down: **Shift**. Then, position pointer at end of text and click	
Remove selection		Click: In any white space	
Shading *(to add)*		Click: [🖊▼] on the Formatting Tool Bar *and/or* Click: [A▼] on the Formatting Tool Bar	**Format, Borders and** **Shading, Shading** Select: From the **Fill**, **Style**, and **Color** sections as appropriate Select: The area of text to apply the shading to in the **Apply To** box or Select: **View, Toolbars,** **Tables and Borders** to use the Tool Bar method
Shading *(to remove)*			Repeat the above menu commands but select the **None** option
Small capitals	Select: The text to be changed Press: **Ctrl + Shift + K**		**Format, Font** Select: **Small caps** in the **Effects** section
Sort (rearrange) items			Select: The items or text to be sorted Select: **Table, Sort**
Spaced capitals	Press: **Caps Lock** key. Leave one space after each letter. Leave three spaces after each word		
Spellcheck	Press: **F7**	Click: [ABC✓] on the Standard Tool Bar	**Tools, Spelling and Grammar**
Standard Paragraph Files *(to create/store)*	Key in: The portion of text to be saved as a standard paragraph file Save: It in a separate file using normal **Save** procedures		
Standard Paragraph Files *(to insert into document)*	Position the insertion pointer: Where you want the standard paragraph to be inserted Select: **File** from the **Insert** menu Select/key in: The appropriate filename		

Action	Keyboard	Mouse	Menu
Standard Paragraph Files To create/store standard paragraphs: To insert standard paragraphs into your document:	Key in: The portion of text to be saved as a standard paragraph file Save it in a separate file using normal **Save** procedures Position the cursor: Where you want the standard paragaph to be inserted Select: **File** from the **Insert** menu Select/Key in: The appropriate filename		
Status Bar			**Tools, Options, View** Select: Status Bar option
Styles *(using)*	Select: The text to be formatted For **Normal** style: Press: **Ctrl + Shift + N** For **Heading 1** style: Press: **Alt + Ctrl + 1** For **Heading 2** style: Press: **Alt + Ctrl + 2**	Select: The text to be formatted Select: The required style from the **Style** drop-down menu on the Formatting Tool Bar	
Subscript	Press: **Ctrl + =** (equals sign) To revert to normal text: Press: **Ctrl + spacebar**		**Format, Font** Select: **Subscript** in **Effects** To revert to normal text: Select: **Subscript** again
Superscript	Press: **Ctrl + Shift + +** (plus sign) To revert to normal text: Press: **Ctrl + spacebar**		**Format, Font** Select: **Superscript** in **Effects** To revert to normal text: Select: **Superscript** again
Switch on and load Word		Double-click: **Microsoft Word Icon**	Select: **MS Word from Start**
Symbols	*See:* Inserting special characters/symbols		
Symbols as graphics			Position the cursor: Where you want the symbol to appear **Insert, Symbol** Select: The appropriate Font Click: The required graphic symbol Click: **Insert** Click: **OK**
Symbols/Accents/Fractions			**Insert, Symbol** Select: The required font Click: On the required symbol Select: **Insert, Close**
Tabs *(to add/set)*	Click: The **Tab Alignment** button at the far left of the horizontal ruler until the type of tab alignment you want is displayed: ⌊ left-aligned tab ⌊ decimal tab ⌋ right-aligned tab ⌊ centred tab Click: On the horizontal ruler at the place where you want to set the tab stop		**Format, Tabs** Enter: The appropriate position and alignment for each tab required
Tabs *(to delete/clear)*	Click: The tab marker Drag: It off the horizontal ruler		**Format, Tabs** Select: The appropriate tab stop Select: **Clear**
Tabs *(to move)*	Click: The tab marker Drag: It to the left or right on the horizontal ruler		Format, Tabs Select: The appropriate tab stop and follow the instructions above under *(to delete/clear)* Set the tab stop in its new position following the instructions above under *(to add/set)*

Action ☞	Keyboard ⌨	Mouse 🖱	Menu 📄
Tables *(to apply ruling/borders)*		Click: [▦] on the Formatting Tool Bar	Select: The table cell(s) to apply ruling to **Format, Borders and Shading, Borders**
Tables *(to add/set/delete tabs inside a table)*	Select: The column in which you want to edit the tab settings Make any tab stop changes in the normal way (see Tabs)		
Tables *(to move between tabs in a table)*	Press: Ctrl + Tab	Click: At the required position	
Tables Insert table		Click: [▦] on the Standard Tool Bar	**Table, Insert Table**
Tables and borders		Click: [▣] on the Standard Tool Bar	**Table, Draw Table**
Text Box		Click: [▦] on the Standard Tool Bar	**Insert, Text Box**
(to add)		Click: [▦] on the Drawing Tool Bar	Drag the cross-hair cursor across the screen until the text box is the required size
Text Box *(to format)*		Click: The text box Press: The right mouse key Select: **Format Text Box** Select: From the options on the **Format Text Box** dialogue box as appropriate	Click: The text box **Format, Text Box** Select: From the options on the **Format Text Box** dialogue box as appropriate or **View, Toolbars, Picture** to format the text box using the Picture Tool Bar
Underline text Single underline Double underline	Press: **Ctrl + U** Press: **Ctrl + Shift + W** Press: **Ctrl + Shift + D**	Click: [U] on the Formatting Tool Bar	**Format, Font, Underline**
Undo mistakes, typing or actions	Press: **Ctrl + Z**	Click: [↶] on the Standard Tool Bar To undo sets of actions, drag down the **Undo** drop-down list; select: The group of actions you wish to undo	**Edit, Undo Typing**
Units of measurement			**Tools, Options, General, Measurement Units** Select: Desired unit from drop-down menu
View magnified pages		Click: [100%] on the Standard Tool Bar Click: **Magnifies** on Print Preview	**View, Zoom**
View – normal view	Press: **Ctrl + F2**	Click: the [▣ Normal] **Normal View** button at left of document window	**View, Normal**
View – online view		Click: the [▣ Online L] **Online View** button at left of document window	**View, Online**
View – outline view		Click: the [▣ Outline] **Outline View** button at left of document window	**View, Outline**
View – page layout view		Click: the [▣ Page Layout] **Page Layout View** button at left of document window	**View, Page Layout**
View – Print Preview	Press: **Ctrl + F2**	Click: [🔍] on the Standard Tool Bar	**File, Print Preview** Select: **Zoom** or **Full Page**
Widow/orphan control			**Format, Paragraph, Line and Page Breaks**